THE ELECTRONIC FINANCIAL MARKETS OF THE FUTURE

THE ELECTRONIC FINANCIAL MARKETS OF THE FUTURE

and survival strategies of the broker-dealers

LAUREN LIEBENBERG

palgrave
macmillan

First published 2002 by
PALGRAVE MACMILLAN
Houndmills, Basingstoke, Hampshire RG21 6XS and
175 Fifth Avenue, New York, N.Y. 10010
Companies and representatives throughout the world

PALGRAVE MACMILLAN is the global academic imprint of the Palgrave Macmillan division of St. Martin's Press, LLC and of Palgrave Macmillan Ltd. Macmillan® is a registered trademark in the United States, United Kingdom and other countries. Palgrave is a registered trademark in the European Union and other countries.

ISBN 0–333–99860–X

This book is printed on paper suitable for recycling and made from fully managed and sustained forest sources.

A catalogue record for this book is available from the British Library.

A catalog record for this book is available from the Library of Congress.

Editing and origination by Aardvark Editorial, Mendham, Suffolk

10 9 8 7 6 5 4 3 2 1
11 10 09 08 07 06 05 04 03 02

Printed and bound in Great Britain by
Antony Rowe Ltd, Chippenham and Eastbourne

CONTENTS

LIST OF FIGURES

Figures

LIST OF SCREEN SHOTS

LIST OF TABLES

ACKNOWLEDGEMENTS

Firstly, I am indebted to two of my colleagues for their invaluable contributions to this volume. Satyajit Das – at whose instance this was written – has afforded me the benefit not only of his incisive strategic mind, but his eminent reputation in the financial markets as well, and has provided me with unwavering support and guidance throughout the process. I am equally grateful to Tracey Rossini for her inestimable contribution to the actual strategic constructs in this book. Her suggestions were always judicious, often inspired, and have enhanced the final product immeasurably.

I would also like to acknowledge Rand Merchant Bank itself who, in the first instance, has allowed me to write this, but who, more significantly, has created the kind of rare environment in which freedom of speech, thought, and spirit flourish. It is only this entrepreneurial zest that has made an analysis of this nature possible.

Finally, I would also like to take the opportunity to thank the editorial and publishing teams at Aardvark and Palgrave Macmillan respectively. I am especially grateful to Andrea Hartill, Jacky Kippenberger and Linda Norris – their dedication and absolute professionalism under the most onerous of deadlines is quite extraordinary.

LIST OF INSTITUTIONS (ACRONYMS)

Basle Committee	Basle Committee on Banking Supervision; Basle
BIS	Bank for International Settlements; Basle
BMA	Bond Market Association; New York
CBOT	Chicago Board of Trade
CEE	Central European Economies
CME	Chicago Mercantile Exchange
Davos	World Economic Forum; Davos; Switzerland
DTCC	Depository Trust and Clearing Corporation
EMU	European Monetary Union; Frankfurt
EU	European Union; Brussels
G7	Group of Seven (largest industrialised nations)
G10	Group of Ten (central bank governors and finance ministers from 11 largest industrialised nations)
G22	Group of Twenty Two (informal representatives from developed and developing economies)
GSTPA	Global Straight Through Processing Association
IFC	International Finance Corporation; Washington D.C.
IMF	International Monetary Fund; Washington D.C.
ISMA	International Securities Market Association; Zurich
LIFFE	London International Financial Futures Exchange; London.
NASDAQ	National Association of Securities Dealers Automated Quotation

NYSE	New York Stock Exchange
OECD	Organisation for Economic Co-operation & Development; Paris
SEC	Securities and Exchange Commission.
SIA	Securities Industry Association; New York
SWIFT	Society for Worldwide Interbank Financial Telecommunication. An international messaging system for payment instructions.
UN	United Nations; New York
World Bank	World Bank; Washington D.C.
WTO	World Trade Organisation; Geneva

OTHER ACRONYMS

e-Jargon

ASP	Application Service Provider
ATS	Alternative Trading System (electronic in nature)
B2B	Business-to-Business (e-commerce)
B2B2C	Business-to-Business-to-Consumer
B2C	Business-to-Consumer
C2C/P2P	Consumer-to-Consumer or Person-to-Person
ECN	Electronic Communications Network (A type of electronic trading system, predominantly for the US OTC equities market, e.g. Instinet, sometimes used more broadly as a synonym for ATS.)
ISP	Internet Service Provider
STP	Straight-through-processing
VPN	Virtual private network

Strategy Jargon

PESTLE	Model of the Macro Environment comprised of the Political, Economic, Social, Technological, Legislative, and Environmental/Ecological environments
JIT	Just-In-Time (supply chain management)

PART I

EMERGING MEGA-TRENDS

Unprecedented Change: the Cause and Effect

CHAPTER 1

INTRODUCTION

THE TECHNOLOGICAL ORIGINS OF CHANGE

At the confluence of the second and third millennia, we are in the throes of an unprecedented wave of change, the effects of which will be profound. It is no overstatement to proclaim that we are the witnesses to the birth of a new politico-economic world order. To accept this as true, however, to even begin to concede the alleged profundity of this change, we need to trace its source. And while the agents of change in this complex ecosystem of ours are numerous, the present variable of highest significance (in the classic PESTLE model of the macro-environment) is indisputably; technology.

From the Stone Age onwards, technological advances have always catalysed great changes in human society. A tour through any old dusty anthropological museum charts the amazing course of human evolution; a course that is discernible through changes in man's socio-economic structure; from primitive tribes of nomadic hunter-gatherers, through feudal agrarian-based societies, to the urbanisation of the industrial age. Each shift in man's system of production and consumption was driven by new technologies – from the fashioning of the first iron implement and the invention of the wheel, to the construction of great seafaring vessels, the invention of the steam-powered engine, the harnessing of electricity, and telephony. Yet, for all that historical turbulence, it is the rate and magnitude which distinguishes this period of change from all its predecessors. This is speculatively because two distinct technological advances have occurred simultaneously – connectivity and computational power – that feed off one another, amplifying the effect of both.

CONNECTIVITY ON A GLOBAL SCALE: THE NETWORK EFFECT

In the first instance, the convergence of, and powerful advances in, telecommunications and information technology (IT) spawned the creation of 'the network', in the broader sense, and hence connectivity on a scale never before possible. This electronic network – both public (the Internet) and private – now accessible via any access device (including the computer, television and cell phone) has, ostensibly at least, heralded the 'death of time and distance'. It allows people to be in 'virtual' contact in 'real time', '24x7x365', 'any time, anywhere'. Most of us are now 'wired' to the Web, access it continuously, and do not need the concept explained. However, for the purposes of this hypothesis, it warrants stating that global electronic connectivity has taken the process of communication – or the exchange of information – to a new dimension. The Net, as a medium for interaction, is unparalleled.

THE POWER OF COMPUTATIONAL POWER

At the same time that this new medium has generated voluminous informational exchange, so we have acquired the ability to exploit it, through powerful advances in computational power.

To process raw inputs, with reference to micro-economic theory, implies the addition of value to produce a product output. The increase in processing capacity that automation or advances in 'the state of technology' afford is pushing the 'productivity frontier' or supply curve outwards. This equates to ever-increasing levels of efficiency.

More significantly, however, the field of data analytics has enabled us to take raw data as an input and advance up the so-called 'insight hierarchy'; from data, to information, to knowledge, to intelligence, through the application of technology.

The link between, and powerful combined effect of, these two interrelated technological advances and, specifically, how the former (defined by the free flow of information) is capitalised on by the latter (dubbed 'informatics') will become patent.

From a theoretical or hypothetical angle, these two concepts are represented by Metcalf and Moore's 'laws' respectively. Metcalf's law, otherwise dubbed 'the network effect', states that the value of a network is equal to the square of the number of users or, more generically, that the value of a network increases exponentially as the number of people connected to it increases. Moore's law states that processing capacity doubles every eighteen months. Whether these statements are technically valid is irrelevant, the principal is true. These two interdependent technological developments – global electronic connectivity, enabling unparalleled free flow of information, and extraordinary advances in data computational power – are the primary drivers of change in the world today. The combined effect of these powerful, mutually reinforcing forces has been the genesis of the 'networked economy'.

THE EMERGENCE OF THE NETWORKED ECONOMY

At the macro-economic level, the effects of these technological causes of change can be reduced to seven interrelated trends, which together define the new economy. These shifts are outlined in Table 1.1.

Table 1.1 Dimensions of the networked economy

From	To
Connectivity/Network Effects: ***The Free Flow of Information***	
Geopolitical or Localised Markets	Globalisation
Divergent/Vertical Industries	Convergence
Intermediated Markets (presence of brokers, agents, middlemen)	Disintermediation
Closed Markets: (restricted access) Information Asymmetry Price Distortions	Open Markets: (unrestricted access: any buyers, any sellers) Transparency Efficient Pricing (competitive/comparative pricing)
Fixed Pricing or Catalogue Model	Dynamic Pricing or Auction Model
Computational Power Effects: ***The Processing of Information***	
Manual Transaction Processing	Process Automation Operational Efficiency
Dumb Data/Data Dump	Knowledge Value-added 'Info'-mediation
Combined Effect	
Sell-side Power Imbalance	Buyer Empowerment
Inefficiency	Greater Efficiency

CHAPTER 2

FROM LOCALISATION TO GLOBALISATION

The power of the network to connect people is one of the origins of the phenomenon of globalisation. The International Monetary Fund (IMF) defines globalisation as the trend towards increasing interdependence of national economies, through increasing volumes of cross-border transactions in commodities and capital (IMF, 1997). It is a process that is integrative in nature and one which has engendered the convergence of national economies into a 'supranational economy'.

This trend was itself induced by two interrelated trends:

1. First, this revolution in network-based technology has eroded physical barriers to market entry, producing an increase in transnational production and trade in products as well as exchanges of capital.
2. Second, allied to this, the process has been accelerated by the concurrent diffusion of the macro-politico-economic ideology of liberalism, because liberalism informs policy and results in liberalisation or deregulation, effectively lowering regulatory entry barriers and further advancing market integration.

However, these dry economic explanations hardly begin to convey the cataclysmic power of this force, its ramifications, nor how consequentially emotive this issue has become.

IN THE BEGINNING

With the collapse of the Berlin Wall, the 1990s heralded this age of globalisation and the economies of both the developing and developed world burgeoned. As economic integration advanced, it seemed to promise an end to the eternal quest for greater prosperity for all, and the doctrine of neo-liberalism was embraced the world over.

There is substantial statistical data on the corresponding increase in global output growth over the period that globalisation has advanced. For example, according to the United Nations (1998), global output growth (with purchasing power parity-based weights) climbed from 1.1% in 1991 to 4.1% in 1997. Growth rates in the developing economies averaged 5.8%.

Nowhere was this globalisation effect more pronounced than in the markets for money. The statistic that most vividly illustrates the astonishing growth in international capital flows is that of average daily turnover in the international foreign exchange markets. The Bank for International Settlements (BIS) reported in 1998 that this figure was an estimated US$1.5 trillion,[1] which represented a 30% increase on the previous year.

THE OMNIPOTENT

As the volumes of capital traded in the international markets grew to dwarf the total value of OECD exports, as well as their daily equivalent GDP, and to exceed the combined value of their central bank reserves by several multiples, people began to perceive danger. Implicit in these ratios is an erosion of state supremacy that has periodically been made explicit. Black Wednesday, the occasion of Britain's expulsion from the European Exchange Rate Mechanism (ERM) in 1992, which resulted from a speculative assault on the currency, is often cited as the first evidence of a reversal in the balance of power. This was not the last such demonstration, especially in the more vulnerable emerging market regions, and there has been a growing sense that governments are now unable to sanction the markets in order to defend their economic interests. Instead, the markets, potentially divorced from economic fundamentals and indifferent to broader social concerns, are now able to sanction governments.

EXTREME VOLATILITY

This issue of power and control may have been negated, however, were it not for the markets' susceptibility to failure. On the eve of the millennium, the global financial markets were struck by a crisis of systemic proportions,

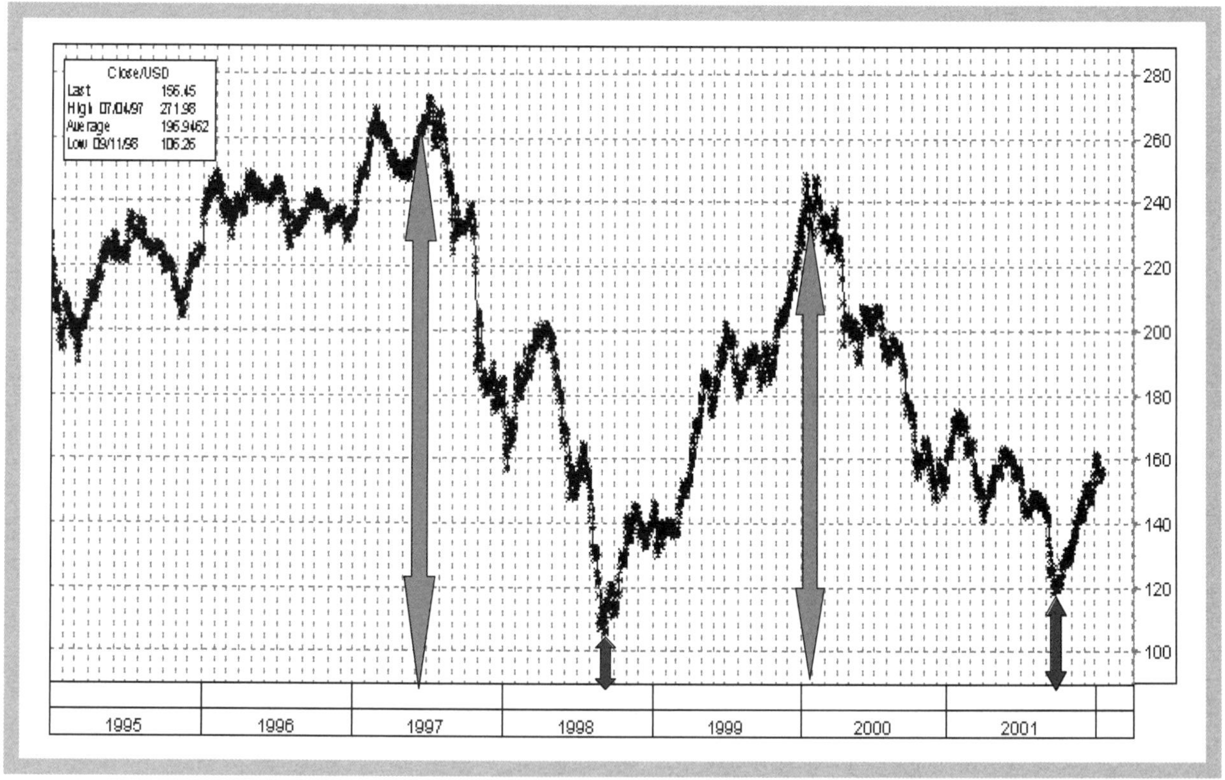

Figure 2.1 FTSE all world all emerging index: 1995–2001

Source: Bloomberg, 2002. L.P. All rights reserved. Reprinted with permission. Visit www.Bloomberg.com

exposing their fragility. The extreme volatility in the markets during 1997 and 1998 was virtually without precedent, as was the virulence with which the crisis affected successive regions. In fleeing hazardous markets, investors fuelled the very crisis from which they fled – as with every financial crisis since the 17th-century tulip crisis, greed mutated into fear, inciting a panic attack. The difference is that, this time, the crisis was experienced on a global scale.

The global financial system may be envisaged as a gigantic circulatory system, sucking capital into the centre and pumping it out to the periphery, either directly, in the form of credits and portfolio investments, or indirectly, through multinational corporations (Soros, 1998). The crisis punctured the arteries. As emerging markets were drained of the capital on which they are highly dependent, the effects were transmitted to their economies. One-third of the global economy entered 1999 in or on the verge of recession, and, apart from Japan, most of the distress was concentrated in the developing world.

In the aftermath of the crisis, 'taming the anarchy of markets that globalisation has unleashed' commanded the attention of the world's top policymakers (Mandel and Foust, 1998, p. 47). Rendering the global financial system safer hit the agenda of every financial and economic forum from Davos to the IMF, the World Bank, G7 and the Basle Committee's AGMs. The G22 was expressly convened for this purpose. Every prominent economist and politician, including Bill Clinton and Tony Blair, opined on the matter. The think tanks at the central institutions of the global economy dedicated themselves to designing a blueprint for a new monetary system – premised on the assumption that the promotion of discipline and the accurate pricing of risk in capital allocation decisions will increase market efficiency and avert failure. The most tangible output of this to date has been the second iteration of the Basle Capital Accord – which has encountered strong resistance from the banking sector.

Yet while all this postulating has been going on, the reversal of surplus capital flows continued unabated, precipitating a bubble-effect in the mature economies. Baby-boomers' – either 'punting' their own capital, or fronted by institutional investors – having fled the Tigers, frantically sought the next high-yield destination and hit upon Silicon Valley. Dot-com mania set in, and with the inevitable bursting of the NASDAQ bubble we have once again been left teetering on the brink of worldwide recession (Figure 2.1).

THE CAUSES OF CRISES

Financial market crises, essentially attributable to inefficiency, or the failure to optimally allocate scarce resources, are directly related to the causes and effects of the globalisation of capital markets.

The virtuous cycle period, which precipitated the last emerging market crisis of the 20th century, was distinguished by external financial sector liberalisation and strong macro-economic performance. In mature markets, low interest rates and high liquidity conditions prevailed. There was a proliferation of institutional investors and a willingness to diversify portfolios to boost yields. This led to surges in private capital inflows to emerging markets. Net (private) inflows (to emerging markets) for the six-year period 1990–96 totalled approximately US$1040 billion, according to the IMF (approximately 3% of their GDP in that period), of which Asia and Latin America received 40% and 30% respectively (Adams et al., 1998). The problems developed when supply began to outstrip demand.

Surplus Capital and the Failure of Market Discipline

John Maynard Keynes is credited with the proposition that recessions are essentially caused by the propensity to save being greater than the propensity to invest. Surplus capital causes asset inflation, and the propensity of the world's mature economies to save, and the resultant persistent savings surplus, is a major contributing factor to the oversupply of capital. Pre-crisis Japan, for example, was unable to profitably invest the 30–35% of its own GDP that it saved, let alone absorb the capital that flowed in from external investors (Smithers, 1999).

Post-crisis surplus savings aggravated by the flight to quality then caused the US and, to a lesser extent, European equity markets to become hugely overvalued. In 1998, Alan Greenspan, chairman of the US Federal Reserve, perturbed by the abrupt reversals, warned that the US financial system, as a result of this panic-stricken flight from risk, could plunge the US and perhaps the world into unnecessary recession (*Financial Times*, 1998). This caution was echoed in many quarters. Yet dot-com euphoria took over and the pattern of greed and folly was repeated.

In the relatively brief period between 1997 and 1999, world stock market capitalisation climbed from about US$11 trillion to over US$30 trillion. At the peak of 'I-mania' some of the NASDAQ 'megacaps', for example, had P:E ratios approaching 1000 (or, since earnings were negative, multiples of infinity). Yet, by the end of the first quarter of 2001, some three trillion had been wiped off the nominal value of America's stock markets (equivalent, though not comparable to, 30% of the country's GDP), and across the globe, paper loss amounted to as much as US$7 trillion (*The Economist*, 2001a). By the end of 2001, the majority of the Internet companies listed on the NASDAQ stock exchange were trading at 90% less than their IPO price. The inevitable bear now stalking Wall Street has placed the world economy in an extremely precarious position. Furthermore, recessions set off by asset price falls do not respond readily to interest rate cuts, because the cost of equity and debt capital rises sharply anyway, as stock prices plummet and a credit crunch sets in.

Basically, the oversupply of yield-seeking capital, and the concomitant voracious appetite for risk, induces a breakdown in market discipline and consequent price distortions. There are two sides to every contract, and on both the borrower and lender – asset and liability – side of the balance sheet, there is ample evidence of this gross imprudence. The net exporters of capital are in no position to simply castigate the net importers for their profligacy.

At the height of the literal Asian gold rush, terms and conditions of borrowers' access to international capital markets had improved dramatically. Credit ratings and terms were highly favourable. Yield spreads on Brady bonds fell, from an average of 1100 basis points over comparable maturity US Treasury bonds in 1990, to 350 basis points by September 1997, and average maturity on new emerging market Eurobond issues climbed from 4.4 years in 1991 to 8 years in 1996 (Adams et al., 1998).

This, in turn, propelled the emergence of large unhedged foreign exchange exposures by domestic borrowers in emerging markets. Asian corporations, in particular, incentivised by relatively higher domestic interest rates and lulled into a false sense of security by ostensibly stable pegged currencies were able to issue large amounts of securities denominated in foreign currencies in addition to acquiring foreign currency syndicated loans from both domestic and foreign banks. The perils of excessive borrowing, especially in foreign currencies, under unsustainable exchange rate regimes and short term, has gained wide recognition in the wake of the crisis.

On the lenders' side, the present Basle capital adequacy standards proved a crude measure of banks' health. For example, since the risk weighting of a loan to a borrower domiciled outside the OECD increases from 0% to 100%, and since short-term lending requires less provisioning, international banks exhibited a tendency to bypass the Basle Accord, by securitising their debt portfolio, and engaging in excessive short-term lending. Of the US$380 billion in international bank loans outstanding to Asia at the end of 1997, 60% had a maturity of less than one year. Thus, the objective of the proposed new standards is to remedy the distortions that induce industrial economies' creditors to indulge in such reckless behaviour in emerging markets.

SPECULATION AND FAILURE OF MARKET DISCIPLINE

Allied to this, is the role of speculation in financial crises. Speculation, engaged in by proprietary trading desks of banks and by hedge funds in particular, has also become one of the most controversial issues in international finance. The value of speculators resides in their willingness to trade risk and provide counterparties to those who are risk averse. All markets are a balance between those in whose interest it is for prices to go up and those in whose interest it is for prices to go down. The speculator is essentially the fulcrum; by assuming a middle position, the (contrary) speculator provides two-way liquidity and a buffer for end-users.

Most hedge funds represent themselves as arbitrageurs; that is, they profit from assets whose prices are temporarily out of line with their fundamental values, by selling overpriced and buying underpriced assets respectively. This is termed market-neutral arbitrage and, in theory, increases market efficiency in the process. However, since opportunities for pure or risk-free arbitrage are extremely limited, most hedge funds' activities are termed expectations arbitrage and incur at least an element of speculation. Julian Robertson, head of Tiger Securities, one of the largest hedge funds globally, concedes that there is no distinction between arbitrage and speculation; that it is a continuum (*The Economist*, 1998).

The case that can be mounted against speculative activity is as follows. First, many hedge funds are classified as highly leveraged institutions, that is, their minimal capital is deployed as leverage collateral, which enables them to gear up immense positions in a given market and literally negate the fundamentals. Short selling on credit or with borrowed scrip (share and bond certificates) is frequently reprehended as empowering speculators to realise their predictions by artificially inflating supply. This power is reinforced through other market weaknesses – by signalling an escalation in selling (albeit potentially non-fundamental), speculators can provoke a genuine investor bail-out to depress asset values further.

Speculators, by definition, are not fundamentally interested in the commodities in which they trade; they do not care whether prices go up or down, and profit from both booms and busts. Moreover, the vested interest they have in volatility, via options, provides them with yet another motive and opportunity for market manipulation.

Second, the imprudence of their capital structures makes hedge funds vulnerable to insolvency, but the extent of banks' exposure to these institutions also makes them prime candidates for bail-outs due to systemic risk. Long Term Capital Management (LTCM), the now notorious hedge fund founded by two Nobel laureates in economics and a former vice chairman of the US Federal Reserve, which became insolvent in September 1998, had liabilities valued at 50 times its equity. The rescue by the US Federal Reserve was reportedly orchestrated by the banks that had lent to it. Alan Greenspan confirmed in his testimony to Congress that had this fund gone bankrupt and liquidated its positions, it would have exacerbated the affected banks' losses and rendered many of them technically insolvent. This, he stated, would certainly have inflicted serious damage on the market and could potentially have impaired the economies of many nations.

Thus, while the jury may be out on the relative costs and benefits associated with speculation, there is at least enough evidence to suggest that they may be guilty of exacerbating ill-discipline and price distortions.

At the centre of this debate on the causes of crises is the Washington Consensus. The

IMF presents the Washington Consensus as a set of neo-liberal economic policies that include trade liberalisation, financial liberalisation, deregulation, privatisation, promotion of inward direct investment, a competitive exchange rate to promote exports, fiscal discipline, and fiscal and monetary policies to tame inflation. Neo-liberalism essentially holds that free markets will discipline governments and produce optimal economic performance. Basic to this orthodoxy is the assumption that markets are efficient – a serious flaw. Markets are certainly more efficient than governments at allocating capital, but both the dot-com-dot-bomb fiasco and the Asian crisis have exposed that capital does not always flow to the most productive investments, information flows are imperfect, markets can be rigged, and investors do not always behave rationally. Capital flowed into emerging economies and then Silicon Valley with little attention to the creditworthiness of the borrowers or the real value of the assets and essentially amounted to a breakdown in pricing discipline in global markets. Washington orthodoxy needs to acknowledge that market failure is endemic in the global financial system.

Capital Mobility and Instability

Second, capital mobility – the fact that vast inflows can suddenly become vast outflows – causes instability.

Once the systemic weaknesses in the emerging markets were exposed (including high rates of unproductive investment, unsustainable asset price increases, high leveraging, lack of transparency, and weak supervisory capacities), the vicious cycle was set in motion – a period characterised by the abrupt cessation or at least severe curtailment of access to international capital markets, followed by reversals of capital flows. This caused large domestic asset price adjustments, which induced large exchange and interest rate adjustments, which induced severe banking sector stress and culminated in decelerated or negative economic growth rates in the affected regions.

The extreme turbulence in emerging market currencies during the crisis was virtually without precedent. Average volatility increased by a factor of 10 in the second half of 1997, compared with the same period for the previous year. When the afflicted Asian currencies reached their low points in January 1998, the Indonesian rupiah had fallen by 81%, the Thai baht by 55%, the Malaysian ringgit by 46%, and the Korean won by 55% (Adams et al., 1998).

As a result, 1997 saw the first major reductions in private capital flows to emerging markets in a decade and a general re-evaluation of emerging market risk. Private capital flows to the four Asian emerging markets in crisis declined by almost US$100 billion during 1997. According to the Institute for International Finance, net capital flows to the 29 largest emerging markets slumped from US$308 billion in 1996 to US$242 billion in 1997 and US$160 billion in 1998. The impact was most acute in the equity markets. The International Finance Corporation's emerging markets composite index fell by 24% in 1998 and underperformed the Standard & Poor's index by over a third. The worst performer was Russia where the market fell by 83%.

During economic crises, the sudden outflow of foreign capital leaves domestic policymakers with two equally unpalatable options: either they must raise interest rates substantially to defend their exchange rates, or they must let their exchange rates collapse. Both policies are highly detrimental to the economy. Capital outflows effectively deprive policymakers of the ability to stimulate the economy through lower interest rates when necessary.

In the open markets of the world today, the free flows of volatile, short-term, 'hot' money can destabilise and exact large tolls on developing economies. It seems that the price of freedom is risk and volatility.

CAPITAL MOBILITY AND CONTAGION

Allied to this issue of capital mobility, in the broader context of globalisation, is that of contagion. A key feature of the recent emerging market crisis was the existence of contagion or spillover effects. In fact, the scale of the crisis is widely purported to have confirmed the suspicion that relatively localised crises can now be transmitted to all emerging markets.

While certain fundamental macro-economic factors help to explain which countries experience crises, there remains an unexplained correlation in the timing of crises. Three channels have recently been proposed to explain the observed correlations between crises in distinct markets:

- *Trade flows and competitiveness effects.* A depreciation in one country will cause a deterioration in the competitiveness of those counties with whom it trades most or with whom it directly competes in third markets. This, in turn, makes the currencies of the affected countries susceptible to speculative attacks. During the recent crisis, the trade partner effect was demonstrated by commodity price dynamics. East Asian economies are major importers of raw materials, so the economic slump in the region caused considerable deflation in the price of oil and other commodities. *The Economist*'s commodity price index fell by 30% between mid-1997 and mid-1998, to its lowest level in real terms for over 25 years. This severely hurt the more vulnerable commodity producers reliant on primary commodities for export income.
- *Financial linkages.* This is demonstrated by the dynamics of three major emerging markets in the recent crisis. Prior to the crisis, Korean banks, in order to maintain

profitability, accumulated substantial amounts of high-yield Brazilian and Russian government debt. Brazilian banks simultaneously invested substantially in Russian debt. When Korean banks experienced severe liquidity problems, they began selling off their Brazilian and Russian assets, leading to falls in asset prices in these markets and knock-on sales of Russian debt by Brazilian investors. Thus, if markets are insufficiently deep, that is, sales by one group of investors cause price changes, the pattern of security holdings can lead to shocks in one country being propagated into other countries, regardless of fundamentals.

- *The 'wake-up call'.* According to this hypothesis, if one country experiences major problems, then such an event will induce investors to re-evaluate other countries. If investors identify the same weaknesses in other countries, their credit ratings are reduced and the crisis spreads. The best measure of this re-evaluation of risk is the increase in average yield on emerging market government bonds, from three percentage points above US Treasuries in mid-1997 to 15 points by mid-1998. Higher costs of capital inhibit growth and inflate government debt-servicing costs.

Information Asymmetries and Distortions in the Price of Risk

Asymmetries in the distribution of information are one of the primary causes of distortions of risk measurement and pricing and, therefore, the misallocation of resources. The issue of access to accurate data, in both the public and private sector, levels of disclosure and transparency is a recurring theme in international finance.

Evidence of market opacity abound: Thailand and South Korea's secret sales of foreign exchange reserves in the forward market made a mockery of their official reserves. South Korea may, speculatively, have avoided an exchange rate crisis if investors had had more accurate data on its short-term debt burden, and Indonesia's economy may not have submerged if its private corporations had been obliged to disclose their unhedged foreign liabilities. Given a macro-economic environment in which critical information was conspicuous by its absence and where corruption was rife, the US$500 billion invested in the region between 1993 and 1997 seems highly imprudent. International investors were apparently oblivious to the lack of transparency and the regulatory shortcomings.

INFORMATION ASYMMETRIES AND MASS PSYCHOLOGY

A lack of information not only partially causes skewed valuations, but plays an incendiary role in turning a correction into an excessive overcorrection. Many analysts have observed the dynamics of 'herding', in which investors are importantly influenced by the behaviour of other investors. Such herding behaviour is typically most prevalent in situations in which there are deficiencies in information and the behaviour of creditors is viewed as revealing important information about borrowers' creditworthiness. The withdrawal of one capital supplier may provoke an unwarranted stampede by others.

Herding is clearly an instinct that speculators would try to exploit. It may also exacerbate contagion. Due to a lack of information, investors cannot adequately distinguish between the financial positions of different borrowers. Thus, there is a tendency in times of market stress to assume the worst-case scenario and rapidly adjust portfolio positions on borrowers that are regarded as being in similar conditions – such as all emerging markets or all dot-coms.

The relative weighting of fundamental and non-fundamental causes of contagion is of consequence because it implies very different policies. The assumption that crises are spread predominantly by a 'demonstration effect' presumes that investor sentiment changes and confidence is lost due to changes in perceptions about the creditworthiness of borrowers that are independent of fundamental factors. This infers that relatively healthy economies can suddenly become seriously ill, not because of some internal development, but because of an external shock, in the form of a withdrawal of international investment. The term 'relative' refers to economies that do exhibit mild systemic weaknesses, but are merely vulnerable, in that they may have avoided a crisis had international conditions not deteriorated to such an extent.

On these grounds, it has been claimed that the risk of infection, to which open economies expose themselves, outweighs the benefits of liberalisation. Second, this notion of contagion also influences the debate on helping the sick among the emerging economies to recover. If such contagion exists, helping the sick also helps the healthy to ward off the disease in the future. Measures to curb infection become an international public good, serving a much broader interest than that of merely bailing out the borrowers and lenders most directly affected. However, those who claim that fundamental factors are invariably the cause of financial crisis, reject such public-good policies due to the increased risk of 'moral hazard' or imprudence due to the existence of a public safety-net.

This type of dynamic relates to the very psyche of markets. A great many 'eco-psychologists' have delved into this collective psyche in a bid to understand the behaviour of markets. In *Manias, Panics and Crashes* Kindleberger (1989) contends that markets function as a collective and at a very base level: contagious emotionalism prevails over rationalism, causing cycles of collective overoptimism, risk propensity and euphoria to alternate with cycles of collective overpessimism, risk aversion and panic, which degenerate into herd-like stampedes. His thesis concludes that markets are inherently manic, volatile and inclined to wild cyclical fluctuations. Bloch (1997) refers to the classic works on mass psychology, including Freud et al.'s *Crowds and Power* to explain cyclicality, and contends that markets are in essence nothing more than measures of mass psychology, oscillating between greed, fear and sheer boredom. Bloch holds that the essence of the speculative booms and troughs of the business cycle is a 'psychologically perceived pseudo-reality which over-rides the fundamentals underlying the trend'. Soros's theories on reflexivity and fallibility expounded in *The Crisis of Global Capitalism* (Soros, 1998) also pivot on this issue.

The so-called linguistic dimension is critical to the phenomenon of mass psychology. The financial and economic media tend to emphasise sensationalism rather than providing balanced and rational analysis, which provokes the mass psyche, reinforcing trends and intensifying the destabilising effects thereof.

With reference to the preceding review on speculation, for example, it is interesting to note the asymmetries in media reportage on speculation. The case for the defence (because it is a trial by media) is presented on the basis of reason and facts, which contrasts starkly with the hype associated with the anti-speculation lobby. Mahathir Mohammed, Malaysia's Prime Minister, for example, demonises speculators as 'the agents of evil' (Chote, 1998), and Jacques Chirac, President of France, indicts them as the 'AIDS of the world economy' (*The Economist*, 1995b, p. 5). Lascelles (1998, p. 42) describes them as 'sinister figures lurking in the shadows ... whose evil machinations bring markets crashing down, enriching the few and impoverishing the many'. The fact that he is being derisive hardly matters. Given the relative power of emotionalism over rationalism in mass psychology, whether speculators are guilty as charged or not is irrelevant; they are represented (or misrepresented) as such in highly sensationalistic terms and are judged accordingly. The very public failures by governments to defend their currencies against speculative attacks, and the high costs thereof, in terms of depleted reserves and devaluation, tend to add weight to the claims, regardless of whether the currencies were overvalued in the first place.

IDEOLOGY AND GLOBALISATION

This brings us full circle to the very issue of globalisation and, specifically, the globalisation of the capital markets. Political sensitivity levels are running high. A 1998 IMF report entitled *The Demise of the Nation State* unequivocally concludes that globalisation will, in time, reduce the degrees of freedom and power of national governments (Tanzi, 1998). However, in the realm of political ideology, the language tends to inflammatory rhetoric. The intensification of anti-liberal sentiment is vividly illustrated in the following chronological excerpts from *The Economist*. In 1995 (b, p. 5) the journal paraphrased the following ominous warning intoned by the anti-liberalists:

> Beware the insidious new enemy of the democratic state that has been secretly amassing power: the electronic army of currency, equity and bond traders. Market vigilantes are now judge and jury of economic policy, meeting out cruel punishments to those they deem non-conformist. In the economic arms race, governments' cache has been plundered.

In 1997 (p. 57) the anti-liberalists' prose had become apocalyptic:

> Globalisation will widen inequality, exacerbate poverty and increasingly lead to social exclusion. These costs will mount even as globalisation succeeds in its own right, at a time when government's capacity to respond is draining away. Its failure to act will undermine the foundations of the democratic state, challenging its very legitimacy. As the remorseless advance of market forces plunges capitalism into a new crisis, Marx will have the last laugh after all.

The orthodox libertarians vehemently deny these allegations, not only on the basis of reason and fact, but on emotive grounds as well. First, they refute the charges of infringement on the powers of the state. *The Economist* (1995a), in an article entitled 'The Myth of the Powerless State', submits that the emasculation of the state is a fallacy. It asserts that governments have actually seized more economic power in the last century than ever before. The statistic cited as evidence of state encroachment is the growth in state share of output in the industrial economies, from less than one-tenth at the turn of the last century, to over half by 1996. In a subsequent survey in 2001, the journal exposes the growing tax burden as another measure of this encroachment. Over the last decade, government takings as a percentage of GDP have actually grown to an average of just under 45% in the G7. Sweden's bureaucrats, at the one extreme, managed to extract 57% of GDP – a sarcastic 'savage' reduction of three percentage points since 1990. In the US – purportedly the nadir of 'private affluence and public squalor' – Uncle Sam managed to collect an average of US$30,000 per household adding up to roughly US$3 trillion last year. As the journal takes pains to point out; 'the depredation of rampant capitalists on the overall ability [of governments] to collect taxes and do good works are invisible to the naked eye' (*The Economist*, 2001b).

Second, free marketeers invariably substitute the insurgents' assumption of a Platonic state, in which government is perceived as the selfless servant of the public good, with the assumption of a leviathan state that acts in its own self-interest. They therefore perceive moderate shrinkage of state supremacy under duress as a positive development. And, in countering the anti-market backlash, they too freely resort to populist rhetoric. *The Economist* (1997, p. 56) concludes a report on 'The Future of the State' with the following incendiary statement:

> In the West, it seems, original sin has been superseded; instead people come into the world with an original burden of obligation to social enterprise, a debt to their fellow citizens that is not of their own making and that can never be discharged ... It is a kind of bondage. It augurs well for big government.

SUMMARY

In the final analysis, financial crises are essentially caused by the dual effects of capital market inefficiency and capital mobility. Inefficiency, that is unproductive investment, or the failure to optimally allocate resources, is attributable to the oversupply of capital (due to surplus savings over investment) and the lack of perfect information (one of the preconditions of market efficiency). Capital mobility is consequent upon the liberalisation and globalisation of capital markets. Because capital flows are reversible, the distortion of the forces of supply and demand, and therefore risk and asset prices, is eventually corrected, or overcorrected – again because of imperfect information.

Contagion or the spreading of crises relates to globalisation and the causes of financial and economic crises on two levels. The interdependence of economies is consequent upon financial and physical sector liberalisation. Crises in the financial sector are transmitted to the real economy and then retransmitted from one economy to the next, via financial or economic linkages. Second, capital mobility and lack of transparency provide the impetus for investor herding and stampeding, which accelerates transmission.

It may be surmised that speculators exploit this to a certain extent by relying on the lack of transparency and capital mobility in order to provoke herd-like stampedes and thereby deflate asset prices to realise a profit. The shock waves from speculation, in particular, tend to be transmitted from market to market. In this way, speculators capitalise on the deficiencies in the system that cause crises and are themselves a cause of crises or the escalation of crises.

Finally, as capital markets are subject to failure, the gains from short-term capital mobility may not compensate for the risks and costs. In the absence of perfect information, mass psychology substitutes: investors tend to panic, stampeding herd-like in and out of markets on rumour, at considerable cost to the real economy.

Despite the conflicting evidence and difficulties in separating correlation from causality, it does seem clear that liberalisation and globalisation produce real economic growth, if unevenly distributed, but these gains have been at least partially offset by the ever-increasing amplitude and frequency of the business cycle or wave. The IMF, for example, has used regression analysis to measure the empirical relationship between financial liberalisation and financial fragility in 53 countries over a 15-year period. A positive, significant coefficient indicates that financial liberalisation increases the probability of a banking crisis, especially if the institutional environment is weak. In the survey, almost three-quarters of its members had experienced significant banking sector crises over this period (Demirguc-Kunt and Detragiache, 1998; Lindgren et al., 1996). The World Bank has reported over 90 severe banking sector crises over the last two decades, almost all of which were accompanied by recessions (Caprio and Klingebiel, 1996).

FOOTNOTE: REGIONALISM

Regionalism is a countervailing trend to that of globalisation and is an inevitable response to the phenomenon of globalisation and intensified international competition. Regional integration is now a salient feature of the world political and economic order. It is positioned between the extremes of unilateralism and universalism, and may be defined as mutual co-operation among states, based on democratic and free-market principles, for the purpose of region building or development. Power and identity are therefore migrating from the national to the regional level.

There are now over 80 regional trade agreements in existence, granting members preferential access to one another's markets. The process of regionalisation has also led to the formation of the Triad: the world's three most powerful regional economic superblocs – the European Union (EU), the North American Free Trade Agreement (NAFTA) grouping, and the Asia-Pacific Economic Co-operation (APEC) grouping.

Regionalism has, however, also come under fire from a number of fronts. First, it negates comparative advantage and causes inefficient trade diversion through preferential tariff structures. Second, regionalism impedes globalisation and liberalisation. Although such initiatives provide excluded countries with an incentive to liberalise, the tendency to discriminate through external protectionist tariffs is anti-liberal and likely to lead to inter-trading bloc competition. The Big Brother phenomenon or inclination of the Triad states to protect and advance the interests of their respective satellite states (MERCUSOR in NAFTA's case and the CEE states in the EU's case) is at the expense of peripheral developing economies outside their jurisdiction, including African states. The theoretical and empirical evidence on the issue is, however, inconclusive.

The most advanced regional system to date is the EU. The process of economic integration, which began with a common market, culminated in 1999 in the conversion to a common currency by 11 member states. The launch of the euro, and the accompanying European Monetary Union (EMU), is certainly unprecedented and potentially risky, and the success or failure of this experiment will have major ramifications for the evolution of the global political and economic system.

In conclusion, globalisation has imposed certain costs on individual nations, in the form of increased pressure to become super-competitive at the expense of social interests, and constraints on the autonomy of governments in policy formulation. Regionalism is perceived as a means of meeting the competitiveness demands while minimising the diminution of national sovereignty. However, the direct transference of power to the regional level is strongly resisted by many nation states. In addition, the acceleration of economic integration is also perceived by many as artificial and therefore liable to fail. The success or failure of the EMU will have major repercussions for the credibility of regional solutions to global problems.

CONCLUSION

Over time, the issue of globalisation has become increasingly controversial. To its fiercest critics, globalisation – the march of international capitalism – is a force for oppression, exploitation and injustice; to its proponents, it is the most effective force for reducing poverty known to mankind. Orthodox liberals, clutching their copies of *The Sovereign Individual* and *The Borderless World*[2] like neo-Bibles, are juxtaposed with insurrectionists' indictments on capitalism as 'Darwinian savagery', and the escalation in riotous violence at each successive gathering of the central institutions of the global economy; the IMF, the World Bank and the G7.

Furthermore, it is clear that in targeting the World Trade Centre on September 11 2001, the terrorists were striving not merely to kill the maximum number of Americans, but to destroy one of the West's most potent symbols of capitalism. The links between the perils of globalisation and anti-western rage are more than tenuous. The end of the Cold War era was hoped to be the end of the bipolar world-view that dominated it, and the emergence of a new a multipolar world-view, in which geographical contours would replace ideological ones. Sadly, it seems, we have reverted to ideological schisms. *The Economist* (2001c), in its inimitable derisive tone, laments this change in perception:

> Is there no limit to the crimes for which globalisation must be held to account? Not only does it oppress the labourers of the rich West, undermine the welfare state, emasculate democracy, despoil the environment, and entrench poverty in the third world; we all knew that already. In addition, we now find, it is a utopian scheme for global ideological conquest – like Stalinism – minus the compassion. Truly, the idea that people should be left free to trade with each other in peace must be the most wicked and dangerous doctrine ever devised.

Predicting where this will end is beyond the scope of this book. Whether the intrinsically hegemonic nature of global institutions and the geopolitical vulnerability of those on the periphery of the protection of the Triad will serve to marginalise them further, or whether liberty will lead to greater democratisation and equality of prosperity, is unknown. However, predicting the future structure and dynamics of financial markets must be undertaken in the context of this broader issue of globalisation and the globalisation of the markets for money.

At a minimum, it warrants noting that while so many cite the dot-bomb debacle as evidence – an exposé – of the Internet's relative insignificance as a medium, it is ironic that it is in fact proof of its power. It is the Internet that liberated and mobilised capital to such an extent, that gave birth to the day-trader phenomenon, that led to a re-enactment of the 1929 stock-market-cum-race-course, that ultimately caused the crash. The fact that the trading occurred in an electronic marketplace, the NASDAQ, and in primarily e-businesses only makes the irony sweeter.

Notes

1 Reduced to US$1.1 trillion per day by 2002 due to emergence of the EMU.

2 Davidson, J.D. and Rees-Mogg, W.R. (1997): *The Sovereign Individual*, Simon & Schuster; Ohmae, K. (1999): *The Borderless World*, revised edn, New York: HarperCollins.

Acknowledgement

This chapter is an updated excerpt from Liebenberg, L. (1999) *Implications for South Africa of the Redesign of the International Monetary System*, University of the Witwatersrand, Faculty of Management, South Africa, Johannesburg.

CHAPTER 3

DERIVED EFFECTS

To return to the structure of this hypothesis, globalisation is itself but one of the seven generic trends induced by the interconnected technological advances discussed in Chapter 1, and the remainder are reviewed briefly below. The disproportionately lengthy preceding discussion on the issues stemming from globalisation, although something of a digression, is nevertheless warranted, since globalisation is the most significant of the trends – to the future of wholesale financial markets and the networked economy itself. It encompasses and precipitates all others. Essentially, as localised, geopolitical markets in every sector of the economy have internationalised, a number of other trends have emerged.

NETWORK EFFECTS

From Divergent Industries to Convergence

In the growing tertiary sector of the economy, products and services are generally intangible. The so-called knowledge industries' primary asset is knowledge, which of course doesn't really exist in any corporeal sense. Intellectual capital resides in the organisation's human and structural capital (its computer systems). As a result, in this digital age, almost any 'product' can be reduced to bits and bytes, ones and zeros. Consequently, a blurring of the boundaries between previously distinct vertical industries has begun to occur. A spate of mergers, acquisitions, joint ventures and other alliance structures have been announced recently – essentially in support of strategies to encroach on territory previously deemed beyond of the outer limits of core competence, synergy, and sound diversification – from telco-technology sector convergence, which spawned the Internet, to old media-new media convergence, à la Times Warner-AOL, retail banking to retailing and vice versa. Across the board, there has been this realignment of industries to support a more hybrid structure.

From Intermediated Markets to Disintermediation

The Internet's unparalleled advantages as a visual (data as opposed to voice) medium to connect and facilitate fully or semi-automated bidirectional exchange of information, bandwidth constraints notwithstanding, represent the greatest threat to intermediaries in every market. It took no time for sellers to advance from one-way 'brochureware' or content-based marketing sites – the proverbial shop window – to two-way transactional sites – the actual shop – and hence to potentially bypassing the middlemen. And while the rate at which this disintermediation process is occurring is slower than predicted, adoption rates of new technologies (from the telephone, television, telefacsimile and so on) are accelerating. The efficiency gains that will accrue to both buyers and sellers will eventually entice them away from their estate agents, travel agents, stock brokers and so on. The Internet will eventually serve to abridge supply chains in every industry, engendering 'frictionless' markets. The classic *Death of a Salesman* has come to pass.

From Closed Markets to Open Markets

Allied to the above is the fact that once buyers and sellers are directly connected and are able to transact, albeit through some migration path using a hybrid intermediary or channel structure, it almost by definition creates a marketplace where trading occurs. The natural extension of this, of course, is a trend away from proprietary, closed, electronic channels from a seller to multiple buyers (the one-to-one or one-to-many model), towards non-proprietary, open markets connecting multiple buyers to multiple sellers (the many-to-many or any-to-any model).

This shift from by bilateral to multilateral interactions has partially been accelerated by the very intermediaries so endangered by this development. Agents of all types have identified that there are no barriers to prevent them from reinventing themselves as electronic intermediaries, for this process of disintermediation is in effect more about electronic reintermediation. The electronic intermediary simply substitutes more efficiently and effectively for the old middleman lodged between disconnected buyers and sellers. Subsequent to this has been a move towards consortia-owned e-markets, comprising either multiple sellers or buyers or both from the relevant industry or industries. In the multi-seller-owned model this has been christened 'co-optition', that is, competing product producers or providers now sell their brands on a common platform.

Across every industry there are a plethora of such e-markets. In the so-called B2B arena or wholesale markets, these e-markets or exchanges tend to be either horizontal or vertical. Horizontal markets trade in so-called generic goods, that is, goods purchased by all industries, such as stationery, and are known as indirect materials or MRO (maintenance, repair and operations) procurement sites. Ariba and Commerce One are the two dominant MRO sites currently. Vertical markets trade in goods specific to an industry and are known as direct materials sites, that is, component materials procured from suppliers in the product production or manufacturing process, the costs of which form part of the cost of sales item on the income statement. Two prominent examples are Covisant, an automotive industry supply-chain optimisation initiative owned by a consortium of manufacturers, and Quadrem, a prominent mining industry hub.

In the B2C arena, the consumer or retail markets, the proliferation of hubs or portals across single or multiple product segments is staggering. Certain portals, often the ISP or browser-linked portals, such as Yahoo!, or the pure shopping malls, sell a range of retail products from a range of retailers. Others, like a shop, focus on one product and sell a range of competing brands, or focus on a specific need and sell a range of core and complementary products to meet that need. For example, a motoring portal might sell the models of a variety of makes, plus vehicle finance and insurance from a number of banks and insurers, plus other value-added services such as AA membership, online motoring magazine subscriptions and so on. All these virtual models co-exist, just as they do in the real world. However, the attractiveness of the open market to the buy-side is undeniable – in terms of the ability to perform product and price comparisons at a single location, and thereby eliminate the traditional price sensitivity versus time or convenience trade-off. It is probably the buy-side who will continue to promote this trend. While, once again, the first generation attempts at these e-markets proved premature – encountering very low market receptiveness – eventual preference for this model is inevitable.

Finally, it warrants noting that there is nothing ostensibly prohibiting or inhibiting a B2B2C or end-to-end hub, whereby, for example, an automative hub enables trade between manufactures and both their suppliers and their customers; however, this has not really materialised to date. Dell, for example, has effectively accomplished this on a proprietary basis, to the extent that a customer can define a specification online and activate a fully JIT-configured production process. However, internal supply-chain integration systems, even those extended to the end-user distribution channel, should not be confused with open industry markets. There are no equivalents in this space, probably for the simple reason that the nature of the transactions on the volume-value continuum are so polarised.

From Fixed to Dynamic Pricing

The next natural extension in this re-evolution of markets is the trend away from fixed pricing – what has become known as catalogue pricing in e-jargon – to dynamic pricing or the generic auction model.

With buyers and sellers now directly connected and (in terms of the purchasing decision-making process) with buyers empowered to compare the prices of the products from multiple suppliers (and to make a choice on the basis of price-sensitivity relative to other factors, such as quality), pricing has become appreciatively more transparent. As the level of transparency has increased, so has the degree of elasticity.

As the markets, in which the buyers and sellers of a commodity trade, become more open, by definition so do the forces of supply and demand, which are then better able to reach equlibrium. Without intermediaries' stranglehold on information, the whole price discovery process, for it is now more about discovery than formation, is more transparent and elastic. Prices are able to respond sensitively to changes in the relative levels of supply and demand, which has led to a trend away from rigid, fixed-price catalogues, towards flexible, auction-type pricing and trading models on the Internet.

For example, eBay started life as an online classifieds and quickly evolved into a C2C and now B2C auction site. Such auction sites have multiplied in recent years across the wholesale and retail markets and are particularly prevalent in the big commodities sectors such as natural gas, coal, chemicals and so on.

Clearly, the at least partial elimination of information distortions (in terms of supply, demand and, therefore, price) as open, transparent markets emerge, and the ability to dynamically set prices where fluctuating supply and demand levels intersect at the micro-level, is enhancing the efficiency of markets in the aggregate.

COMPUTATIONAL POWER EFFECTS

From Manual Processing to Automated Processing

Linking the connectivity and data exchange technologies to the data processing capacity advances, process reengineering, generally via automation, intended to optimise efficiencies, has produced phenomenal economic gains across every industry. The ability to automate both internal and external processes (such as procurement) has shifted the productivity frontier outwards at a previously inconceivable rate. Dell, Cisco and some of the other technology companies have epitomised this new super-efficient model.

From Dumb Data to Knowledge

Finally, as alluded to above, in this new age of information overload, we have also begun to acquire the capacity to turn this dump of dumb data into real knowledge and even a form of artificial intelligence. In every industry there has been some attempt at employing or deploying data screening or filtering applications, so-called info-mediation applications, to deliver only targeted marketing to the buy-side of a market, as well as data processing or computational applications, in order to gain inferences from data. Many of these data analytics systems are based on fairly advanced mathematics and have spawned the field of 'informatics' in e-jargon. In almost every instance, the inferences that these applications are designed to draw, the 'what does the data mean?', are for the purposes of enhancing predictive capacity. Much of human, and particularly commercial, endeavour is spent in crystal ball gazing, and advances in computational power are aiding and abetting that quest.

For example, in the retail market, online banking and investing has been a proverbial 'killer app', and more recently, a key differentiation strategy to avoid the discount price wars that are raging has been the provision of a host of personalised value-added services. These generally take the form of tools or toolboxes designed to enhance the consumer decision-making process and alleviate the burden of self-service, while simultaneously capitalising on the customer empowerment trend. No more force-feeding the customer, these applications are based on so-called CRM systems – 'know your customer's needs, even predict your customer's needs, so that you can better meet your customer's needs' (at least, better than the competition). Sites such as SmartMoney.com and FinancialEngines.com try to present Joe Bloggs with a balance sheet – 'my net worth' – and then help him restructure it optimally, based on his risk propensity, income, assets and liabilities and even lifecycle stage. It's a short step from there to highly targeted product marketing. Capital One Financial Corp. has emerged as a pioneer in this field and makes an interesting short case study (Fishman, 1999).

The telephones at Capital One ring more than one million times a week, and more than one million times a week, this is what happens (before a caller hears the first ring). The instant the last digit is punched, high-speed computers go into overdrive. Loaded with background information on one in seven US households and with exhaustive data about how the company's millions of customers behave, the computers identify who is calling and predict the reason for the call. After reviewing 50 options for whom to notify, the computers select the best option for each call. If a call is routed to a live agent, the computers also pull and pass along a concise but rich profile on the person who is calling. They even predict what the caller might want to buy – even though he or she isn't calling to buy anything – and then they prepare the customer-service rep to sell that item, once the original reason for the call has been addressed. All these steps – the incoming call, the data review, the analysis, the routing, and the recommending – happen in just 100 milliseconds. That's one-tenth of a second, or one-eighth of the time that elapses between the beats of a human heart.

The history of 'intelligent call routing' (a term that Capital One coined) – with its tiers of computer-enabled decision making – is a case study in how a culture of innovation can take small problems or modest ideas and turn them into breakthroughs. In this case, the problem had to do with a margin-guzzling phone bill. The solution, proposed by the techies, was founded less on pure automation to increase operational efficiency, and more on the discipline of artificial intelligence. The aim was to develop a system that could predict the reason for each call and thereby, answer the question before the caller asked it. It was a lengthy and costly process to analyse the calling patterns, to determine which events in a customer's credit-card life would predict a call, to write the decision-tree software, buy the switches and so on. However, the system went into effect in June 1998, and prediction-success rate is now at about 70%. What's more, it just keeps getting smarter. For example, if a customer routinely calls from her boyfriend's phone – the number for which is not on file at Capital One – the computer will eventually figure out that his number should be associated with her account.

A routine problem in search of a quick solution led to a new way of doing business. This calling system has become a competitive advantage for Capital One, making possible both lower costs and more efficient service, but it has spawned far more than that. For example, Capital One has applied its scientific methodology to its vast databases of customer behaviour to design new products. It now offers 6000 different kinds of credit cards, each with slightly different terms, features and benefits, and each requiring a slightly different monthly statement. It does not, however, confuse its customers with choices, but instead tries to determine what each customer wants and deliver the most simple solution. One reason why Capital One has attracted millions of customers is that it's able to present itself a little differently to each of those customers. Essentially, its scientific method of relentless testing and learning has produced a product innovation machine and enabled it to deliver mass customisation or personalisation.

Next Capital One began selling other products (auto insurance, auto loans, mortgages, cellular services, long-distance service, discount catalogues and buying-club memberships) to customers who called. Using an analysis of each customer's buying habits and demographics, the system is able to offer the right product, at the right price, to the right customer, at the right time. Today half of all new Capital One customers buy something other than a credit card within their first year as a customer. Most credit-card companies, including Capital One, have long tried to 'cross-sell' to their customers – often by using inserts in monthly statements to tout everything from calculators to cruises. Capital One only attempts inbound cross-selling, and believes that every interaction is a selling opportunity.

Finally, its systems have proved effective, not only as customer acquisition and cross-sell tools, but as a powerful retention tool as well. If you call to close your account, you'll encounter a subtle measure of what Capital One thinks of your business – because the system will do a real-time analysis of your current and potential value as a customer. People worth keeping are routed to a live, highly incentivised, retention specialist-type agent, who can offer the potential defectee a range of computer structured deals to prevent just that. People who Capital One is not unhappy to be rid of are routed to a voice-response unit and allowed to close their account using their touch-tone phone. Meanwhile, more capabilities are in development.

The company was founded in 1994 and its growth rate has been phenomenal. It now ranks among the ten largest issuers of credit cards in the United States. For Capital One's cofounders – Rich Fairbank and Nigel Morris – a pair with no previous hands-on experience in the banking industry, the credit-card business has been a grand experiment in using information technology to figure out what people want to buy and how Capital One can sell it to them. Ultimately, the secret of Capital One's success is its credo that credit cards are not banking products, but a source of information. Fairbank and Morris contend that theirs is not a credit card strategy but a revolution in marketing that can be applied to any business.

In October 2001, Capital One reported another record quarter and reaffirmed its 3% full year growth target amid the global economic slowdown. It stated that its vast database, which is now being used more to asses credit risk on consumers, once more enabled it to limit losses and lend across the range of borrowers at competitive rates, a factor analysts see as crucial in tough times.

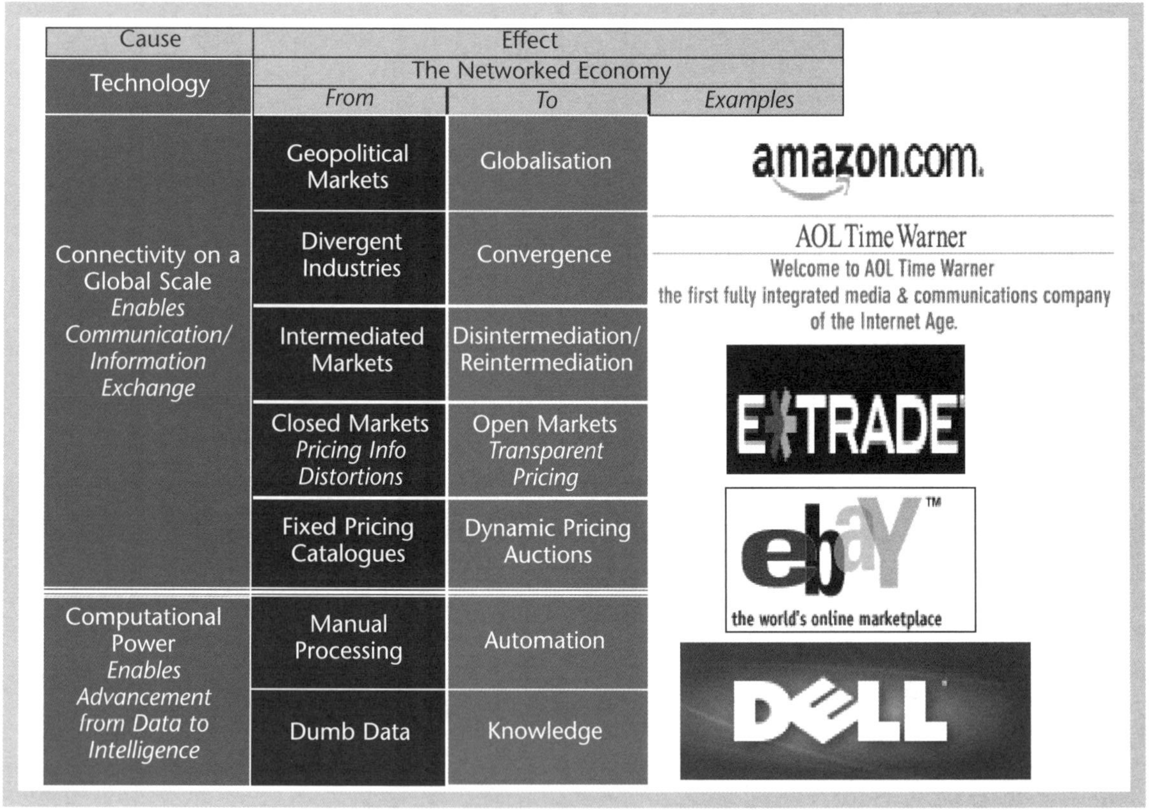

Figure 3.1 Unprecedented change: part I

Fairbank asserted that its database, offering real-time information on spending, payment and borrowing patterns provides a priceless window on the economy at a critical time. In January 2002, Capital One reported a 39% rise in its fourth quarter profits, again defying the effects of the weakening economy.

While Capital One is at the forefront of this trend, advances are being made across the board. As the vast wealth of data that is being captured and stored electronically has begun to be mined, it promises great advancements in efficiency and effectiveness across the spectrum of industries. The potential applications are endless – from forecasting to intelligent agents – and we are only beginning to explore the possibilities.

CONCLUSION

These powerful interrelated effects, represented matrix-style in Figure 3.1 below, are shaping tomorrow. Despite the volatility, as we look to the future, the underlying trend is irreversible. Electronic network-based markets and economies will come to dominate. Gartner, a prominent international technology research and consulting firm, has forecast that global B2B Internet trade, which amounted to US$433.3 billion in 2000, will exceed US$8.5 trillion by 2005. They have many cohorts. The potential of this medium to conduct trade has hardly begun to be exploited.

CHAPTER 4

NETWORKED FINANCIAL 'SUPERMARKETS'

Continuing our discussion of emerging mega-trends, we will now extend our model from the macro-level to the micro-level. The preceding appraisal of the impact of the Internet in the macro-environment – which has presaged the networked economy – provides a basic template in our causal model of the effects of these technologies on the markets for money and capital. As emphasised, every industry is exhibiting these seven generic trends, but the actual manifestation thereof is distinct to the industry. Thus, in the banking sector we are able to perceive a localised manifestation of these effects. However, before exploring these, let us conduct a brief overview of existing market structure. The model presented below, adapted from an excellent model developed by the BIS (2001), elucidates the current market structure.

MARKET ARCHITECTURE

All financial markets are structured around a number of key dimensions, which can be used to discriminate between various types of trading systems.

Market Access
(Centralisation vs. Segmentation and Degree of Intermediation)

The concept of market access refers to the way in which various market participants (buyers and sellers) are able to access the market to trade. This relates to the degree of segmentation that exists in the market, as well as the degree of intermediation.

In certain markets, there exists a relatively high degree of centralisation, such that, at least in respect of a certain geographic product market, trading takes place at a central location and intermediation between buyers and sellers may only be necessary for those not physically present.

By contrast, in other less centralised (but less geographically constrained) markets, end-users typically do not trade directly with each other, but do so through intermediaries. In such markets, segmentation between the inter-dealer market and the dealer-to-customer market usually exists, that is, there are two distinct markets for a given product and several tiers of intermediaries.

Allied to this is the role played by a specific type of intermediary known as a market-maker. In such market structures, there is frequently a mandatory liquidity provision role on the sell-side, performed by specified dealers or market-makers.

The Trading System
(Basis of Interaction, Degree of Continuity and Standardisation)

In all types of markets, the system and processes under and by which trading takes place act as a nexus between market participants. The nature of the trading system can be defined in terms of the way in which buyers and sellers communicate, the degree of continuity of trading, and the level of standardisation.

The way in which market participants interact or interrelate can typically be classified as either bilateral or multilateral. Bilateral interaction generally allows for price negotiation and the establishment of relationships. Multilateral interaction generally does not allow for price negotiation or the establishment of relationships (however, it does not prevent actual trades from being executed bilaterally between individual market participants). It usually refers to the pooling of trading activity, and implies that orders are executed at the best price available, irrespective of the counterparty.

Allied to this is the degree of continuity, that is, whether trading is continuous or periodic. In a periodic trading system, orders are batched and cleared at periodic intervals. Trading protocols also differ according to the type of orders allowed (limit, market, stop, off-market and so on), and rules regarding trading (the minimum tick size, trading halts, openings and closings and so on).

Price Formation and Transparency
(Degree of Anonymity)

First, prices can either be determined within the system (the system provides price discovery) or taken from outside the system (the system does not provide price discovery).

Second, price formation can be *order-driven* (prices follow orders) or *quote-driven* (orders follow prices). Under order-driven price formation, orders are sent to a central location and prices are derived from the interaction of these order flows. Under quote-driven price formation, market-makers quote prices at which they are willing to buy and sell securities. The willingness of customers to transact at these quotes determines market prices, although prices for larger trades are typically negotiated bilaterally. Prices can result either from multilateral interaction between market participants (quotes competing in a central location) or can be predominantly bilateral (fragmented price formation).

Allied to this is the issue of transparency or the amount and extent of pricing information that is disseminated. Under full transparency, systems would provide timely information, both pre-trade (for example best bid, offer and depth) and post-trade (for example last trade price and volume), and disseminate it widely (to all market participants). However, actual systems offer various degrees of transparency. This, in turn, relates to the degree of anonymity; whether the identity of counterparties is disclosed, either pre- or post-trade.

Based on these interdependent features of market architecture, two highly illustrative archetypes can be distinguished. The architecture of centralised markets – order books – and decentralised markets – over-the-counter (OTC) or dealer markets – can typically be summarised as in Table 4.1.

To explain this structure of the more complex OTC markets more fully, the interaction of the various market participants in OTC markets prior to the introduction of electronic trading systems is schematically summarised in Figure 4.1.

In practice, of course, a hybrid structure often exists. For example, in the US, equity shares are traded at stock exchanges as well as in the OTC market. At exchanges, such as the New York Stock Exchange (NYSE) and the American Stock Exchange, buyers and sellers of securities meet in one central location to execute trades. Trading on the NYSE, the largest organised stock exchange in the US, is, however, structured around an intermediary called a specialist. For each stock one specialist has an exclusive franchise, functioning as both broker or agent and dealer. As broker or agent, he acts as a match-maker – matching buy and sell orders and maintaining the limit-order book, which records all the unexecuted limit orders received from brokers. As dealer, the specialist periodically posts his own price quotes on the market and trades from his own inventory, providing liquidity when the normal order flow is inadequate. Orders are executed manually by the specialist. The specialist's limit-order book contains proprietary information to which others have very limited access.

Table 4.1 Dimensions of archetypal centralised and decentralised market architectures

	Centralised markets: Exchange/Order book model	Decentralised markets: OTC/Quote/Dealer model
■ Access ■ Segmentation	■ Unrestricted access ■ No segmentation	■ Restricted access ■ Segmentation between the inter-dealer and dealer-to-end-user market
■ Market-makers/Dealers	■ Often present but not necessary (Dealers may participate by quoting two-way prices, but generally they have no special role in providing liquidity)	■ Necessary for trade execution
■ Counterparty/Credit	■ Centralised: Central counterparty/Credit facility ■ Lower credit and settlement risk ■ Central clearing and settlement process	■ Decentralised: Bilateral credit limits (Dealer principal) ■ Higher credit and settlement risk ■ Bilateral clearing and settlement process
■ Interaction	■ Multilateral ■ No negotiation	■ Typically bilateral ■ The price of larger orders is negotiated
■ Continuity	■ Continuous or periodic	■ Generally continuous
■ Trading protocols	■ Standardised	■ Not standardised
■ Price formation	■ Centralised, usually order-driven, within the system (Although some market participants may, in effect, quote continuous prices by maintaining limit orders in the book) Participants submit bid-offer orders to the exchange. The central element is an algorithm, which matches orders	■ Fragmented, quote-driven Dealers post bid-offer quotes to the inter-dealer broking system. Prices are determined when a quote is hit by another dealer
■ Transparency	■ Potentially high	■ Limited
■ Anonymity	■ Usually anonymous	■ Not anonymous, but disclosure limited
■ Examples	■ Some stock and futures exchanges	■ Large parts of the fixed income, forex and derivatives markets

In the OTC market, by contrast, dealers at multiple locations trade shares of a stock with anyone who accepts their price. The OTC market is organised by the National Association of Securities Dealers (NASD), which facilitates trades

PARTICIPANTS

- *End-users* provide the underlying supply and demand that ultimately determines prices, (although fluctuations in dealers' inventories may affect short-term price dynamics). End-users range from private traders or investors to institutional investors, large corporations' treasuries, dealers' independent proprietary trading desks and so on.

Various classes of intermediaries can be distinguished by the type of services that they provide:

- *Dealers* take positions and trade for their own account as their primary business, but usually have assumed a mandatory liquidity provision responsibility in the market. As such, they make markets for their customers, the end-users, by quoting bid and ask prices, and acting as the principle or counterparty in resulting trades. In the process of seeking to profit from a bid-ask spread and exploiting pricing anomalies, they add liquidity to markets and thereby assist their customers in trading and hedging.
- *Inter-dealer brokers* (IDBs) are conduits for the orders or quotes of dealers and do not take positions or trade for their own account.

PARTICIPATION PROCESS

- Traditionally, when an end-user needed to transact in traditional foreign exchange or fixed-income markets, he incurred a search cost of telephoning one or more of the dealers with whom he had a credit line. A price would be negotiated and a trade executed at the best price available.
- If the dealer did not want to keep the acquired position, she would either have to find another customer with whom to conduct an offsetting transaction or she would have to go to the inter-dealer market. To do this, she could either directly find another dealer to do an offsetting transaction, or go through the inter-dealer broker system. The voice-screen broker would post the bid/offer prices for trade sizes at which dealers were willing to trade onto a network screen viewable by other dealers and broke the trades telephonically. The first type of interaction is bilateral, but the inter-dealer broker channel can be characterised as a multilateral interaction, since all quotes are pooled on a common platform and are thus in direct competition with each other.
- Apart from providing price discovery and execution of transactions (provision of liquidity and immediacy of execution), dealers provide other services to their customers, such as research (economic, fundamental, technical), trading expertise, information about the current state of the market and clearing and settlement services.

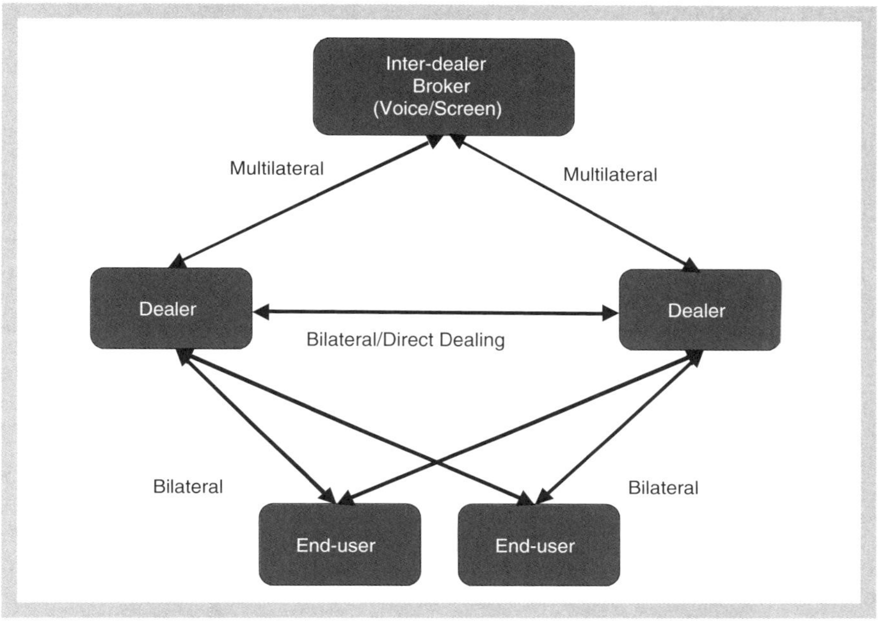

Figure 4.1 Interaction between market participants in OTC markets prior to electronic trading

Source: Bank for International Settlements, *The Implications of Electronic Trading in Financial Markets*, 2001

mainly through its NASDAQ automated quotation system. The OTC market mainly involves trading in stocks not listed on an exchange. All purchases and sales of shares occur through a dealer but there are multiple dealers for each share. Thus, a broker with access to the NASDAQ system can identify the dealer with the best quote before making a sale or purchase. This multiple-dealer structure is a key feature distinguishing the OTC market from the NYSE and its single-specialist structure. As in a traditional exchange, a dealer's limit-order book generally contains proprietary information not available to individual investors.

Thus in one regional product market (US equities) we can discern both an exchange-based and dealer-based market and, furthermore, can discern elements of the archetype of each (especially in terms of access and intermediation) in both.

Armed with this very basic knowledge of how markets are structured and function, we can present a high-level overview of the impacts of technology derived from the macro-economic model.

GLOBALISATION

■ Emergence of Borderless Virtual Markets
■ Massive Volume Growth

With reference to our earlier discussion on globalisation and the globalisation of capital markets, the rise in global trade volumes provides ample evidence of this trend; however, it is more tangibly evidenced by the emergence of multilateral electronic trading networks. We will return to the various forms that these e-markets are taking in due course but, for the moment, suffice it to say that these virtual markets have served to dramatically extend the scope of markets globally.

Why this is possible should be self-evident. Electronic trading networks are both location-neutral, that is, free of geophysical constraints, and allow for continuous multilateral interaction. For trading purposes, the common physical location of users is no longer necessary as long as they can connect to the system. However, unlike traditional location-neutral trading, such as telephone-based dealer markets, these networks allow for continuous multilateral interaction (telephone-based systems are bilateral almost by definition). Consequently, electronic trading systems facilitate cross-border trading and cross-border alliances and mergers between trading systems to a greater extent than traditional markets. Furthermore, electronic systems are scalable, that is, the capacity of the network can be increased with relative ease.

CONVERGENCE

■ On All Fronts: Between Inter-dealer and Dealer–customer Segments of OTC Markets, Between Product Markets, Between Types of FIs, and Between Markets and FIs or Market Participants Themselves

The interaction between market participants in a typical OTC market, such as the foreign exchange or fixed-income markets, is very interesting. The present structure of these markets is a function of their history, which predates the emergence of interactive networks. When these markets extended their reach beyond that of the traditional exchange floor in search of liquidity, they were subject to the voice and data technology constraints of the time, that is, the telephone and non-interactive (information only) screen-based systems. As a result, they exhibit a highly fragmented structure.

These OTC markets are typically segmented into an inter-dealer and dealer-to-customer market. One of the main effects of electronic trading systems may be to merge these market sectors. Electronic trading makes it technically feasible for the market structure to move to a centralised model, where end-users can access the market directly to transact. As a result, the current segmentation observed in OTC markets between the inter-dealer market and the dealer-to-customer market may slowly be eradicated.

In addition to driving centralisation, electronic trading may promote product market convergence. For example, many of the electronic trading networks in OTC product markets have diversified, or plan to diversify, their product range, and many of the (physical) commodities e-exchanges now trade their derivatives as well, so that the major end producers (or utilities) and consumers do not have to pay a separate visit to the bank or insurer to meet their hedging needs.

Finally, distinctions between different types of financial institutions (FIs) are also blurring. For years, mergers and acquisitions have been creating institutions that combine different specialisations: retail and investment bank, stockbroker and trader, insurer and fund manager, and so on. Now, with the emergence of electronic communications networks (ECNs) and other types of electronic trading networks (explained below), broker-dealers are effectively becoming exchanges, and, with the subsequent alliances formed between them and traditional exchanges, distinctions between market participants and the market itself are blurring.

DISINTERMEDIATION

■ Death of the Middleman: Inter-dealer Brokers and Market-makers

The technical ability to directly connect buyers and sellers is obviously accompanied by a process of disintermediation. Although technical feasibility has not yet led to a significant degree of convergence between the two market segments in OTC markets, the intermediaries in the sell-side market have come under very real threat. Traditional inter-dealer (voice) brokers are steadily being replaced by electronic systems. (This does not necessarily imply that brokerages are going out of business as they may reinvent themselves as e-brokerages.) Furthermore, electronic trading makes the direct dealing relationships redundant, that is, the interaction in the inter-dealer market is becoming increasingly multilateral. The dotted lines in Figure 4.2a and the eventual outcome depicted in Figure 4.2b indicate the diminishing importance of the direct trading channels and the traditional inter-dealer broker channels.

Furthermore, in traditional exchange-traded markets, such as equity markets, brokers and market-makers (and the accompanying sales function) are being marginalised, as buy-side participants can directly connect to the electronic exchanges.

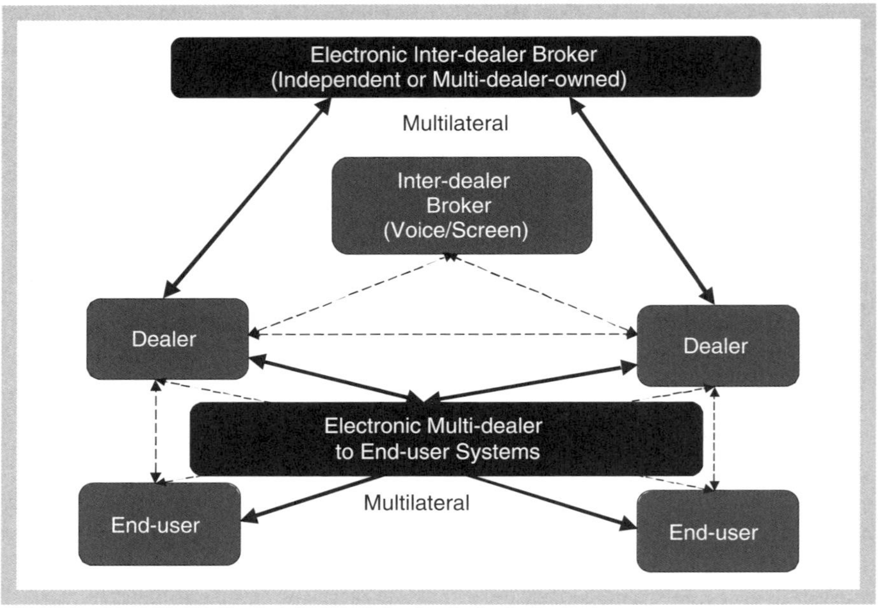

Figure 4.2a Interaction between market participants in OTC markets post introduction to electronic trading

Source: Adapted from: Bank for International Settlements, *The Implications of Electronic Trading in Financial Markets*, 2001

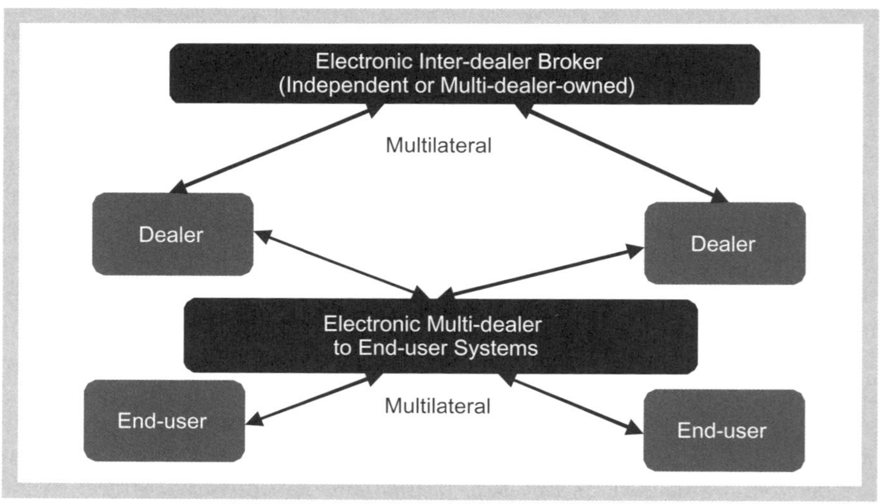

Figure 4.2b Interaction between market participants in OTC markets post introduction to electronic trading

Source: Adapted from: Bank for International Settlements, *The Implications of Electronic Trading in Financial Markets*, 2001

OPEN MARKETS, PRICE TRANSPARENCY AND ANONYMITY

■ Reduced 'Price Impact'

As markets open – that is, as trading is centralised and middlemen are cut out – pricing information, at least in theory, becomes more ubiquitous. Transparency has two aspects. *Pre-trade transparency* refers to the availability of information about bids and offers. In an OTC market, this means firm or indicative quotes by the dealers. On an order book, it may mean just the best bid and offer orders available, the full depth of the book showing amounts at each price, or something in between. *Post-trade transparency* refers to the public and timely transmission of information on past trades, which may include price, volume and execution time.

Electronic systems automatically capture all aspects of both pre- and post-trade information, thus making a greater extent of transparency possible than in traditional trading. Also, because information technology enables the simultaneous bundling of various information sources, it makes links between related markets explicit to market participants. Furthermore, the pooling of market information on joint platforms enables market participants to make a better assessment of the depth of the market.

The improved access to (or lower cost of obtaining) information – facilitated by information technology and further enhanced if markets become more centralised – ostensibly reduces information asymmetries and thus erodes the advantages of those who benefit from them, such as market-makers.

Furthermore, electronic trading systems used in inter-dealer markets are designed in such a way that they provide little information as to the identity of who is intending/willing to trade. Many market participants believe that as markets become more multilateral, it will become easier to assume and unwind positions anonymously in electronic systems. If multilateral trading platforms evolve into central order books with central clearing, then trading could be completely anonymous, pre- and post-trade. The degree of anonymity helps to reduce costly market impact (or the impact of a sizeable trade on price) incurred through leakage and front-running by those in the know.

DYNAMIC PRICING

■ Shift from Quote-driven to Order-driven Price Formation (Exchange Model)

■ Spread Compression

The main impact of electronic trading on the nature of price formation in OTC markets is through centralising trading on a common platform, as can be witnessed in the inter-dealer foreign exchange and government bond markets. Consequently, electronic trading systems enable better price discovery,[1] whether following from quote- or order-driven price formation. However, there is a pronounced shift towards order-driven price formation. Although electronic trading systems provide price discovery, it may be fragmented in a market where several competing electronic trading systems operate, unless these systems are electronically linked.

Electronic systems also posses the interim potential to at least increase the speed with which price information is relayed to the customer market from the inter-dealer market. In addition, the customer may enjoy a tighter bid-ask spread on the electronic trading system. This implies that price information and spread charged are integrated over the customer and the inter-dealer market, even if these markets are segmented with respect to customers' access.

AUTOMATION AND DATA ANALYTICS

- **Automated Pricing and Trading**
- **STP – 'The Holy Grail'**
- **Unbelievable Advances in Data Analytics – Risk Management**

Electronic trading is potentially integrative in nature, that is, it will facilitate the integration of disparate systems across the different elements of the trading process. Therefore electronic trading not only affects front-office activities, but back-office functioning as well.

The automation of the trading process has important consequences for the operational efficiency of markets. Increased operational efficiency provides scope for reducing the cost of trading. A large part of this scope is thought to relate to lower order processing costs. Electronic trading makes it possible for trades to be passed straight through to the middle and back offices by linking order management, pricing, execution, booking, verification, confirmation, clearing, settlement and reporting of trades, with market risk management and operational risk management procedures. This is known as straight-through-processing, or STP. STP potentially eliminates the need for intermediate manual intervention, such as data input or capture, and so has the potential to reduce the overhead costs for back offices. It also has the potential to minimise errors in trade reporting, thereby further reducing costs and rendering risk management more effective. In general, increased computational speed allows the simultaneous processing of large amounts of trade-related information, thus enabling integrated credit, market and operational risk management solutions. Market participants are well aware of the benefits of STP, although the general view is that major cost reductions can only be realised when STP is fully implemented. This is more likely if dominant electronic trading systems emerge over time and/or market standards are adopted.

Operational efficiency will also improve because of the automation of other trade-related processes, thus enabling a further reduction in the associated overhead costs. Whereas previously human traders were involved in the pricing of all individual transactions, dealers in, for example, the plain-vanilla fixed-income and FX markets now use pricing engines for smaller transactions with customers. They also encourage customers to use single- and multi-dealer trading systems for routing their trades.

Finally, electronic trading systems automate the collection of pre-trade and post-trade information, for example obtaining quotes and instructing execution. By greatly increasing the amount and timeliness of information, the new systems provide greater efficiency and reduce search costs, that is, the costs of searching for the best price.

SUMMARY

In sum, the effects of electronic trading systems on all dimensions of market structure – market access (through disintermediation and convergence), the trading and pricing system, and transparency – are engendering a shift towards centralised exchanges on a scale never before possible and enhanced market efficiency.

All these developments are diagrammatically represented in Figure 4.3 which shows the cause and effect relationships of technology on the macro-economy and markets for money in terms of our seven generic trends.

Notes

1. The only exceptions being those so-called crossing networks tht match orders using prices from outside the system, such as equities crossed at exchange closing prices.

Cause	Effect		
Technology	The Networked Economy		The Networked Markets
	From	*To*	*Impacts*
Connectivity on a Global Scale *Enables Communication/ Information Exchange*	Geopolitical Markets	Globalisation	– Multilateral e-Trading Networks – Massive Volume Growth
	Divergent Industries	Convergence	Convergence between OTC inter-dealer-customer markets, products, participants, and so on
	Intermediated Markets	Disintermediation/ Reintermediation	Death of the Middleman: inter-dealer brokers and market-makers
	Closed Markets *Pricing Info Distortions*	Open Markets *Transparent Pricing*	– Better Price Discovery – Reduced 'Price Impact' – Spread Compression
	Fixed Pricing Catalogues	Dynamic Pricing Auctions	Shift to Exchange Model: from quote-driven to order-driven price information
Computational Power *Enables Advancement from Data to Intelligence*	Manual Processing	Automation	– Auto-pricing and Trading – STP – 'The Holy Grail'
	Dumb Data	* **Knowledge** * **Buyer Empowerment**	Unbelievable Advances in Data Analytics – Risk Management

Figure 4.3 Unprecedented change: part II

CHAPTER 5

eVOLUTION OF MARKET STRUCTURES

THERE IS (SOME) METHOD TO THE MADNESS

The unprecedented changes wrought by global electronic connectivity *materially* manifest in the financial markets in the continual emergence of new market structures. These, as we have said, generically take the form of electronic trading networks. In recent times, the markets have been besieged by a virtual legion of these systems, assuming a myriad of 'explanatory' acronyms and jargon – from electronic communications networks (ECNs), alternative trading systems (ATS), to institutional portals – which has left many prospective electronic traders feeling completely bewildered (see Figures 5.1 and 5.2). However, closer analysis does uncover some distinct models and imposes some order on the chaos that seems to reign currently.

AN eVOLUTION

The plethora of electronic marketplaces can be differentiated on the basis of their origins, as we are essentially witnessing the technology-accelerated evolution of market structures. Somewhat ironically then, the basic assumption, previously alluded to, is that the ultimate trend is towards the virtual equivalent of the old-fashioned market square or the floor of the physical exchange. Geographic limitations aside, this was and is the most efficient form of marketplace – a central location where buyers and sellers can meet to trade,

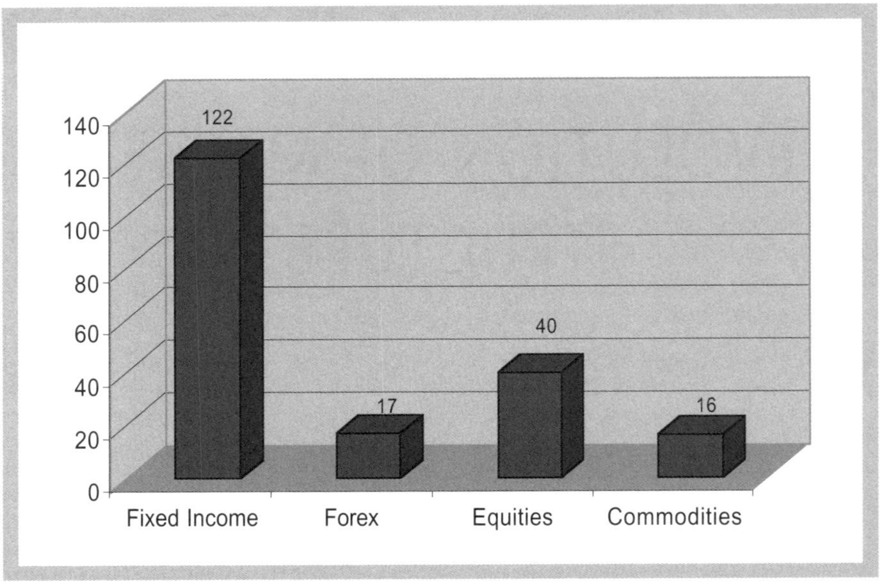

Figure 5.1 Proliferation of e-market platforms by product (as at June 2001)

Source: TowerGroup/SIA: *Technology Trends in the Securities Industry*, 2001

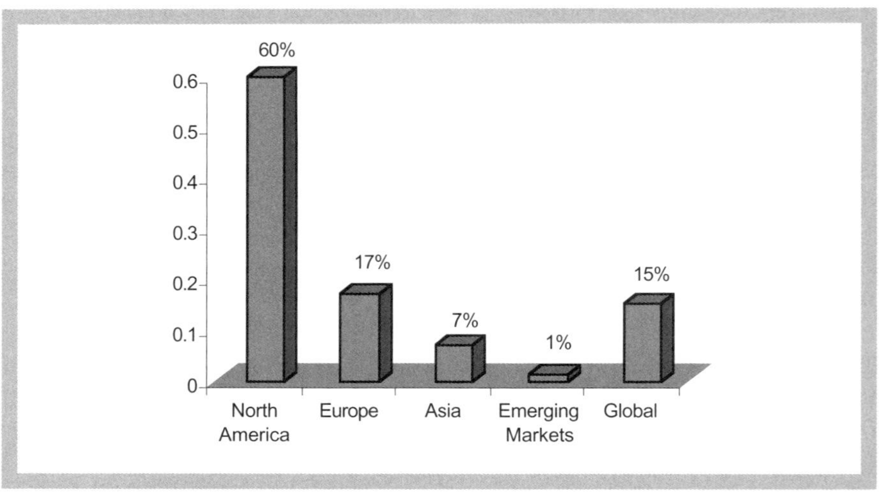

Figure 5.2 Proliferation of e-market platforms by geography (as at June 2001)

Source: TowerGroup/SIA: *Technology Trends in the Securities Industry*, 2001

and thus, a single place where supply and demand intersects without the need for intermediaries – brokers, agents, or other middlemen. Technology is simply enabling the equivalent thereof without the physical constraints of time and distance. We will now proceed from this very abstract, conceptual principle to the presentation of the stylised classification system developed from it.

FUNDAMENTALS OF MARKET THEORY (OR MARKET THEORY 101)

All electronic trading networks can broadly be classified as one of the following five types:

- Single-dealer systems
- Multi-dealer systems
- Inter-dealer systems
- Crossing systems
- Electronic exchanges.

So, what distinguishes one from another? As we have said, we can start with their origins, and specifically their product origins. Clearly, a market, any market, is designed to trade one or more products (and if plural, there will be some form of common denominator across the product range), and the market structure, trading system, processes – the very price formation mechanism – will all, to some extent, be a function thereof. For example, a shopping mall of shops is designed to trade consumer or retail goods between retailers and consumers and is designed accordingly.

While this may seem like an echo of your Ecos 101 (first-year economics) class, it is frequently extremely useful to return to basic economic or market theory in order to gain deeper insight into current developments – to understand their causes, effects and to try to predict the future. Thus, in the markets for money, while we variously refer to instruments, asset classes, securities and so on, we are still ultimately talking about products, and can in the first instance separate markets by product.

Over time, and for various reasons alluded to, certain types of products, such as interest rate or fixed income, money market and currency, have tended to be traded in OTC markets, while other products, such as equities, commodities and their derivatives, have tended to be traded on exchanges. These two broad product-based classifications of markets exhibit distinct characteristics. We have already examined these distinctions in some detail, but the obvious warrants stating: in OTC markets, buyers and sellers are generally separated, that is, not directly connected, and trading is, therefore, highly intermediated. Allied to this, buyers and sellers are segmented and segregated.

Typically, the investors – the buy-side of the market – interface with the sell-side – the banks or broker-dealers – via their sales desks, who in turn interface with their market-makers, who in turn are intermediated by inter-dealer brokers; the so-called IDBs. To the uninitiated, basically this means that the inter-bank or inter-dealer market – the sell-side to sell-side market – is separated from the sell-side to buy-side market, with an inter-dealer broker intermediating between dealers, and the dealer acting as the broker for the investors (via the salesman and market-maker). By contrast, exchange-traded markets do not exhibit such a high degree of segregation and intermediation.

OVERVIEW OF THE EVOLUTIONARY PROCESS

Thus, in the technology-induced trend towards a vast virtual exchange(s), it should be clear that markets currently based on the exchange model merely have to e-enable themselves, while OTC markets are obliged to follow an evolutionary path – albeit an accelerated one. As such, the first three trading networks – single-dealer, multi-dealer, and inter-dealer systems – generally only occur in OTC markets and form part of this evolutionary process.

In the multi-tiered intermediary structure that exists in OTC markets, inter-dealer systems are in effect electronic or *e-brokerages* connecting banks, while single- and multi-dealer systems are in effect electronic *distribution channels* connecting the banks with their customers. Furthermore, there is a pronounced, if recent, trend away from closed, proprietary, single-dealer distribution systems, towards open, non-proprietary, multi-dealer systems, and, as a continuation or an extension thereof, a trend towards inter-dealer trading among the multi-dealers on the platform or vice versa. There is nothing to prevent this natural convergence between the previously distinct market segments and the disintermediation of the broker or e-broker. Electronic marketplaces effectively enable the direct connection of all forms of buyers and sellers, and the death of the middlemen in the process, and hence, one should add, the increased efficiency of the price discovery process and the market as a whole.

That said, while certain of the multi-dealer systems have hinted at their intention to simultaneously perform the inter-dealer function, and thus merge the previously segregated markets, none has yet aggressively embarked on such a drive. In addition, inter-dealers could potentially start targeting the end-customers – the institutional investors, asset managers, money mangers, mutual funds and trusts and so on – but have either refrained or been prevented from doing so by regulatory barriers. However, this natural progression has manifested in the emergence of so-called crossing or cross-matching systems – new entrants that have effectively leapfrogged the previous e-market forms. These trading systems can be buy-side to buy-side, sell-side to sell-side, or sell-side to buy-side, and therefore represent the greatest threat to inter-dealer brokers and broker-dealers (in terms of the sales and market-making function). Crossing networks are ultimately starting to resemble the traditional exchange, with the exception of how they deal with risk, which brings us to the final stage of the evolutionary cycle.

Traditionally, exchanges provided some form of centralised insurance or hedge against counterparty credit and settlement risk, from which their e-counterparts initially abstained. However, recently there have been several initiatives to provide such a centralised credit-limit system, probably because it has the potential to become a lucrative business in due course.

Finally, without going into any depth at this juncture, it should be clear that in the traditional exchange-traded markets, such as equity and commodity markets, only the last two models are really applicable, and the evolutionary prelude to the true electronic exchange is much condensed.

This evolutionary process is summarised diagrammatically in Figure 5.3.

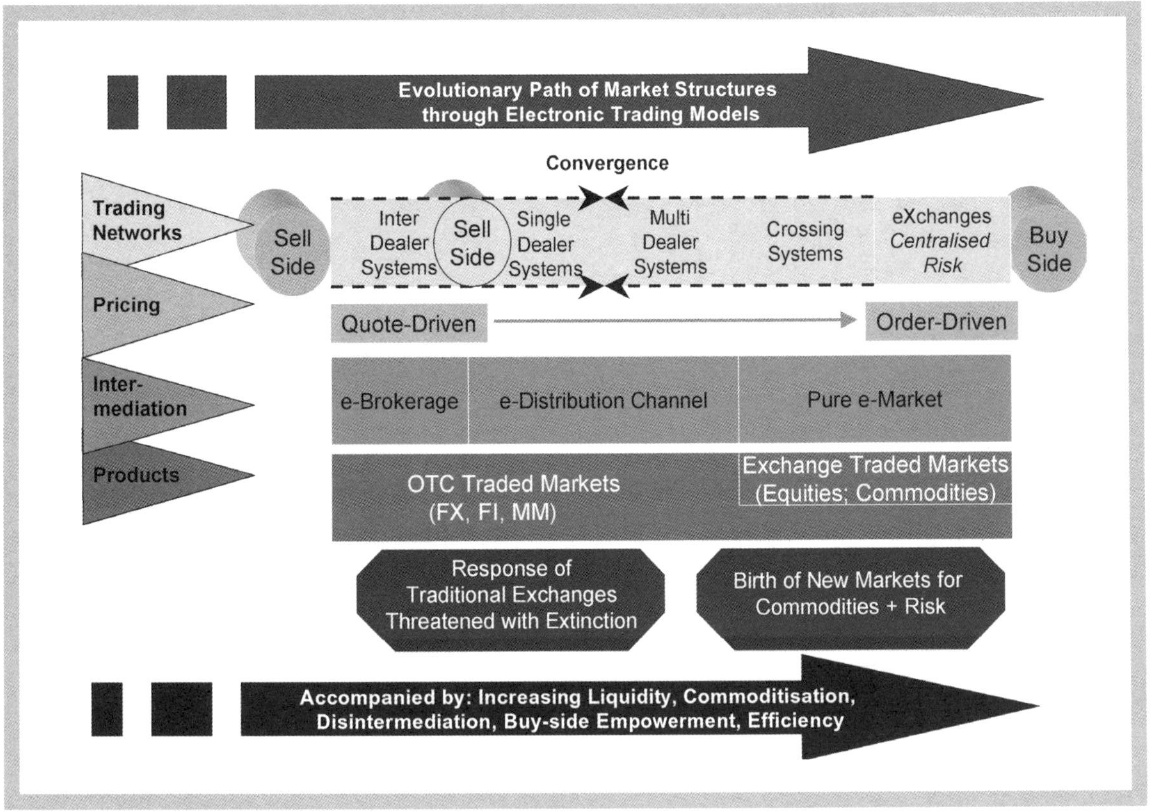

Figure 5.3 eVolution of market structures

CHAPTER 6

A VIRTUAL TOUR OF THE e-MARKETS OF TODAY

SINGLE-DEALER SYSTEMS

Definition

Single-dealer, closed, or proprietary trading systems basically function as e-distribution channels, which enable investors to access quotes and execute transactions with one specific dealer. The dealer in most cases acts as the principal in each deal. These systems commonly cover forex, bond and money markets. Access may be offered through a variety of mechanisms, although in recent years there has been a pronounced shift toward Internet access. While the trading models vary, these systems generally operate by posting indicative prices but trading occurs on a request-for-quote (RFQ) basis. Quotes are either manually or computer generated. Almost all banks have developed some form of proprietary dealing system. Solutions such as GenIdeal from UK systems vendor AVT also provide this functionality.

Advantages

The advantages that ostensibly accrue to a bank in developing this capability include enabling:

- the penetration of new market segments, such as smaller or more remote customers, who previously could not be serviced cost efficiently.

- trades in low-margin vanilla products to be executed with minimal human intervention, thereby lowering transaction costs and operational risks (by reducing the margin for error). It also optimises the productivity of the sales function. Typically, this type of business is very low margin, so an electronic system frees the salesforce to concentrate on higher margin business and on marketing the electronic system to new clients.

Examples

While proprietary single-dealer distribution channels might seem second rate in comparison to multi-dealer distribution channels-cum-markets, some of them are performing extremely well. For example, in Q1 2000, Goldman Sach's electronic bond trading system, WebET, handled US$70 billion or 75% of Goldman's Treasury trades. Over the course of 2000, Merrill Lynch's e-commerce platforms, including its proprietary portal MLX, the Liquidity Management System and the Client Connectivity Application, generated trades in debt and equity products valued at US$1.9 trillion (see Screen Shot 6.1).

MULTI-DEALER SYSTEMS

Definition

Multi-dealer, open or non-proprietary trading systems basically provide an e-distribution channel for multiple sell-side banks to their customers, which enables the buy-side to access and compare quotes, and execute transactions with multiple dealers, from a single screen. The multitude of prospective counterparties serves to concentrate liquidity. The dealers generally act as principals in transactions. These systems, with reference to the preceding discussion on OTC market evolution, commonly cover forex, bond and money markets. Again, while trading models vary considerably, these systems generally display indicative quotes (often the best bid or ask price for a given security), but the actual trading process is generally RFQ-based.

Advantages/Disadvantages

The advantages accruing to banks participating in this type of market structure are very similar to the closed model, in terms of efficiency gains and a potentially expanded customer base; however, the additional benefits of this open model to the buy-side clearly come at the expense of the banks. The

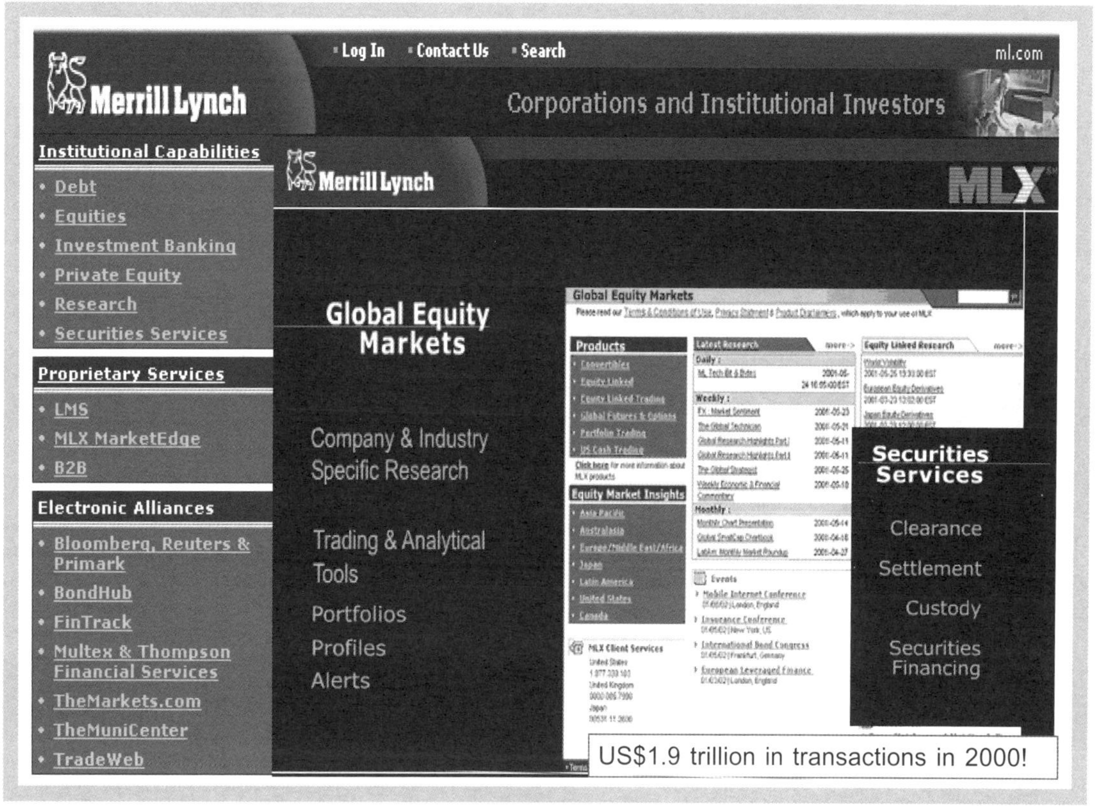

Screen Shot 6.1 Merrill Lynch's sophisticated suite of electronic products and services

Source: www.ml.com

transparent and dynamic competitive pricing model inevitably leads to further spread compression (unless the dealers collude to prevent this).

Examples of Multi-dealer Systems

Examples of these types of systems abound. However, the actual penetration rates of these electronic systems in the dealer-to-customer market, although growing, is not nearly as high as in the inter-dealer markets.

Examples of Forex Multi-dealer Systems

In general, the (dealer to buy-side) forex market is migrating online at a slower pace than other markets. A significant proportion of the buy-side market is still not ready to hang up the telephone and sacrifice a measure of comfort in favour of the anonymity of the more efficient computer. Basically, inertia and psychological barriers to trust are still impeding the online transition. Nevertheless, online trading increased significantly in 2001, albeit off a low base.

According to recent electronic-FX studies performed by a variety of research firms, buy-side institutions and corporations now collectively trade up to 10% of their total volume online worldwide. Penetration, at 15%, is higher among institutions, who represent 40% of the forex market, but 75% of total volumes, according to Greenwich Associates (*eFX*, 2001). Moreover, among the one in seven professionals who do trade online, the percentage of their total trades conducted online, which grew from 13% in 2000, to 19% by 2001, is projected to double to 42% by 2003. According to Celent Communications, at current rates, the proportion of all trading that will be conducted online is predicted to reach 50% by 2004 (see Figure 6.1).

Interestingly, in the surveys conducted recently, online traders ranked faster execution, convenience, reduced error occurrences and access to research higher than price improvement as the major benefits derived from online trading. However, many cited economies realised from a reduced headcount in addition to operational efficiency. The hunt for liquidity is much less protracted when one mouse click delivers multiple quotes, and therefore demands less manpower.

FXConnect, owned by fund manager goliath State Street, currently dominates the e-FX landscape. FXConnect went live way back in August 1996 and, as of August 2001, was generating an average daily trading volume of US$5.75 billion. FXConnect is part of State Street's Global Link trading platform. Global Link was originally a proprietary platform, but in March 2000 the portal began opening itself to other banks. It now connects over 25 banks to 400 asset

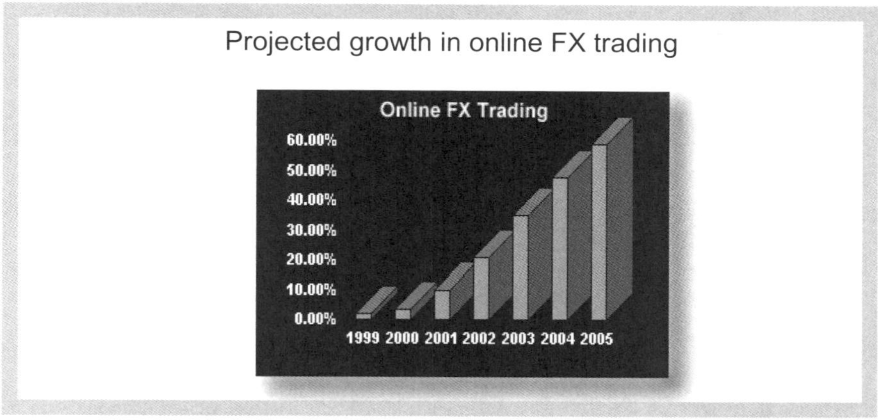

Figure 6.1 Projected growth in online FX trading
Source: McCormick, 2001

managers. The umbilical cord to the giant State Street mothership and integration with the multi-asset class trading capability of first-mover Global Link (which covers equities, futures, money markets and funds) gives FXConnect a real edge. (Although it warrants noting that Global Link's bond product, BondConnect, has failed.)

Currenex is another prominent e-FX system, which launched in March 2000. It has grown daily trading volumes from US$370 million at the end of 2000 to over US$1.36 billion by August 2001. Interestingly, Currenex qualifies as one of the few remaining independents, with roughly 90% of its equity held by a mix of employees and venture capitalists. Currenex claims that its killer app is its credit model. The system allows customers to set up a credit line with a prime broker and then trade with all the banks with whom the prime broker has an inter-bank relationship.

Finally, attention should be called to two new blips on the e-FX radar (although one of the two was rather short-lived). Atriax and FXall were the latest entrants into the forex market, having only launched in June and May 2001 respectively. Both qualified as true multi-dealer-owned multi-dealer sites, and their coincident and much-hyped launches led to intense competition, not least for airspace in the media. Atriax's investors (Citibank, Deutsche, JP Morgan Chase and Reuters) together represent about 30% of the global forex market, and within six months Atriax had registered over 70 additional banks on the sell-side. Similarly, FXall's seven founders command an aggregate market share of about 25%, but their market or price-makers total just over 30. However, after less than a year, in early April 2002, Atriax, without warning, announced that it would be exiting the market, leaving FXall as the unexpected survivor. At the time that its last rites were read, Atriax was recording

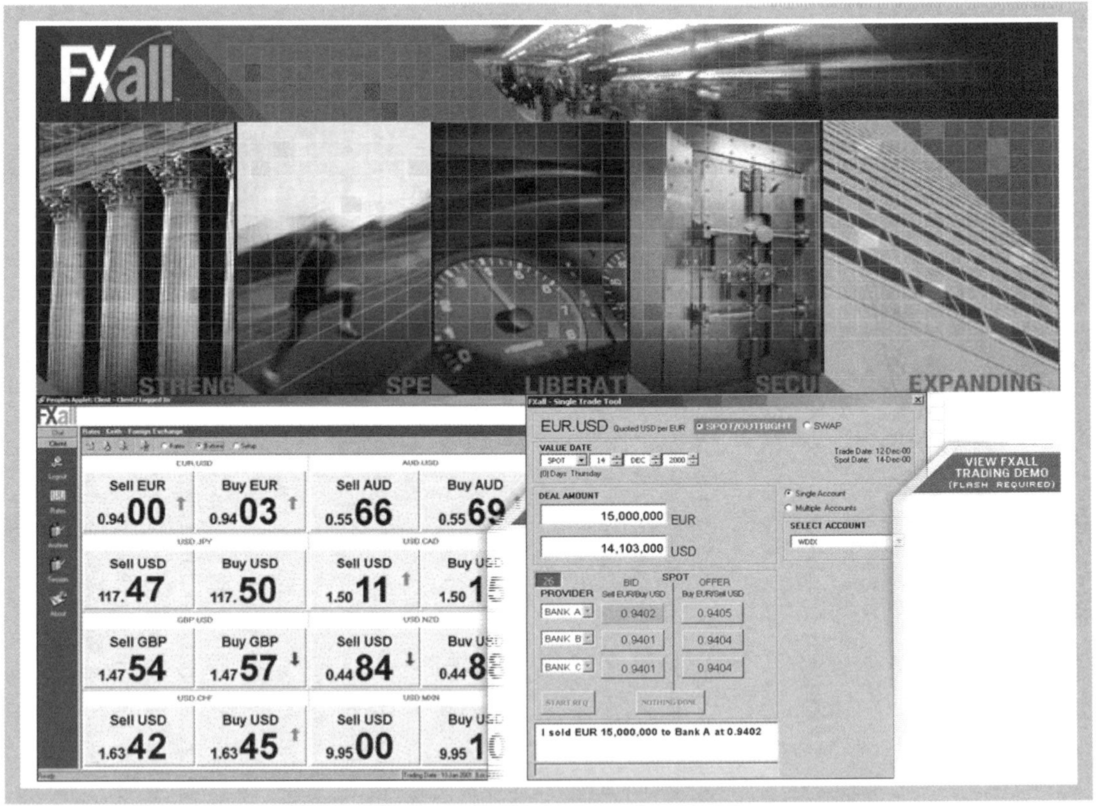

Screen Shot 6.2 The FXall multi-dealer forex trading site

Source: www.fxall.com

Table 6.1 Sample of foreign exchange multi-dealer (to buy-side) systems

System	Type	Products	Ownership Structure	Ownership Composition
State Street's FXConnect	Multi-dealer: RFQ	Spot	Independent	State Street
Currenex	Multi-dealer: RFQ	Spot, forwards and swaps	Independent	Independent
FXall	Multi-dealer: RFQ	Spot, forwards and swaps	Consortium	BoA; Bank of New York; BNP; Citi; Credit Agricole Indosuez; CSFB; JPMC; DKW; GS; HSBC; MSDW; Royal Bank of Canada; Royal Bank of Scotland; Standard Chartered; Tokyo-Mitsubishi; UBS; Westpac
Atriax (now defunct)	Multi-dealer: RFQ	Spot, forwards and swaps	Consortium	Citibank; JP Morgan Chase; Deutsche; Reuters

Note: The bank code key appears at the end of the chapter.

average daily trading volumes of a paltry US$220 million, while FXall was recording US$200 million. Although this is a tour of live (not dead) sites, Atriax, whose failure is both so recent and so high profile, should be counted (see Screen Shot 6.2).

FXall is a simple 'e-telephone' (as was Atriax), that is, it is an online RFQ system that mimics the telephonic RFQ system. However, it has focused on systems integration to give it an edge. FXall's interface to banks' rate engines enables providers to stream prices from their own rate engines over the platform and enables customers to receive a price within 3 seconds 90% of the time. FXall also provides integration to client treasury and portfolio management sysyems and offers a range of content. FXall was voted best overall multi-bank portal for research, trading and straight through processing in the Euromoney Forex Poll 2002, and was selected as multi-bank portal in Global Investor's annual survey. By its first anniversary, it had registered over 200 buy-side customers and its sell-side investor base had grown to 17, who command an aggregate market share of over 80% of the dealer-to-customer FX market.

The key features of these systems are summarised in Table 6.1. Note that almost all these markets now trade both spot and derivatives, such as forwards, swaps and options.

Examples of Fixed-income Multi-dealer Systems

In the fixed-income market, the uptake of electronic trading is reaching significant levels. For example, approximately 20% US Treasury market transactions are now transacted electronically. Given that, as a fiduciary, the buy-side has an obligation to seek approximately five bids and offers from competing dealers, the attractiveness of multi-dealer systems, which deliver these quotes instantly without human intervention, is obvious. According to Greenwich Associates (Oakley, 2001), even in Europe, the number of tier one institutions trading fixed-income products online rose from 25% at the end of 1999 to 30% by the end of 2000. Numerous multi-dealer systems are currently operating in direct competition with each other. It is estimated that perhaps only three will survive longer term. Some of the major contenders are presented below.

Launched in 1998, TradeWeb is deemed the dominant system 'du jour', and is arguably the most successful electronic trading network in the OTC markets today (see Screen Shot 6.3). Initially it focused on the highly liquid US government bonds but has since diversified its geographic and product range. In fact, Treasuries now account for less than half of TradeWeb's total volume. As a simple RFQ system with bilateral credit limits, TradeWeb constitutes an exact replica of the existing market model, which has proved phenomenally successful. With 18 of the world's leading dealers as market-makers and 1000 of the largest buy-side institutional investors as customers (including 200 of the top 250 in the US), over US$10 trillion has been traded in the market since its inception and its growth rate has been exponential. While it took four years to do US$8 trillion in total trading volume, it took three years to do US$3 trillion and one year to do five (US$5 trillion). Approximately US$20 billion and up to US$47 billion is transacted through its system daily, and it is estimated to have captured approximately 15% of the dealer-to-customer flow in the US government securities market. The scope for future growth is enormous.

By comparison, launched in January 2001, MarketAxess focuses on the less liquid instruments, such as high-grade and high-yield corporate and emerging market government bonds, as well as new issues. It employs a hybrid model, incorporating an adaptation of the name-give-up IDB model (whereby firm rather than indicative prices can be traded on by submitting an order at a posted price) and an anonymous cross-matching system. The anonymous crossing system came into being after MarketAxess acquired the now defunct Trading Edge's BondLink, which acts as the anonymous central counterparty. However, as at the end of 2001, 93% of volume was routed via the disclosed counterparty model in which all trades are customer-to-dealer. It boasts 11 top liquidity providers and over 3000 buy-side customers (although many are smaller investors). After six months of trading, and still in its infancy, it reported a daily trading volume of US$75 million, and a total of just over US$5 billion, and a quarterly growth rate of 58%. MarketAxess even seems poised to usurp Bloomberg's Spread Execution System in corporate bonds. By the end of 2001, there were, on average, 1100 bids and 250 offers on MarketAxess, for example, whereas the anonymous Bloomberg system had only around 120.

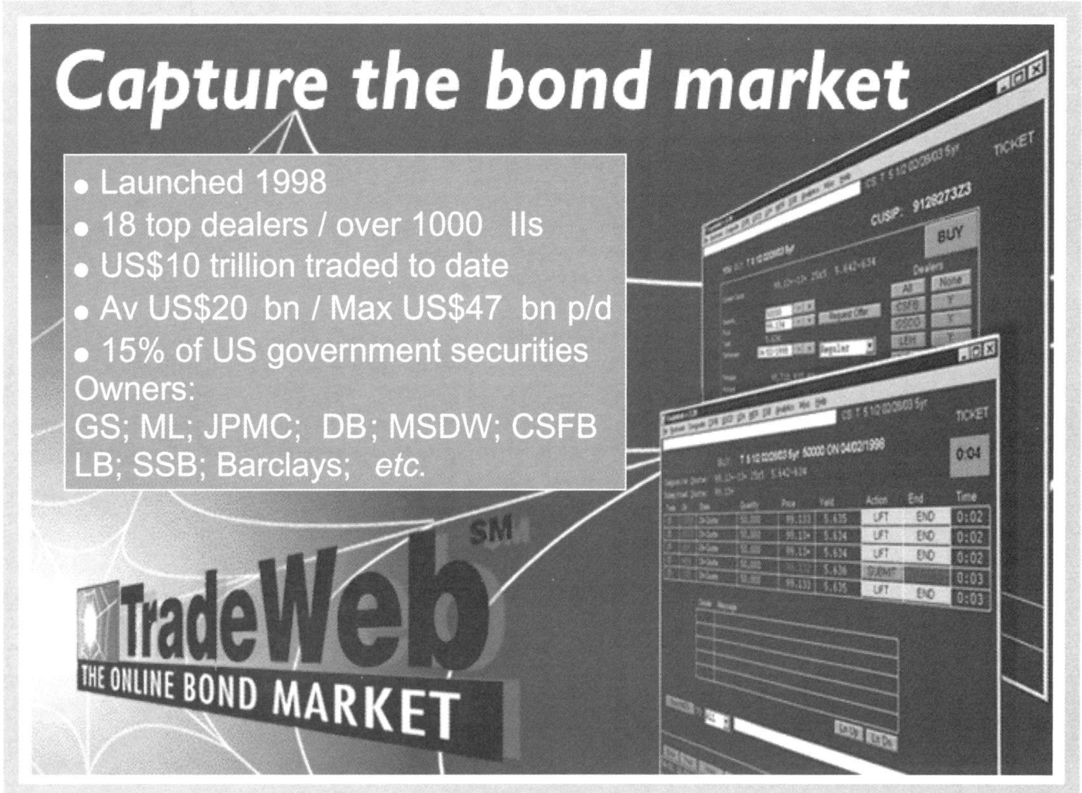

Screen Shot 6.3 The TradeWeb multi-dealer fixed income trading site

Source: www.tradeweb.com

Table 6.2 Sample of fixed-income multi-dealer (to buy-side) systems

System	Type	Products	Target Market	Ownership Structure	Ownership
TradeWeb	Multi-dealer: RFQ	G (UST + ES); A;	Institutional investors MBS; CP	Consortium	Barclays Capital; CSFB; DB; GS; JPMC; LB; ML; MSDW; SSB; other
MarketAxess	Multi-dealer: Both name-give up IDB model + anonymous cross-matching with central counterparty	HG; HY; EM; C; M; EB; A; NI	Institutional + mid-tier investors	Consortium	ABN; Bear Sterns; CSFB; DB; JPMC; LB; SSB; UBS (acquired Trading Edge's BondLink)
BondVision	Multi-dealer: RFQ	G-ES	Institutional investors	Consortium	EuroMTS (ref. Inter-dealer)/ (merged with BondClick)
BondDesk	Multi-dealer: Order cross-matching/ Exchange (Primary Auction)	G; A; M; HG; HY	Primarily retail brokerages	Consortium	ABN; Bear Sterns; BoA; FirstUnion; GS PaineWebber; Capital; Prudential; Spear; Leeds & Kellog; TD Waterhouse; UBS; other

Note: Bank and product code keys appear at the end of the chapter.

BondVision, which launched only in August 2001, trades European sovereign bonds on a simple RFQ basis. BondVision was formed from what EuroMTS (the consortium-owned inter-dealer platform) salvaged from what was left of the infamously unsuccessful BondClick venture. While TradeWeb Europe already dominates Northern Europe in European government bonds, BondVision may yet survive, especially in Southern Europe. In its first week of trading it reported an average ticket size of €15 million and daily trading volume surpassing €500 million, counting one side of trades only (see Table 6.2).

Examples of OTC Derivatives Multi-dealer Systems

In the OTC derivatives markets, the use of this type of electronic trading system has been limited. The counterparty credit risk involved in these instruments is a major hindrance and the reason for their low penetration.

Exchanges do not face this problem if they incorporate central counterparties (which is discussed later), and so because of this, and also because of greater standardisation, electronic trading is more widespread in exchange-traded derivatives. Moreover, no real economic incentives exist for either liquidity providers or even clients to migrate to these types of platform anyway. Electronic trading in OTC derivatives may bypass multi-dealer models and go directly to exchange-based models.

However, the aforementioned multi-dealer forex systems, FXall and Currenex, do trade forex derivative instruments, including forwards, swaps, options and hybrids, as do a number of the bond systems. Furthermore, the soon to be launched interest-rate derivatives focused inter-dealer system, Swapswire (owned by Citigroup, Deutsche Bank, Goldman Sachs, JP Morgan Chase, UBS Warburg, MSDW, CSFB, BNP Paribas and Merrill Lynch), does intend to develop into a multi-dealer-to-buy-side site. If the inter-dealer market establishes e-trading in OTC derivatives, the buy-side could be incorporated later.

INTER-DEALER SYSTEMS

Definition

In terms of the intermediation dynamics discussed previously, single- and multi-dealer systems function as distribution channels, electronically connecting the sell-side to their customers on a one-to-many or many-to-many basis respectively. By contrast, inter-bank systems are electronic intermediaries or brokerages, connecting the sell-side to the sell-side. They supplant traditional telephonic voice brokers in OTC product markets. However, they're little more than a better telephone themselves – mimicking the existing model, whereby tradable prices are posted onto a common platform, but enabling dealers to execute transactions electronically with other dealers without the manual intervention of the broker (price input and telephonic trade execution). In order to meet the competition from new electronic entrants into their markets (owned by independent third parties or consortia of dealers themselves), all the major IDBs have launched such systems, dubbed the fully anonymous brokers' broker.

Advantages/Disadvantages

The mere existence of such electronic inter-dealer brokers should enhance the efficiency of the inter-dealer market (for broker-dealers) – in terms of both market and pricing efficiency as well as operational efficiency or cost. Furthermore, in cases where the dealers own the e-IDB, they pay themselves the increment on the spread previously levied by brokers.

Examples of Inter-dealer Systems

Examples of Forex Inter-dealer Systems

The advance of electronic broking in forex predates the public network and the exploitation thereof in other markets. It began in the early 1990s when first Electronic Broking Services (EBS) and then Reuters' systems began replacing voice brokers in inter-bank trading and, today, two-thirds of the current US$1.1 trillion in daily trading volume in the professional forex market is brokered electronically. EBS and Reuters eventually grew to dominate the inter-dealer market: when EBS launched in 1993, for example, there were over ten voice brokers active in the hub of New York, today there are only three, all of whom are actively pursuing e-strategies.

EBS's Spot Dealing System and Reuters' Dealing 2000–02 are each dominant in certain currency pairs, after EBS usurped Reuters' dominance in certain segments. Participation in both systems is limited to dealers, who anonymously enter bids and/or offers into their terminals. Each user observes both the best bid and offer for a given exchange rate available in the market, as well as the best bid and offer available to that user. The difference between the best market price and the best price available to a given dealer arises from the credit allocation procedure followed by each user. Since dealers will only be willing to take on settlement risk with counterparties for whom they have internally approved credit lines, each participant identifies those subscribers with whom it is willing to trade and the credit limit it is willing to allocate to each. That way, a subscriber will only be matched with counterparties with whom it is willing to deal, and for whom it has available credit lines. Upon hitting a bid or offer on the system, the two counterparties are revealed to each other and settlement occurs (on T+2). If several banks are offering the same best price, their offers are met on the basis of time (first in, first out). The systems provide automated interfaces with banks' internal systems applications to allow a degree of straight-through-processing.

These electronic broking systems have expanded rapidly in recent years, at the cost of traditional means of dealing such as through voice broking or direct dealing. The advance of electronic broking owes much to its lower cost, higher efficiency and, most importantly, greater transparency compared with traditional trading channels. The spot foreign exchange market has traditionally been opaque, because of the difficulty in disseminating price information in the absence of a centralised marketplace. Before the advent of electronic broking, dealers – especially the smaller ones – had to enter into a number of transactions to obtain information on available market prices. By contrast, traders are now able to know instantly the 'best' available market price, without having to go through an uncertain price discovery process. Finally, it warrants noting that the possibility of these info-mediary-owned systems extending themselves into the multi-dealer-to-customer segment should not be discounted, in accordance with the broader convergence trend, which is facilitating market centralisation and access to buy-side market participants. In fact, Reuters' stake in the now defunct buy-side site, Atriax, may have posed some conflicts of interest in this respect.

Examples of Fixed-income Inter-dealer Systems

In the inter-dealer G10 government bond markets, electronic systems are rapidly gaining ground. Several systems are competing for the same business, and since it is not clear which systems will prevail, intermediaries are trying to be involved, as owner and/or user, in several of these systems. Some prominent examples are given below and summarised in Table 6.3.

EuroMTS, with robust technology and good liquidity, has positioned itself as one of the major contenders in the European government bonds sector. Despite the poor performance of exchange-type models in the multi-dealer to buy-side market, it employs just such an order-matching system, acting as an anonymous central counterparty and, as such, has been remarkably successful. It seems that dealers accustomed to the inter-dealer model are more amenable to this shift, which is less dramatic and less risky for them than for institutions. EuroMTS currently has over 400 users or connections and generates an average trading volume of €45 billion a day (counting one side of the transaction). EuroMTS has since acquired a 15% stake in ISMA's CoreDeal (together with several other broker-dealers (including JP Morgan Chase, Morgan Stanley, Lehman Brothers and UBS), as ISMA winds down its stake from 58% currently to 15%). CoreDeal lists over 5000 corporate bonds but lacks liquidity and good technology. The two have established a joint venture and intend to launch the CoreDealMTS bond exchange in early 2002. Government and credit trading will interact, bringing euro-denominated spread trading to CoreDeal customers. Trading will continue to be based on a central counterparty.

While CoreDealMTS will initially serve only broker-dealers, this closed exchange model is well positioned to eventually form an open exchange for dealers, institutional investors and borrowers. The only other real fixed-income exchange is provided through the Swiss Stock Exchange, but it has failed to expand into a broader based market. In the interim, CoreDealMTS

Table 6.3 Sample of fixed-income inter-dealer systems

System	Type	Access	Products	Target Market	Ownership Structure	Ownership
BrokerTec Global	Inter-dealer: exchange model	Proprietary network	G (UST and ES); A; R	Broker-dealers (all Government Securities Clearing Corporation members)	Consortium	ABN; Barclays Capital; CSFB; DB; DKW; GS; JPMC; LB; ML; MSDW; SSB; WDR; UBS
EuroMTS/ CoreDeal	Inter-dealer: exchange model	Proprietary network	G (ES); HG	Broker-dealers	Consortium	BoA; Barclays Capital; DB; GS; JPMC; MSDW; SSB; Soc Gen; WDR; other/ISMA plus 13 banks (ABN; BNP; ING; LB; Dresdner; UBS; and so on
eSpeed	Inter-dealer: IDB model	Proprietary network	G plus other liquid instruments	Broker-dealers	Independent IDB	Public but majority Cantor Fitzgerald
ETC	Inter-dealer: IDB model	Proprietary network; Internet	G	Broker-dealers	Independent IDB	Garban-Intercapital plc
LibertyDirect	Inter-dealer: IDB model	Proprietary network	G (UST)	Broker-dealers	Independent IDB	Liberty Brokerage Inc., a Tullett & Tokyo Liberty plc company
The MuniCenter	Inter-dealer: order-matching; anonymous	Internet	M	Broker-dealers + retail brokers	Consortium	LB; ML; MSDW; SSB; other

Note: Bank and product code keys appear at the end of the chapter.

could even work in tandem with subsidiary BondVision, by trading CoreDealMTS securities on the BondVision platform. However, CoreDealMTS is an inter-dealer exchange, while BondVision is a multi-dealer to buy-side RFQ system, and the two may be incompatible.

The multi-dealer owned BrokerTec Global and Cantor Fitzgerald's eSpeed have also performed well. BrokerTec, owned by 14 of the world's major

Table 6.4 Sample of OTC derivative inter-dealer systems

System	Instruments	Type	Ownership	Ownership Composition
Volbroker	FX options	Inter-dealer	Consortium	Citi; DB; GS; JPMC; UBS. All designated market-makers/ liquidity providers
Blackbird	FX + interest rate derivatives	Inter-dealer	Independent	Derivatives Net (DNI); Minorities: Reuters and Garban
EBS	FX derivatives	Inter-dealer	Independent IDB	EBS
ICOR – not yet live	FX, interest rate (and equity derivatives)	Inter-dealer	JV	Reuters; Icor Brokerage
Swapswire – not yet live	Interest rate derivatives (primarily swaps)	Inter-dealer/ multi-dealer	Consortium	BNP; Citi; CSFB; DB; GS; JPMC; ML; MSDW; UBS

Note: Bank key is at the end of the chapter.

dealers, launched in June 2000 in the US and June 2001 in Europe. It is another anonymous order-matching exchange-type system that has proved successful, generating US$45.2 billion per day and over US$11 trillion in transactions to date. Cantor Fitzgerald's eSpeed is a straight IDB-modelled system, as are both Tullet & Tokyo and Garban's offerings.

OTC Derivatives Examples

Electronic brokerage in OTC derivatives is truly in its infancy, nevertheless there are a number of new entrants into various segments of this market. The lack of history means that the jury is still out on the prospects for individual platforms, as well as for the electronic inter-dealer market in derivatives as a whole. However, as usual, the systems with the highest probability of success are those multi-bank-owned ones that emulate the current model, and which address counterparty credit risk most effectively (see Table 6.4).

CROSSING NETWORKS

Definition

Crossing or cross-matching or order-matching networks are, in principle, electronic marketplaces, connecting the true buy- and sell-side of a market directly, without intermediation, to trade on the exchange basis, of order-driven price formation, such that an algorithm matches market or limit orders posted onto the central order book.

'Disadvantages'

In terms of the format adopted in the preceding appraisal of single-, multi- and inter-dealer systems, where advantages and disadvantages were appraised from a broker-dealer's perspective, there are no advantages of crossing systems. In this context, the collapse of the dealer-dependent market structure, which crossing systems theoretically represent, is hardly advantageous to dealers.

With respect to the intermediation dynamics depicted in Figure 5.3, crossing systems are electronic markets, as opposed to an electronic form of a distribution channel from broker-dealers to their customers or an electronic inter-dealer broker between broker-dealers, and displace both. By potentially connecting the buy- and sell-side of a market directly, without the need for intermediaries, crossing systems represent the greatest threat to intermediaries, and to broker-dealers in that capacity.

In theory, at least, the match-making role performed by broker-dealers and other 'agent' brokers, as well as the principal or capital provision role performed by dealers, has been dispensed with, as has the need for inter-dealer brokers of any kind, since the separate dealer market ceases to exist. However, in reality, the forms that these systems take vary substantially.

History and Emergence of the Hybrid Model

The original versions, with reference to the preceding discussion on the evolutionary cycle, emerged in the exchange-traded markets, and specifically the equity markets – representing their e-enablement. Initially, based on the premise that investors are in fact the ultimate source of liquidity, they operated purely as buy-side to buy-side pre- or off-exchange order-matching systems with no intermediation or obligatory liquidity provision by designated sell-side or price-making participants.

However, liquidity was not sufficient to form continuous markets or to allow for price discovery. Consequently, these systems simply used the primary market to set the price at which their customers could execute a trade. Since exchanges set prices, while crossing networks used those prices to trade cheaply, they were denounced as parasites and accused of increasing market fragmentation.

From this inauspicious beginning as market appendages, crossing networks began to gain independence. Anonymity and the elimination of the broker or broker-dealer from the process yields significant economic benefits. Matching buy or sell orders entered into a common system at the midpoint of the bid and offer spread (1) eliminates any immediate market impact, (2) avoids the bid-offer spread that a dealer would charge, and (3) cuts out the commission paid to the broker. The savings that accrue amount to as much as 80% of a transaction's cost. As a result, certain crossing systems eventually siphoned sufficient liquidity off traditional exchanges to start forming prices internally. (In fact, these electronic trading systems may eventually improve price discovery in traditional markets. For example, as electronic trading systems are typically more transparent than traditional OTC markets, the prices they produce may serve as a benchmark for related markets where price discovery is less transparent, because of fragmentation or limited liquidity.)

Moreover, over time, many of the original protagonists abandoned their dogmatic position on liquidity provision and accepted that institutional investors generally do not place orders of sufficient size and frequency to create liquid markets on a continuous basis, despite the huge assets that they hold. Many 'bastardised' their model to provide for crossing with capital commitment – effectively establishing OTC-style market-makers who would guarantee a two-way price. Quoting a two-way price then becomes the equivalent of maintaining continuous limit orders on the book.

Latterly, cross-matching systems have also emerged in various guises in the OTC product markets, but not quite as the 'final' phase of a linear evolutionary process. In certain instances, the order-book/order-matching or crossing model has been adopted by inter-dealer and, to a lesser extent, multi-dealer to buy-side systems, but these have yet to evolve into true exchanges granting equal access to all market participants. In the simplified and stylised model presented diagrammatically in Figure 5.3, such complexities are not really accommodated, except to the extent that a blurring and convergence between the RFQ and order-book models is provided for, as markets tend towards electronic exchanges.

The greater penetration of crossing systems in the inter-dealer segment (compared to the dealer to buy-side segment) is probably due to relatively less disparity in the price formation and trading models. The difference between auto-matching of contra buy- and sell-side orders and the typical IDB model of posting and lifting prices is less pronounced than between cross-matching and the typical buy-side RFQ model. Crossing systems are more common in the interest rate product market than in forex, and are also quite prominent in the new OTC derivatives markets.

Frequently, to compensate for illiquidity, benchmark pricing is still introduced from outside the system. As an example, the continuously updated prices of the highly liquid bond futures and 'on the run' government bonds tend to be used in pricing engines that provide quotes for a wide range of less liquid fixed-income instruments. Finally, trading is either continuous or takes place in discrete, periodic cross-matching sessions. The discrete model is more appropriate in the illiquid and primary markets. We will return to this in due course.

Ultimately, these systems are developing into replicas of the exchange model, with the final step in this process being the mitigation of counterparty risk. This takes the form of the provision of centralised credit facilities or by acting as a central counterparty as well as the centralisation of clearing and settlement functions. The growing role of central counterparty clearing houses in financial markets has wider implications for financial stability which are beyond the scope of this book. From a narrow trading perspective, however, the removal of concerns about counterparty credit risk may make trading systems more resilient because market participants would no longer be potentially deterred by those concerns, which are likely to increase in times of stress. It should be noted that in stressful times, the robustness of the central clearer becomes a very important issue.

Thus, order-book cross-matching systems occur in a multitude of forms. However, in general, these systems are more open, especially to the buy-side, facilitating buy- and sell-side liquidity provision (even if designated sell-siders perform an obligatory function in this regard). Price formation tends to be more order-driven (with an order-book and matching system), as opposed to RFQ, and, as central counterparty credit risk management replaces bilateral credit limits, they tend to be more exchange-like, in both form and function.

Examples

Examples of Equity Crossing Systems

Electronic trading in the global equity markets on these types of platforms is gaining momentum (see Figure 6.2). Apart from the ECNs (discussed below), one of the major equity crossing networks in the US is POSIT (Portfolio System for Institutional Trading), a non-continuous matching system operated by US brokerage ITG, for both institutional investors and broker-dealers. Annual volume has exceeded more than 7.8 billion shares and it accounts for over 3% of the traded volume on US exchanges. POSIT is currently used by more than 500 major institutions and broker/dealers. It claims to save its clients over US$1.2 billion annually. In 1998, it started crossing in Europe.

A number of other major initiatives have recently been launched in Europe. E-Crossnet, a venture backed by 19 of the world's largest institutional investors including Merrill Lynch Asset Management, Mercury Asset Manage-

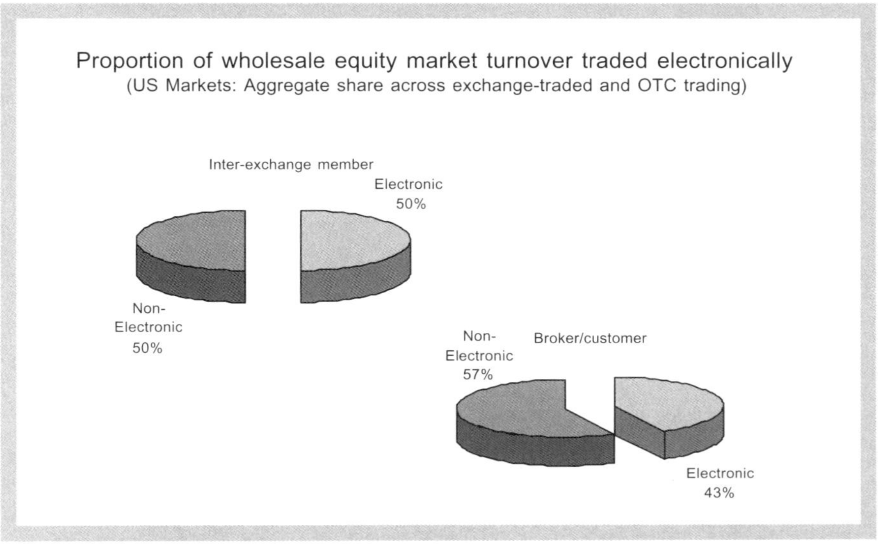

Figure 6.2 The rise of online equities trading

Source: Reserve Bank of Australia (2001) *Electronic Trading in Australian Financial Markets*, Reserve Bank of Australia, Bulletin, December

ment and Barclays Global Investors, was launched in 1999. Fund managers in the network who want to buy or sell European shares no longer have to place their orders on an exchange but can deal directly with other fund managers. The E-Crossnet joint venture is the first to be owned purely by buy-side investors (see Screen shots 6.4a and b).

Virt-X, a joint venture between the SWX Swiss Exchange and TradePoint, a JP Morgan and Morgan Stanley-owned electronic crossing network, was launched in mid-2001. It is the first joint venture between a traditional stock exchange and an ECN. The trading model encompasses a continuous electronic public limit order book with opening, intra-day and closing single price auctions and full anonymity. Facilities are also available to support liquidity providers and off book and block trading requirements. It offers straight-through-processing from trading to clearing and settlement. SWX moved all trading of 29 of the most important Swiss stocks from the Swiss market index to the new platform, which also offers blue-chip trading with 600 other European equities from the 30 most important indexes. Already 109 members have joined. UBS will play a market-making role in 450 stocks. Other prominent supporters include Merrill Lynch, CSFB and Morgan Stanley. Virt-X's stated objective is to secure a 10% market share in European equity trading in its first year. It intends to provide a central counterparty for cross-border trading in 2002 (see Table 6.5).

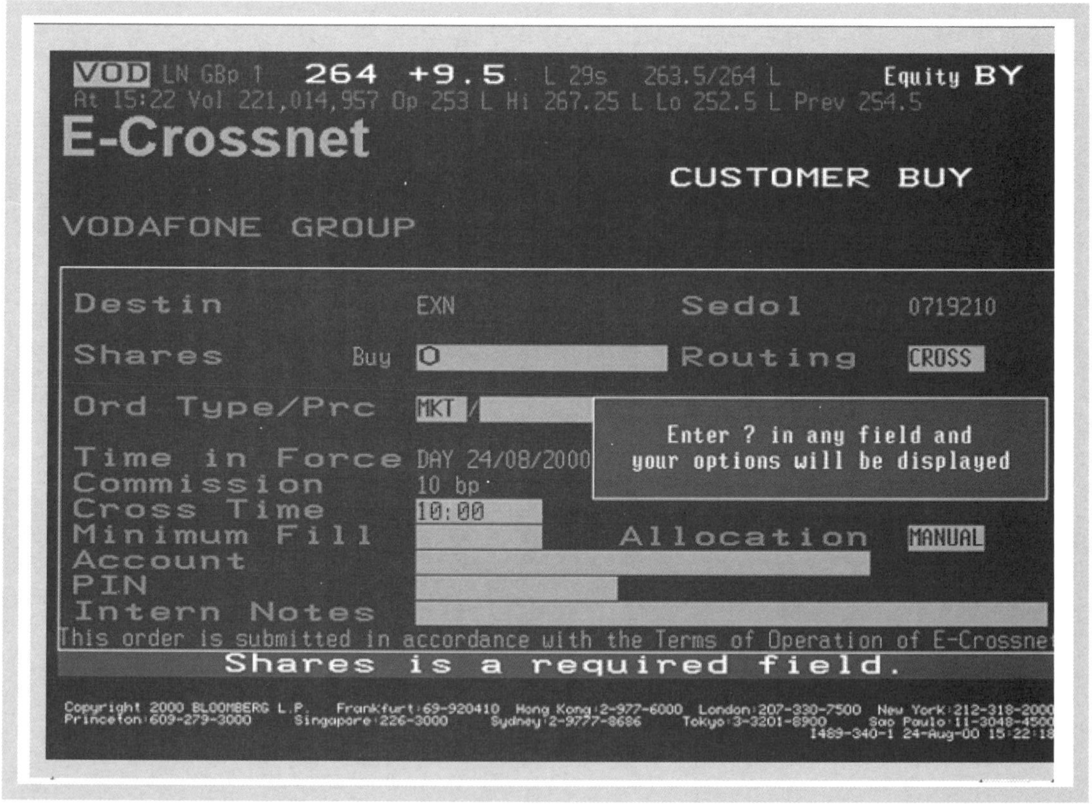

Screen Shot 6.4a E-Crossnet buy ticket

Source: Bloomberg 2002. L.P. All rights reserved. Reprinted with permission. Visit www.Bloomberg.com/www.ecrossnet.com

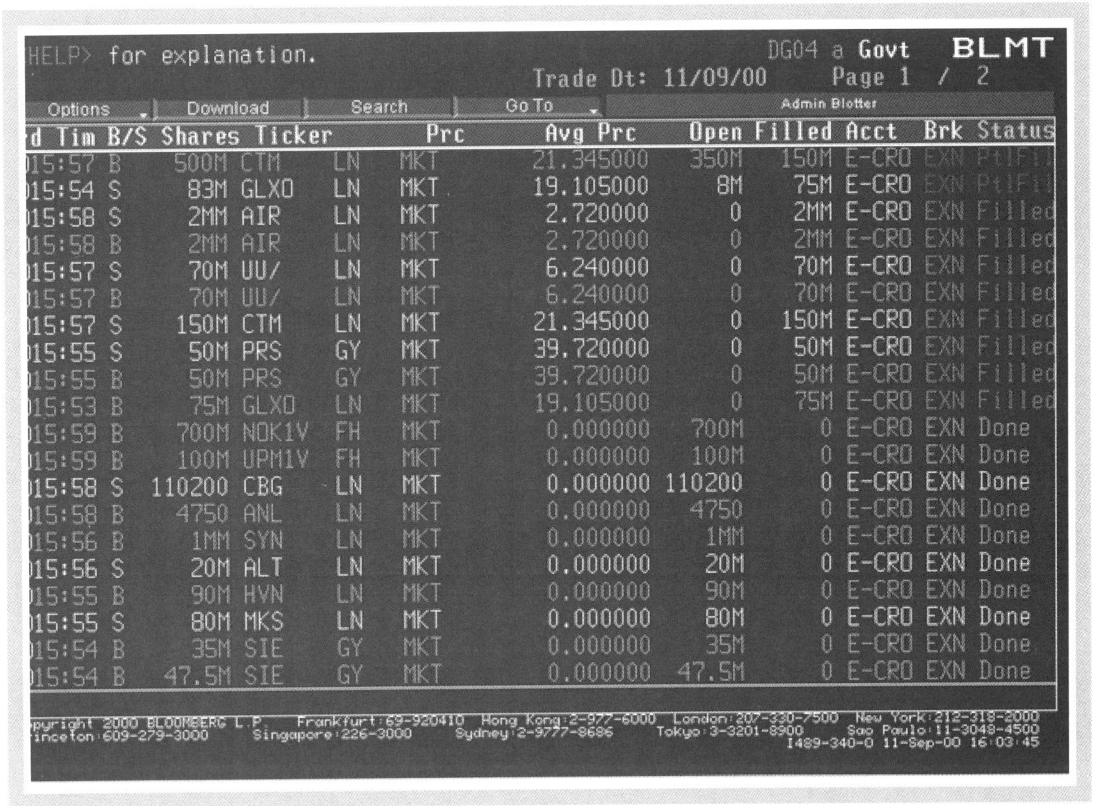

Screen Shot 6.4b E-Crossnet blotter (Bloomberg)

Source: Bloomberg 2002. L.P. All rights reserved. Reprinted with permission. Visit www.Bloomberg.com/www.ecrossnet.com

Table 6.5 Sample of equity crossing networks

System	Products	Target Market	Ownership Structure	Ownership
POSIT	US and European equities	Wholesale: Institutional investors + broker-dealers	Independent	ITG Brokerage
E-Crossnet	European equities	Wholesale: Institutional investors + broker-dealers	Consortium (buy-side)	Merill Lynch Asset Management; Mercury Asset Management; Barclays Global Investors
Virt-X	European equities	Wholesale: Institutional investors + broker-dealers	Consortium/JV	JV between SWX Swiss Exchange and TradePoint
NASDAQ Europe (formerly EASDAQ)	European equities	Wholesale: Institutional investors + broker-dealers		NASDAQ
Jiway	European equities	Retail brokers	Independent	OM Gruppen (previously J.V. with MSDW)

Examples of Crossing Systems in OTC Markets

Fixed Income and Forex

In OTC markets, the inter-dealer and the dealer-to-customer markets are still largely segregated. Although it is technically feasible, so far the market has not moved to an open network in which end-users and intermediaries have equal access. Thus, there are no true examples of e-exchanges in these sectors. However, in the fixed-income multi-dealer to buy-side space, MarketAxess and BondDesk have incorporated an anonymous CCP-based order-matching system and do enable buy-side to buy-side trading, while in the inter-dealer space, both EuroMTS and BrokerTec also employ an order-driven crossing system and may potentially open themselves to the buy-side. In the non-interbank forex market, MatchbookFX.com is similarly order-driven.

Derivatives (Old and New)

In exchange-traded commodities and equities derivatives markets, the futures and options exchanges themselves have enhanced their own technological and

Table 6.6 Sample of new OTC derivative crossing networks

System	Instruments	Type	Ownership	Ownership Composition
Creditex	Credit derivatives	Cross-matching	Consortium	DB; JPMC; CSFB; BoA; MSDW; Soc Gen; UBS; DKW
CreditTrade	Credit derivatives	Cross-matching	Independent	CreditTrade Limited; minority shareholders include JPMC, Internet Capital Group, Prebon Yamane

Note: Bank key is at the end of the chapter.

electronic trading capabilities to such an extent that they have raised formidable entry barriers to new e-markets. However, in the OTC derivatives market, including forex and fixed income, but even more so in the new product markets, crossing networks are establishing a presence. Forex and fixed-income derivative instruments tend to be traded on the spot platforms, but a few examples of pure derivatives crossing systems for newer instruments are presented in Table 6.6.

ELECTRONIC COMMUNICATIONS NETWORKS (ECNS)

Introduction and Definition

Electronic communication networks (ECNs) are, without a doubt, the most important form of electronic cross-matching network to have materialised to date, and have had a profound impact on the structure and dynamics of those equity markets in which they occur. The advent and impact of ECNs therefore warrant further elaboration (see Screen Shot 6.5).

While the term is applied generically nowadays, strictly speaking ECNs are a distinct component of the markets, primarily trading in the OTC equities market in the US. ECNs are basically private electronic networks that display and match orders for equities received from their customers, setting prices for trades in the process. Although they all have different strategies, the basic model is the same: ECNs post the size and price of orders that they receive from their subscribers onto their internal order book and automatically execute when a match is identified. Orders are matched on a strict price/time priority basis. By definition, market orders get the highest priority, while limit orders (minimum or maximum price orders) are prioritised on the basis of the price that the investor is willing to trade at. Investors willing to buy at the highest price get top priority for buy orders, and sellers willing to sell at the lowest price get the highest priority. If two limit orders are received at the same price, the order that was received first receives the highest priority. The

refresh | island home | disclaimer | help

QQQ

GET STOCK

QQQ go

Island Top 20 Active Stocks

#	symbol	mkt	shares matched	last trade price	net change
1.	QQQ	AM	264,906	38.0500	+0.0700
2.	CSCO	NM	160,415	19.2500	+0.2400
3.	WCOM	NM	143,057	10.6700	+0.2700
4.	JDSU	NM	97,362	7.0700	+0.1100
5.	BVSN	NM	74,884	2.1400	-0.0700
6.	SUNW	NM	71,532	10.7000	+0.0600
7.	VRTS	NM	60,596	44.0000	-2.1500
8.	NXCD	NM	41,180	0.2400	+0.0100
9.	MFNX	NM	38,831	0.4300	0.0000
10.	FDRY	NM	37,335	6.5600	-0.9300
11.	ORCL	NM	37,240	16.5500	+0.0500
12.	EXLT	NM	36,440	10.1300	+1.2400
13.	ARBA	NM	30,420	5.2500	+0.0700
14.	OPWV	NM	28,674	6.8700	+0.0900
15.	SEBL	NM	26,232	35.1600	+0.2300
16.	IDPH	NM	25,976	56.7520	-2.7580
17.	AMZN	NM	25,328	14.0400	-0.1800
18.	BRCD	NM	22,918	35.2500	+0.1900
19.	PALM	NM	20,348	4.0000	+0.0400
20.	RAZF	NM	19,601	0.1900	+0.0100

as of 9:17:38.86 important information

LAST MATCH		TODAY'S ACTIVITY	
Price	38.0500	Orders	9,233
Time	9:17:58	Volume	267,906

BUY ORDERS		SELL ORDERS	
SHARES	PRICE	SHARES	PRICE
1,300	38.0400	100	38.0500
2,000	38.0300	400	38.0600
500	38.0200	1,000	38.0700
1,600	38.0200	400	38.0700
800	38.0140	400	38.0800
1,000	38.0100	1,000	38.0800
800	38.0090	800	38.0800
1,600	38.0060	1,000	38.0800
800	38.0050	100	38.0900
1,000	38.0000	2,000	38.0900
3,000	38.0000	500	38.0900
2,000	38.0000	2,000	38.0900
1,000	38.0000	900	38.0990
700	38.0000	1,000	38.1000
1,000	38.0000	3,200	38.1300
(35 more)		(54 more)	

Screen Shot 6.5 The Island ECN – book view

Source: www.island.com

price is set at the level that allows the greatest number of shares to be traded. What distinguishes ECNs from most other crossing networks is a unique structure to compensate for illiquidity. If no match is identified, the order can be posted externally on NASDAQ as soon as it becomes the best price. This unique advantage is a function of their history, which is expanded upon below.

ECNs function as a hybrid between a broker for counterparties, a broker-dealer or market-maker, *and* an exchange, and their gain has been at the expense of NASDAQ, the exchanges and their middlemen. First, in a certain sense, ECNs function like a broker – acting as the agents in a transaction (by matching orders and disguising trades). However, as mentioned above, they can also post their best unmatched bids and offers onto the NASDAQ Quote-Montage, a privilege previously enjoyed only by the market-makers. Thus, they also perform one of the key functions previously only performed by dealers, and are in fact registered as broker-dealers. (Of course, the other distinction remains – market-makers act as principals in transactions, committing their own capital and competing with one another to attract orders in NASDAQ stocks, while ECNs do not.) Finally, since they make it possible to price and execute a trade, and to cut out both middlemen, they function very much like an actual electronic stock exchange (although from a strictly regulatory perspective, most ECNs do not have exchange status). ECNs make money like an exchange by charging a fee for each transaction in the form of a low commission. By contrast, market-makers are not permitted to charge fees, but generate profits from the spread between the bid and offer.

History

ECNs first entered the equity markets in the mid-1990s to display customer buy and sell orders publicly. However, it soon became clear that these networks could directly match orders and thereby execute transactions. Their rise can be attributed in large part to certain regulatory developments, which created a favourable environment for the networks' entry into the OTC equity market.

Prior to 1994, a NASDAQ dealer had discretion over public limit orders, and could refuse to execute an order that represented a better price than he presented. Needless to say, in the absence of direct competition from public limit orders, dealers could potentially post lower bid or higher offer prices for stocks, earning excess profits at the expense of investors. Then, after a scandalous incident in 1994, in which NASDAQ dealers were taped harassing colleagues who had been squeezing the bid-ask spread (in other words, enforcing a price-fixing scheme), the Securities and Exchange Commission (SEC) stepped into the breach. The perpetrators were punished with a US$1 billion antitrust civil settlement – the largest in history. However, more significantly, to thwart such anti-competitive practices, in 1997, the SEC enacted new Order Handling Rules, which were designed to set the industry back on the righteous path towards the Platonic ideal of the National Market System. The new Order Handling Rules included the order display rule, which compelled dealers to take public limit orders into full account.

The rules give a dealer three possible courses of action: limit orders must be fully reflected in the dealer's quote, or the orders must be immediately executed against the dealer's inventory, or they must be forwarded to another dealer or ECN. Thus, the rules have led to greater transparency and heightened interaction of limit orders – an outcome that in turn has spurred the development of ECNs, whose liquidity is based largely on limit-order flow.

More importantly, the SEC also gave ECNs complete access to the NASDAQ. Prior to 1997, although dealers would occasionally place on proprietary systems (Reuters' Instinet being the only system of any consequence at the time) orders that were better priced than their public quotes, these systems disseminated very little price information to the public. Suspicious of these private networks, admission to which was reserved to institutional investors and market-makers, who could then trade in secret, the Commission adopted its quote rule. This obliges dealers to display publicly their most competitive quotes and prevents a dealer from posting a more competitive quote in an ECN unless the price is viewable by, and accessible to, all market participants. By 'forcing' Instinet to post its quotes on the NASDAQ's trading bulletin board, known as a Level II screen, the SEC ended ECN privacy, and inadvertently opened a gateway to the public marketplace.

Opening the NASDAQ to ECNs proved to be a crucial step in their evolution: a network with such access needs to provide only one party to a transaction; the counterparty can come from anywhere else in the system. By contrast, a proprietary system needs to attract both a buyer and a seller to complete a transaction.

Day-trading firms, which for years had sought greater market access to NASDAQ, rushed to set up ECNs. Island ECN (largely owned by the online brokerage Datek), Attain, Archipelago and NexTrade, for example, all started off handling day-trading orders. Not to be left out, brokerage firms and other traditional players backed their own stable. REDIBook was launched by the NYSE specialist Spear, Leeds & Kellogg, for example, while Strike was started by Bear Stearns. There are currently nine licensed ECNs connected to the NASDAQ, up from the initial four approved by the SEC in 1997. These are presented in Table 6.7 and their rankings in Figure 6.3.

Table 6.7 The NASDAQ ECNs

System	Products	Target Market	Ownership Structure	Ownership
In order of magnitude				
Instinet	Unlisted US equities	Wholesale: Large institutional investors; broker-dealers (more recently); retail brokers	Independent	Reuters
Island	Listed + unlisted US equities	Retail brokers	Independent, but consortium of venture capitalists	Datek (majority); Louis Vuitton Moet Hennessey; Bain Capital; TA Associates; others
Redi-Book* *to merge with Archipelago	Unlisted US equities	Retail brokers	Consortium	Spear, Leeds & Kellog; BOA; Charles Schwab; CSFB; DLJ; Fidelity; LB; TD Waterhouse; others
Archipelago*	Listed + unlisted US equities	Wholesale	Consortium	E*Trade; GS; Instinet; JPMC; ML; others
B-Trade (supplanted Bloomberg TradeBook)	Unlisted US equities	Wholesale: Institutional investors + broker-dealers	Independent	The Bank of New York
Brut (merged with Strike Technologies)	Unlisted US equities	Wholesale: Institutional investors + broker-dealers	Consortium	26 Equity partners incl: ABN; BS; CSFB; E*Trade; GS; Herzog Heine Geduld; Hull; Knight Trading; LB; ML; MSDW; Prudential; SSB; SunGuard Data Systems
NexTrade	Listed + unlisted US equities	Wholesale: Institutional investors + broker-dealers	Independent	NexTrade Holdings Inc.
Attain	Unlisted US equities	Retail brokers	Independent	Domestic Securities Inc.
MarketXT (formerly Eclipse)	Unlisted US equities	Retail brokers	Independent	Tradescape Corp.
GlobeNet			Independent	GlobeNet Capital Corp.

Note: Bank key is at the end of the chapter.

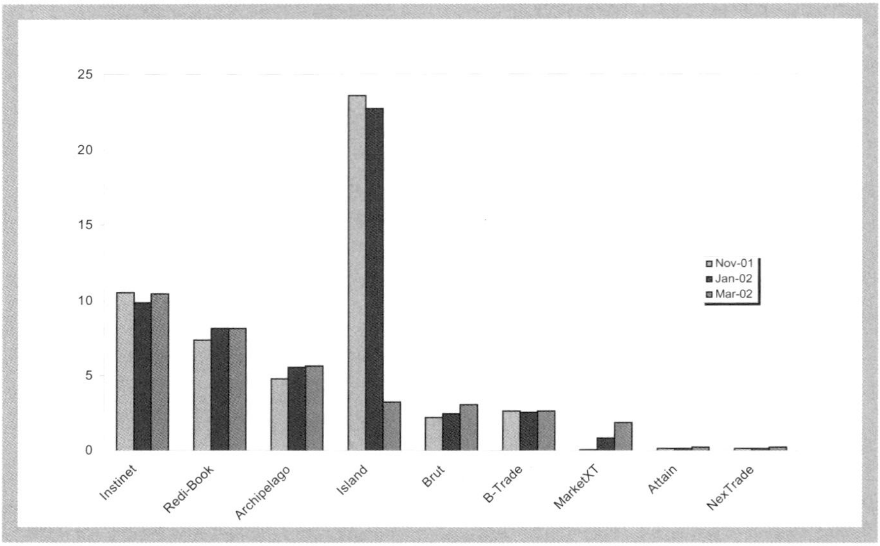

Figure 6.3 The NASDAQ ECNs: profiles

Source: The NASDAQ Stock Market, Economic Research Department, Monthly Market Data: www.marketdata.nasdaq.com, accessed April 2002

Competitive Advantages and Economic Benefits

ECNs are very attractive to investors and, to a lesser extent, other market participants (including brokers and broker-dealers). ECNs (as a type of broker-dealer) enable large investors and retail investor brokers to avoid using market-makers, and are far more cost efficient. Instead of shopping around, making repeated phone calls and negotiating for prices, an investor or broker can simply place its orders, or a portion of its orders, into an ECN and, if the other side can be found, those orders will be matched automatically. ECNs' average commission ranges from 0.0015 of a cent to 4 cents a share. By contrast, market-makers' spread is typically between 0.0625 and 0.25 of a point or between 6.26 cents and 25 cents per share.

Thus, although ECNs function as a dumping ground for unwanted limit orders for broker-dealers, overall, the growth in ECNs has come partially at the expense of market-makers, who have seen their spreads narrow and an ever-increasing proportion of their order flow handled through ECNs, rather than manually. Dealers on the NYSE and the NASDAQ have had average operating margins of 55% and 25% respectively. ECNs are steadily eroding these margins. Indeed, since the adoption of the SEC rules in 1997, the average NASDAQ spread – the difference between the bid and offer price – has declined by more than 40%. The emergence of ECNs has very probably contributed to the reduction in trading costs. Since the conversion to pricing stocks in decimals rather than fractions in 2001, NASDAQ spreads have shrunk even further – by as much as 70% on the most heavily traded stocks.

Another of their main advantages is privacy. They enable buy-side firms to buy and sell large volumes of orders anonymously. Internally ECNs post only the size and price of orders, not the identity of the trader. On NASDAQ, orders are identified only by the ECN's name. This is critical in preventing market costs through leakage and front-running. Furthermore, ECN software enables funds to post large, potentially market-moving orders in reserve. Charged with a 100,000-share bid, it might coyly post a bid for 1000 shares that will automatically refresh itself or accept larger offers until all 100,000 have been accumulated.

Swifter trade execution is another potential advantage of ECNs. State-of-the-art technology generally allows the networks to execute orders significantly faster than the trading systems of established market centres. For example, the average turnaround time for an ECN-executed order is 2–3 seconds, compared with 22 seconds for an order processed through an exchange.

The ECNs' continue to develop their systems, displaying an ongoing ability to automate the services that middlemen provide and supplant them in the relevant trades.

ECN's Gain on NASDAQ Market Share

As a consequence, since their inauguration in 1997, ECNs' growth rates have been phenomenal. According to JP Morgan H&Q (Sales, 2001), ECNs accounted for almost 47% of NASDAQ's volume in the third quarter of 2001. The hijacking of NASDAQ's business is also reflected in the networks' growing self-containment. The major ECNs now generate sufficient traffic to match about 60% of their orders internally, up from between 5 and 10% in 1999.

Future Prospects – Achieving Integration in the Securities Market

In the first instance, ECNs exist because of the previously price-driven, dealer-dependent structure of the NASDAQ OTC market, and the growing number of investors who prefer, for reasons previously examined, an order-book structure. This difference between order and price-driven markets has been key to the growth of these electronic trading systems.

However, the ECN model only partially satisfies a greater demand. Ultimately, regulators, marketplaces and certain market participants, specifically investors, are pursuing the elusive holy grail of 'best execution'. Best execution encompasses many aspects of an efficient market and primarily means securing the most favourable prices possible, but it also refers to speed of execution and other factors.

True best execution would, theoretically, only be attainable in a unified global electronic marketplace for all securities, or closely attainable in one for equities. Again, theoretically, this would be based on a virtual central limit order book (CLOB) that would display all orders (and prices) from all markets (executing limit orders on an optimal price-time basis). By ensuring full interaction of all orders, the book would lead to competition among orders, rather than among order handlers. The CLOB would be visible to everyone, allowing investors to evaluate liquidity across the markets more effectively and to seek out the best price across a variety of exchanges and OTC markets.

It is assumed by certain market participants that, eventually, the proposition of a virtual CLOB will be too powerful and compelling to resist, as basic economics dictates that the greater the supply and demand that concentrates in one place, the more efficient the price formation mechanism.

However, others envisage a different route to best execution utopia and have a different interpretation of the term 'virtual' that is, that the market will be virtually single by virtue of connectivity. Currently, a degree of integration has been achieved in the omnipotent US equity markets through something called the Intermarket Trading System. This and other methods of market interconnection enable a broker to identify the best price for clients by investigating whether the NYSE, the American Stock Exchange, the regional exchanges, or the OTC market offers this price. Many practitioners maintain that the current level of market interconnection and price transparency is insufficient to achieve a truly competitive market. However, many contend that the ECNs themselves are already a force for, rather than against, further market integration. Outbound order routing and the full transparency of limit orders achieved by some networks are deemed the prototypes of a truly interconnected market more effective than any monolithic CLOB. Thus, the fate of the ECNs depends on their ability to position themselves as the basis of this new model.

Affecting ECNs' more immediate prospects is a technological-regulatory development in this vein called SuperMontage. In early 2001, the SEC unanimously approved the NASD's proposed new trading system, SuperMontage. SuperMontage will in effect function as a quasi-CLOB in OTC stocks and will increase the market's liquidity and enhance transparency. The NASDAQ SuperMontage will centralise the display of the top three levels of orders or quotes on individual stocks, rather than just the single best bid and offer quote (as per the QuoteMontage). Consequently, participants will be able to get a better sense of the depth of interest in and prices of a security. ECNs and dealers can voluntarily enter quotes on SuperMontage. SuperMontage is intended to link the fragmented markets created by the nine ECNs and dozens of dealers.[1]

Although the SEC overrode opposition from the ECNs that compete with NASDAQ in approving the proposal, it did make a proviso that partially addresses the ECNs' objections, but which still serves the regulator's broader interests. The Commission stipulated that an alternative display facility be developed. The alternative system will give ECNs an opportunity to display their single best quotes on NASDAQ screens without going through the much larger SuperMontage. The best quotes from the ECNs currently aren't displayed on NASDAQ screens unless they are the best in the US marketplace. This other market will compete with SuperMontage and overall will increase the probability of spreads narrowing.

Strategies: To Increase Liquidity

Consolidation

As alluded to above, in economists' terms, stock exchanges tend to be natural monopolies, because investors will gravitate toward the largest exchange, to find both liquidity or the maximum number of counterparties willing to trade at the best possible price. Thus, whether the market ultimately supports a sort of oligopoly of interconnected electronic exchanges or an actual CLOB monopoly, the ECNs' best chances of survival reside in pursuing effective strategies to attract liquidity, that is, more orders onto the book. The implied starting point for some ECNs is to contradict their own brand name, such as Island and Archipelago, which insinuate, somewhat paradoxically, that they are separate from the ocean of liquidity.

Exchange theory aside, operating a trade matching engine is not the best business proposition. In fact the business case is rather weak; margins are razor thin, and it is therefore highly volume dependent. As fixed costs are disproportionately high, efficient infrastructure capacity utilisation and realising scale economies are the most critical success factors for ECNs.

Strategies to generate volume have stretched to 'paying for liquidity' (that is, employing simple but costly discount pricing strategies, such as Island's rebating of 0.1 cent of its 0.25 cent-per-share fee to anyone who placed an order), however, mergers and acquisitions rank among the more prominent.

At the one end of the spectrum, several ECNs have sold minority stakes to various types of financial institutions, who are then incentivised to divert orders their way. At the other, are full blown mergers (invariably a euphemism for an acquisition) between ECNs or between ECNs and exchanges. For example, Sunguard's BRASS Utilities' system, Brut, merged with Strike Technologies', while more recently, REDIBook has announced a merger with Archipelago. Archipelago has also partnered with the Pacific Exchange. It has even been rumoured that two of the biggest trading rivals, Reuters' Instinet and Island, may merge, which would undoubtedly pose the biggest threat to date to the NASDAQ market itself.

More broadly, consolidation in the sector was and is inevitable. As with many new technology-driven industries, there has been an initial boom and a proliferation of new entrants, and a period of rationalisation will follow – in alignment with the overarching direction of change; convergence. It is probable that only four or five ECNs will continue to thrive or even survive in the end, while the others will either exit the market or be acquired by brokers who want their own online execution services.

However, while bigger players will undoubtedly continue to swallow up some smaller players, until the optimum level of integration is realised, there will be opportunities for niche providers. Even among current ECNs, there is wide variation in offerings and markets targeted. Some of these differentiation strategies are covered below.

The market will probably grow by niche players merging, and by continuous and non-continuous markets moving together, or through interfaces between different systems. In the current environment, there is still some opportunity for new differentiated models to add liquidity to the markets. While no one knows for certain what the electronic trading landscape will look like in the future, providers of specific, customised services are likely to have a role to play, even in a consolidated market.

Target Market/Relative Competitive Positioning/Differentiation

Most ECNs are regulated as brokers and, as brokers, they receive orders from customers. ECNs typically do not serve individual investors, but instead focus on other brokers and institutional investors. However, ECNs do distinguish themselves from each other by targeting different markets. Island, for example, the second biggest ECN, tends to focus on retail brokers and traders, including day traders, while Instinet, the biggest of them all, has focused on institutional investors. ECNs also differ in terms of their trading systems. Some networks, for example, handle limit orders exclusively and are destination-only ECNs (that is, orders do not leave the network until they are cancelled). Other ECNs take both market orders (orders to buy or sell a stock immediately at the best available price) and limit orders, and routes them to the NASDAQ in search of the optimal price. These outbound-routing ECNs actively seek liquidity outside their networks: when the national best bid or offer – the best price available in the entire market – can be obtained from another dealer or network, outbound-routing ECNs send their orders there. Archipelago, for example, offers its subscribers outbound order preferencing, allowing them access to other ECNs. Interestingly, destination-only ECNs often consider outbound-routing networks some of their best customers.

ECNs also differentiate themselves in other ways. For example, each ECN that routes orders to other market centres has its own method (or algorithm) for selecting the centre that is likely to provide a particular combination of speed, quality, price and certainty of execution. Some ECNs batch orders for short periods and conduct regular 'call markets' to establish a stock price, while still others engage in price discovery continuously. Furthermore, ECNs vary in the type of information they provide investors: some post their limit-order books on the Internet, while others grant individual investors more limited access to price information. These different approaches to price discovery, quality of execution and order information are likely to attract diverse clients with diverse trading needs.

ECNs are also at the forefront of the highly publicised push towards after-hours trading. Having already created global 24-hour markets in, for example, foreign exchange, the ECNs are optimistic that technology can do the same in

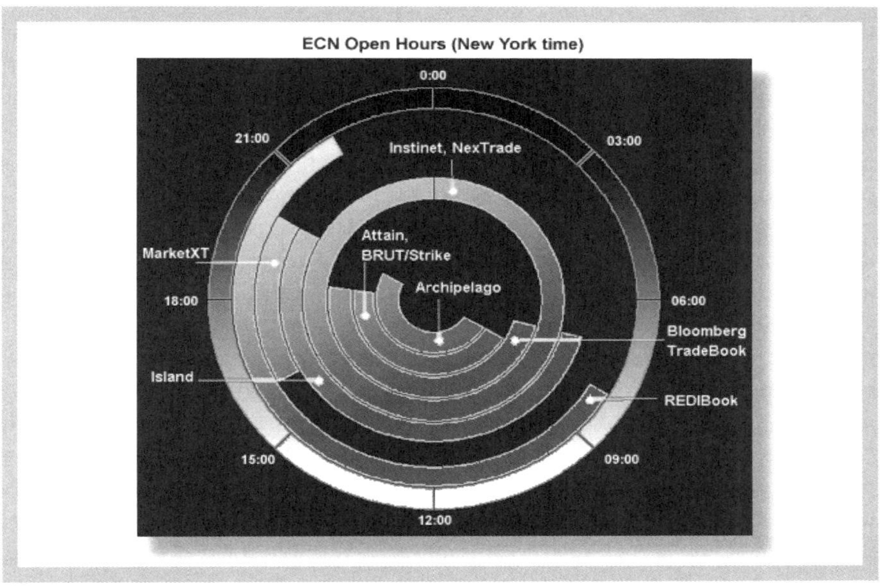

Figure 6.4 ECNs and the push towards after-hours trading
Source: Celent, May 2000

equities. Up to 40% of online orders are nocturnal, which results in an increasingly chaotic start that strains the capacity of the current system and distorts prices. Thus for ECNs, for whom extending hours is relatively easy given their low staff complements, the prospect of increasing volume by absorbing some of the night-time overhang is irresistible. The ECNs have formed a consortium to share after-hours trade data so that they can continue to operate. Some ECNs already operate after dark, such as Island, which trades 8:00am to 8:00pm weekdays, and Instinet and NexTrade, which never close (see Figure 6.4).

Expansion – Acquire Exchange Status

Discounted pricing, trading model differentiation and acquisitions or mergers are all strategies to reach a critical mass of investors. Another is to extend the product range. To date, ECNs have largely been limited to the OTC market and are still struggling to gain even a small piece of the listed share action, transacted by auction-driven US equity exchanges. Indeed, they have collectively only succeeded in securing a negligible and stagnant 4% of the NYSE's trade volume – due to its invincible centralised liquidity position. However, legislation that came into effect in 1998, enabling ECNs to apply to be regulated as exchanges themselves, has now made it conceivably more feasible to boost their share of the listed equities pie and even to target the Big Board itself.

ECNs that convert to exchanges will be subject to more scrutiny but will also be granted new freedoms. As mentioned previously, equity markets in the United States were interlinked in the late 1970s through a National Market System, which comprises the Consolidated Quotation System (NCQS) and the aforementioned Intermarket Trading System (ITS). The NCQS displays stock quotes in each participating market centre. Brokers at one exchange can then commit to buy or sell the stock at another exchange through the ITS. This system represents a major disadvantage to ECNs, because they can be linked to the ITS only via the National Association of Securities Dealers' (NASD) gateway to the network: the Computer Assisted Execution System. Since this system interface was designed for dealers, it is not very suitable for pure matching engines, such as ECNs. For example, it prescribes that any broker/dealer that participates in ITS must maintain two-sided quotes for any orders it enters into the system. ECNs only match trades on behalf of their customers and do not commit their own capital to match trades because they do not trade on behalf of their own account. The rule therefore forces an ECN to compromise its pure agency model. If it does not have a buy and a sell order for a given stock, it is obliged to submit its own quote for one side of a trade, compelling it to potentially take a proprietary position and incur risk. The system is also relatively slow.

Designation as a fully fledged stock exchange will overcome these problems. First, as an exchange, an ECN can become a self-regulatory organisation. Currently, ECNs are subject to the regulatory apparatus of the NASD, with whose members many ECNs compete. In addition, by becoming an exchange, an ECN would gain unrestricted access and connectivity to the ITS and representation on the NCQS. Furthermore, ECNs would have a say in the governance of this system and could influence the direction of investments in system upgrades.

There is, of course, no consensus on whether to pursue such offensive strategies. Island, Archipelago and NexTrade were among the first to take up the gauntlet and submit applications (as was Virt-X in Europe). Archipelago has now received approval to operate as a self-regulated exchange and is poised to strike at the NYSE Goliath. Through its partnership with the Pacific Exchange, Archipelago is set to become the first ECN to make the exchange transition. The Archipelago Exchange's ArcaEX trade-matching engine will shortly replace the Pacific's equity floors, and the former ECN will, for the first time, be able to compete for listed order flow with the NYSE and American Stock Exchange, as ITS equals. Exchange status also generates additional revenue sources, such as listing income.

However, other ECNs, including the likes of Instinet, TradeBook, Brut, Attain and MarketXT, have decided to maintain their existing status as NASD-regulated broker-dealers. Eventually, however, ECNs are likely to become targets of the exchanges themselves.

SUMMARY

In the final analysis, one cannot clearly distinguish these systems. They exist along a continuum, and exhibit a hybrid structure. For example, some OTC product multi-dealer to buy-side and inter-dealer systems employ a central order-book/order-cross-matching model, with an anonymous central counterparty, and can accommodate buy-side to buy-side trading. However, some buy-side/price-taker crossing systems have resorted to reincorporation of sell-side/price-makers who commit capital and act as principals in transactions to enhance liquidity. In these cases, the distinction between orders and quotes is becoming indistinct. (The best bid quote is the equivalent of the best buy limit order, while the best offer quote is the equivalent of the best sell limit order.) Ultimately, the great liquidity debate is as yet unresolved. Advocates of the dealer market model defend the dealer's role of liquidity provision, because investors provide liquidity only as a by-product of portfolio trading, while proponents of the exchange or order-book model allege that investors are the ultimate source of liquidity or, at least, cite the obsolescence of liquidity providers in highly liquid stocks.

It is also simplistic to chart this evolutionary path – the market may well allow certain online models to co-exist even with offline models. Voice-supported models will still be necessary for the less liquid markets where instruments are thinly traded. Reuters-owned Instinet, for example, is a global agency brokerage that operates on NASDAQ as an ECN, but elsewhere uses technology combined with traditional voice brokerage to offer customers higher speed and liquidity and lower transaction costs in both equity and debt markets.

Finally, to some extent it is also premature to try to predict how these immature market structures will evolve at all. As electronic trading in electronic markets is in the infancy of its lifecycle, its structure is far from static. The ultimate Darwinian survivors in this dynamic environment are as yet unknown.

Note

1 NASDAQ's screens currently only display the single best buy and sell quotes, so dealers trying to fill a large order have to find the next best quotes on ECNs.

Product Code

A	Agency bonds
ABS	Asset-backed securities
C	Convertibles
CP	Commercial paper
EB	Eurobonds
EM	Emerging market bonds
G	Government bonds
-ES	-Euro Sovereign
-UST	-US Treasury
HG	High-grade corporate bonds
HY	High-yield corporate bonds
I	Indications
IRS	Interest rate swaps
M	Municipal bonds
MBS	Mortgage-backed securities
NI	New issues
R	Repurchase agreements
Res	Research publications

Bank Code

ABN	ABN Amro
BoA	Bank of America
BNP	BNP Paribas
BS	Bear Sterns
Citi	Citigroup
CSFB	Credit Suisse First Boston
DB	Deutsche Bank
DKW	Dresdner Kleinwort Wasserstein
GS	Goldman Sachs
ING	ING Barings
JPMC	JP Morgan Chase
LB	Lehman Brothers
ML	Merrill Lynch
MSDW	Morgan Stanley Dean Witter
SSB	Salomon Smith Barney
UBS	UBS Warburg
WDR	Warburg Dillon Read

PART II

UNPRECEDENTED CHANGE
The Impact!

CHAPTER 7

LIQUIDITY: THE RISING TIDE

The overall effect of technology on market structure, that is, the trend towards virtual exchanges on an unparalleled scale, is concurrently producing a number of key effects on the way in which markets function. The key implications are in terms of liquidity and, by association, buy-side empowerment and overall market efficiency.

The impact of electronic trading on liquidity is multidimensional and calls for an in-depth exploration. In principle, centralised electronic trading will enhance liquidity and, therefore, efficiency. However, there are powerful countervailing forces, rooted in the present liquidity power structure, which are retarding the rate of evolutionary change and changing the contours of the future. This pivotal liquidity dynamic is an expression of many other market dynamics including intermediation, commoditisation and counterparty risk. These aspects of liquidity are explored below.

We have previously made the arbitrary assertion that single-dealer systems form an evolutionary prelude to their multi-dealer counterparts (which, in turn, will cede to true exchange-based systems). Why the former will yield to the latter is essentially because of the market's thirst for liquidity, which rises in direct proportion to the number of dealers. Let us examine this assertion and some of the allied implications.

CLOSED VS. OPEN MARKETS: ARE DIFFERENTIATED PRODUCT OFFERINGS AND MARKET POSITIONS SUSTAINABLE?

The primary differentiators between single- and multi-dealer systems, apart from the obvious in terms of number of dealers, are, at least currently, in terms of product range and target market segment. Both single-dealer and multi-dealer portals offer commingled data and trading functionality. However, single-dealer sites, such as Merrill Lynch's MLX.com, offer their clients access to a range of value-added services across a range of asset classes. By contrast, multi-dealer sites provide more basic content and focus mainly on trading a single-asset class or instrument, such as bonds, derivatives or foreign exchange. Furthermore, single-dealer portals primarily target small to medium-sized corporate or institutional investment firms (who are generally single-banked), while multi-dealer portals primarily target the bigger clients (who are frequently multi-banked). Proprietary Web-based channels at least potentially allow the big-time investment banks to reach a huge segment of the market that they previously had difficulty reaching, due to the cost of a direct line.

Thus, there may be a case for the market's ability to support both single-dealer and multi-dealer portals. The differences between these two categories of portals are analogous to the differences between portals that commingle quotes from multiple airlines and portals that link directly to a specific airline. Some people like to access a multi-airline portal to search for the cheapest prices, while others may go to a direct-airline portal to, for example, check their frequent flyer mileage or purchase an entire holiday package including accommodation and transport. And, similar to these airline portals, multi-dealer and single-dealer institutional portals should be able to co-exist.

The problem with this 'differentiated' positioning is that it is not really sustainable:

- It may be true that the multilateral and automated nature of electronic trading networks, compared to the bilateral and manual nature of the telephone, provide banks with a cost-efficient mechanism to access new customers. However, this is by no means only true if the system is proprietary. There are few barriers, cost or otherwise, in this new high-tech environment, to prevent even the proverbial 'rats and mice' from eventually graduating to multi-bank 'relationships', using the term loosely. Perhaps at the very bottom of the market – at the SME and SoHo level – the money market, forex and other needs are so basic, that these customers will continue to engage in only one primary *commercial* banking relationship. However, in general, the Internet is the great leveller: size no longer counts (at least not as much). And many of these developments favour the buy-side, serving to empower the universal customer.
- Furthermore, in terms of content, there is nothing to prevent open portals from matching, or even exceeding, the level of value-add offered by the proprietary sites. To stress test this hypothesis, let us look at some trends

emerging in retail financial services. Often there are remarkable parallels between developments in retail and wholesale markets, with the wholesale markets lagging behind slightly. For whatever reason, B2C e-commerce has a headstart, and therefore provides a valuable precursor to B2B e-business.

In their infancy, online banking and trading sites offered basic transactional functionality, supplemented by basic information, with minimal value-added services, such as advisory services. As they evolved, these sites added ever-more technically advanced functionality, such as wallets, access to multiple exchanges, so-called 'after-hours' trading, access through mobile devices, and a full package of content (including stock quotes, news, technical trends (graphs and data), and so on) to equip Joe Bloggs to make his own decisions. However, red-hot growth in demand led to intensified competition, and as the execution-only sites began to mirror one another, allowing for differentiation only on price, price wars began to rage. Under these conditions, e-brokerages, particularly, realised that they had saturated the first generation segment of investors, the so-called 'day traders', who were typically techno-savvy with a high-risk propensity, and that the needs of the second generation were quite different. This mass market of more cautious investors rejected the burden of self-service and demanded more hand-holding. As a result, both banks and brokerages began to focus on an alternative value proposition – customer intimacy. They started introducing personalised financial management tools, geared around 'my net worth' and optimising that net worth, incorporating risk propensity, income, assets and liabilities, all linked to lifecycle stage (for example student banking 101 to retiree), and so on. Having realised that no market segment valued the transaction component, which has become commoditised and low margin, even the discount brokers started adding tools and toolboxes to optimise the investor's portfolio – be it a 'white-knuckle' or 'blue-chip' mandate. The best-of-breed providers now purport to be able to calculate the prospective investor's risk profile, the principal they are able to invest, and the optimum return – delivering a customised financial proposition tailored to each individual's changing profile over time. Finally, online financial portals realised that the customer's accounts (transactional banking, such as cheque accounts; assets, such as unit trusts; liabilities, such as mortgages; and insurance and assurance policies, such as retirement annuities) were probably sourced from different financial institutions, and that a single point of access to all 'my accounts' was a compelling value proposition. These portals also realised that in restructuring the balance sheet, the best-of-breed products may not necessarily come from their own stable. Enter the open finance model. A handful of banks in Europe and the US have pioneered open finance. Credit Suisse, with its Fund Lab and Insurance Lab, have introduced Web users to open finance by enabling them to choose best-of-breed branded products from dozens of external suppliers. Citibank's 'My Accounts' offering presents the balances and statements from multi-bank accounts. Many competitors, such as ABN Amro with Money Planet, have already stated their intentions to follow suit. There is now growing evidence that this model will end up in pole position.

What does this reveal about the likely fate of proprietary and non-proprietary institutional portals? It would indicate that content will continue to advance up the evolutionary tree, from market data to portfolio optimisation, but that the portfolio optimiser application will probably have to be open in terms of bank account linkage, and will probably still have to link to the open pricing and trading engines.

- In addition, while the multi-dealer portals currently focus on a single instrument, there is nothing to prevent them from extending the product range in time. Already all the OTC market sites have proposed expanding their territory – from fixed income to money market to forex to their derivatives or vice versa.

Thus, the essential problem with this product-market positioning is that it reduces single-dealer sites to a mere alternative to the phone in accessing all the broker-dealer's services. They're basically a new medium with which to communicate with the bank. As such, while such a site might save the inconvenience of having to telephone several different departments, they do not offer any significant value-added services.

THE OPEN MARKET ADVANTAGE: MULTI-DEALER LIQUIDITY

By contrast, the multi-dealer portals currently have one significant advantage over the likes of MLX: liquidity. And this is not just in terms of price, that is, the ability to access quotes from multiple banks simultaneously, but product too, that is, one of the most substantial benefits that the central marketplaces or exchanges offer is an online gateway to a huge inventory of stocks or bonds. Despite the sophistication of single-dealer click-and-trade sites, multi-bank sites effectively do the same thing except that posted prices are generally indicative only and a trade is executed on a firm quote. Request-for-quote systems might be e-mail on steroids, but they work. The bottom line is that multi-dealer sites give investors what they want – a single screen of competing prices. Single-dealer sites do not. Perhaps prematurely, given the newness of the technology, the proof is in the transaction volumes. Although actual data on transaction volumes is scant, initial trading levels would indicate that single-dealer sites, with a few notable exceptions, are struggling. Many are now predicting that without sufficient liquidity, a single-dealer portal will ultimately drift into extinction.

TIMING: A REPRIEVE FOR THE SINGLE-DEALER

Perhaps the single-dealer species, lacking the liquidity advantages of the new multi-dealer breed, and with few other sustainable advantages or protective barriers, does face eventual extinction. However, this is a longer range forecast. In reality, the average CFO has yet to even start trading with individual banks over the Web, and many smaller treasuries do not even have access to Reuters or Bloomberg dealing screens, far less to state-of-the-art Web pricing and execution. Nor is the average institutional investor any more technologically savvy. Six out of ten institutional investors in the US have yet to trade a bond online, for example.

Technology constraints (ability) and low levels of sophistication (willingness) imply that market receptiveness for aggregated Internet access is low. The question is; are banks and technology companies clambering to meet a need that doesn't really exist? And in doing so, are they rushing to squeeze their own margins and further commoditise their services in an already highly competitive market?

It seems, at a minimum, that the rate of change is often *overestimated*. Surprisingly, given the typical organisation's resistance to change, the window of opportunity today is often perceived to be narrower than it is and organisations yield to a false competitive imperative of speed. This is probably because e-ventures are often driven by techies who are early adopters in their personal capacity and non-representative of the mass market. The dire consequences of techie-driven business decisions are now known to many a defunct portal; from FX-oriented CFOWeb.com to derivative-oriented TreasuryConnect.

That said, most market participants share a common vision of the future, one where end-users can reach whichever banks they want through a single e-channel, providing access to pricing and execution, as well as portfolio and risk management advisory services. The market will probably eventually coalesce on a relatively small number of open sites in order to concentrate liquidity and achieve maximum efficiencies. The majority of end-users will opt to connect to the system that is most appropriate to their market segment. Single-bank e-trading may well be relegated to history.

EQUITY AND LIQUIDITY: THE POWER OF LIQUIDITY PROVIDER CONSORTIA

Allied to this is the issue of ownership. As stated above, liquidity is by far the highest weighted factor contributing to a portal's success or failure. It supersedes all others because it is fundamentally about the 'network effect'. A market will clearly live or die by the volume of buy- and sell-side trades and traders that it secures. However, the key is not just to open the gateway to multiple sell-side liquidity providers, but to sell them equity too. Ownership, in fact, contributes most to the generation of liquidity. Those with an equity stake have a major incentive to provide the market with liquidity, and *who* those stakeholders are, is therefore a key determinant of the market's ability to secure maximum transactional volume.

Mortality rates support this proposition. For example, of the 14 or so fixed income hubs that have gone belly-up since their number peaked at over 80 by the end of 2000, all but two were independents. By contrast, the undisputed winner in interest rate products is multi-dealer-owned TradeWeb.

The death of CFOWeb.com, a one-stop trading and data centre targeted at CFOs, corporate treasurers and fund or trust managers, was one of the first high-profile failures. It provided 'case study' proof that it takes more than cutting-edge technology and savvy marketing to build a winner. While CFOWeb offered its clients access to real-time quotes, news, market data, research, analytics and so on, as supplementary to online trading, all from one central location, the clients, it seems, only ever logged on to feast on data. Before its untimely demise, Integral, CFOWeb's parent, while admitting that it was no hotbed for trading, defended the portal as not primarily about trading in any event. They asserted that it was more about the provision of a suite of aggregated and integrated value-added functions, from content in the pre-trade realm, and confirmations and settlement in the post-trade realm. However, when the kitty ran out, Integral conceded that these offerings were intended as 'attractors' to boost transaction volumes, and that it had failed due to the lack of strong financial backing and liquidity. The barrier to liquidity, or the key, is multi-bank or, by default, liquidity provider ownership. The actual death knell was tolled following the formation of two very large, multi-dealer consortia: Atriax and FXall. Integral decided that the liquidity quotient of these bank-owned consortiums posed too large a threat to CFOWeb's success. Without distribution capability and critical mass, it couldn't survive as a marketplace and the plug was pulled.

Interestingly, Integral agreed to build an enhanced version of CFOWeb's trading engine for Atriax. Backed by such Wall Street titans as Deutsche, Citibank and JP Morgan, Integral presumed that Atriax simply had greater potential for liquidity than CFOWeb had. It is ironic that the demise of

CFOWeb, and its ultimate rebirth through Atriax, was followed by the eventual demise of Atriax too, leaving FXall to mop up. One way or another, though, early precedent does indicate that the winners in this industry will be the multi-party consortia, not the independents.

This has been a pervasive trend. Once upon a time, developing new and innovative stand-alone trading platforms, to establish one's technology as superior to rivals, was the modus operandi of every broker-dealer on Wall Street, despite the dominance of Bloomberg. More recently, however, there has been a shift towards co-optition, whereby Wall Street's power players are jointly investing in trading platforms that amalgamate the prices and services of several dealers in one central marketplace. For example, while over 50% of the top 20 bond dealers offer a proprietary single-dealer system, by comparison, over 85% have invested in at least one, but usually multiple multi-dealer platforms. This seems to be a sort of concession that the number one priority for any portal is to put together a consortium that can provide liquidity and distribution for the product.

The once alleged threat of disintermediation posed by new independent entrants has been nullified by a lack of liquidity. And, save a few survivors (notably amongst the ECNs), the sites that succeed will ultimately be the ones that banks allow to succeed – their own. The cruel and inescapable truth is that power begets power, and the great Wall Street titans will enter the electronic age on their own terms.

EQUITY STAKES AND HEDGING BETS

The tendency of broker-dealers to pump cash into multiple consortia, rather than putting all their proverbial eggs and liquidity into a single basket, warrants some comment in relation to what this has indirectly exposed about the rate of evolutionary change in markets, and in dealer markets in particular.

Certain names appear on the investor roll of multi-bank-owned e-markets with monotonous regularity, to which Table 7.1 below testifies. Obviously, if those systems in which a given bank has invested can be discriminated between on the basis of:

- product (such as equities or forex or interest rate securities), or
- sub-product (such as sovereign versus high-yield debt), or
- target market segment (such as inter-dealer versus dealer-to-corporate, or retail versus wholesale), or
- target geographic market,

then the investments represent strategic coverage of all bases. Most product markets are too heterogeneous and geographically distributed for an 'everything to everyone' strategy to be feasible in the short term for any one entity with finite resources. For example, in the fixed-income market, AsiaBondPortal (owned by Deutsche, JP Morgan Chase, and UBS Warburg among others) and BondsInAsia (owned by Citigroup, Deutsche and HSBC, among others) might have to battle it out in the Asian region, but are unlikely to be waging war with TradeWeb (owned by Deutsche, JP Morgan Chase, and Citigroup among others) any time soon.

However, many of the ventures in which the same banks have invested are far less distinguishable. What would account for the same banks investing in ventures that undeniably either currently compete head-on or may butt heads in the future? In certain instances at least, one can discern subtle distinctions between trading models which account for these cross-holding patterns. These distinctions relate to the degree of evolutionary advancement. For example, the simple RFQ model may have been rendered more (discontinuous) auction-like in one system, if it has been adapted to resemble the primary market model. Instead of being blind and therefore static, pricing becomes dynamic, if all the banks (and the client) participating in the auction are able to view the 'book' live, that is, to see – albeit anonymously – competing 'bids' and to bid more aggressively until the auction closes. Alternatively, a system may facilitate a shift from quote- to order-driven price formation by permitting investors to trade on posted prices or, even more so, by permitting investors to post a true order onto an order book instead of submitting a request for a price. Or a system may actually start to function like an exchange by permitting investors to apply for a central credit limit with the exchange, which then acts as a principal counterparty.

Potentially, their owners hold or held the view that such differentiation may sustain a demand for several systems in different segments. For example, more advanced systems may only be supportable in liquid instruments, while illiquid product markets may still depend on more traditional liquidity provision. Even if there were some territory encroachment or overlap in terms of instrument coverage, success may still not be mutually exclusive. However, this seems improbable. There were and still are too many consortia sites trying to serve the same market. They cannot all survive.

Thus, the heavyweight banks with deep pockets may simply be adopting a defensive strategy, hedging their bets, so to speak, because they can afford to. As Deutsche, at least, has admitted, no one knows which consortia are going to be the winners. If they knew with any certainty who would gain a foothold where, they'd be making singular rather than multiple investments. In other words, broker-dealers are aware that some of the start-ups in which they're acquiring equity are bound to fail. The position seems to be that technology investments invariably incur such risks. As Roger Bates, chief operating officer of Deutsche Bank's e-Ventures unit stated in an interview with *Wall Street & Technology*, 'You're going to win some and going to lose some ... [But] as long as you're winning more than you're losing, that's a positive gain' (Sales, 2001). This defensive posture implicitly assumed in buying equity in multiple consortia is risky, costly and may lead to conflicts of interest in the future. However, in the aftermath of the online day-trading feeding frenzy which caught many banks off guard, many have vowed never to get caught unprepared by technology innovations again.

REVELATIONS ABOUT THE RATE OF EVOLUTIONARY CHANGE

Already the banks have sustained a few losses in the first round of e-trading, and those losses are quite illuminating in the broader context of evolution. Developments in the US fixed-income arena are a case in point. At the beginning of the new millennium, online bond trading was just ready for takeoff, and four consortia were revving up on the runway: TradeWeb, MarketAxess, BondDesk and BondBook.

As they were initially structured, these sites were definitely not mirror images of one another, but the distinctions were minor. Essentially they were all fixed-income multi-dealer to buy-side trading systems that originated in the North American market. BondDesk targeted the retail segment, however, while the others targeted the wholesale market. And while TradeWeb was positioned in the most liquid product segment, namely government bonds, BondBook and MarketAxess traded less liquid corporate debt.

The accompanying ownership composition shown in Table 7.1 is effectively a list of the usual suspects, each of whom held a stake in at least two of these sites. Several had an equity stake in three or four.

By the end of 2001, TradeWeb was leading the pack by some distance, while BondBook had crashed and burned. Since heavyweight backing was a common denominator, and therefore neutralised as a factor, other factors can be weighted in their contrasting fortunes.

At the outset, the major distinction between the wholesalers was in terms of counterparty identity disclosure; such that TradeWeb is completely non-anonymous (RFQ), BondBook was completely anonymous (order-matching), while MarketAxess is a hybrid (name-give-up IDB model and order-matching).

The now defunct BondBook, launched in early 2001, was by far the most innovative of the three leading US contenders, but met with an untimely end at the end of 2001. Modelled on exchange principles of any-to-any connections, true transparency and absolute anonymity, it proved to be ahead of its time.

Table 7.1 Cross-holding patterns in fixed-income e-market consortia

	TradeWeb	MarketAxess	BondDesk	BondBook
ABN Amro		X	X	
Credit Suisse First Boston	X	X	X	X
Deutsche Bank	X	X		X
Goldman Sachs	X		X	X
JP Morgan Chase	X	X		
Lehman Brothers	X	X		X
Merrill Lynch	X			X
Morgan Stanley Dean Witter	X			X
Salomon Smith Barney/Citigroup	X	X		X
UBS		X	X	X

When its backers pronounced its death sentence, they cited lack of critical mass. Why the masses didn't come is the crux of the matter. Owner broker-dealers were obliged to support the system – by committing capital to make markets and stimulate liquidity – and they incurred penalties if they reneged. However, down on the ground, dealers were reluctant to throw real weight and money behind a platform that allowed clients to trade directly with each other, despite the rationale that it would reduce the balance sheet, free up capital, and usher in a new generation of value-adding salesmen. Furthermore, the dealers resented the anonymous provision of liquidity. Most reckoned that a no-name brand service to clients was nonsensical. Second, the product range was constrained by the fact that traders, who do not like too much price transparency lower down the credit ratings, would only support the exchange model for high-grade credits. Investors, too, proved reluctant to abandon their bilateral relationships and derived credit lines. There were too many unanswered questions about liquidity during volatile periods to risk being a guinea pig with an anonymous central counterparty.

Ultimately, BondBook's model wasn't necessarily wrong, but its timing was. It fell victim to unlucky timing, as harsh economic realities and market conditions (in which liquidity is a non-issue), non-conducive to a behavioural change, conspired against it. The elongation of the time to critical mass could not be absorbed in relation to costs. Developing such a system is unavoidably expensive simply because it's new, but also because of the heavy back-office functionality requirements. (By comparison, under disclosed models, the settlement process remains the transacting counterparties' responsibility.)

What's worse is that BondBook tried to short-cut this by buying the Bank of New York's BondNet exchange technology, which was eight years old and cost over US$60 million to upgrade. (To corroborate this, CoreDeal, which also used the Bank of New York's platform, has since sold out to MTS in order to get the right technology.)

After trading a total of US$10 billion in five months, BondBook's backers were asking themselves whether they could or should be trying to introduce the all-to-all model at this time. After eight months, BondBook's backers decided that the answer was 'no' and cut their losses. The question, 'if not now, then when and how', remains.

TradeWeb, by contrast, is a runaway success story and, by no coincidence, is frankly prosaic by design. It simply replicates the telephone method of trading (ringing up three traders to get the best price) and makes it faster and more efficient online, and doesn't threaten dealers too much. It started with the most pedestrian and predictable of assets – government bonds – and then expanded the product range. (Having established liquidity in US Treasuries and euro gilts, it should be easier to transition into less liquid, high-grade corporate bonds, than to launch into these markets, as others have attempted.) TradeWeb's cumulative trading volume since launch in 1998 hit the US$8 trillion mark by the end of 2001.

Although it is set to dominate in the medium term, MarketAxess may yet prove a formidable rival. MarketAxess predominantly trades high-grade and high-yield corporate debt, as did BondBook, but on a risk-mitigating dual basis (of name and no-name-give-up), and its gain had been partially at BondBook's expense. Since many of BondBook's investors had also invested in MarketAxess, the decision to drop BondBook in favour of MarketAxess seemed wise. MarketAxess's hybrid structure may hold the answer to the question of when and how to introduce exchange-style trading. Although currently over 90% of MarketAxess's trading is conducted via the disclosed model, within three to five years the undisclosed model may yet have its day. Finally, the early success of exchange-styled multi-dealer ventures in the inter-dealer sector, such as CoreDealMTS, and their likely eventual encroachment on buy-side territory, will also reveal much about the immediate future of electronic dealer markets as a whole.

POLITICS IN BUSINESS

Of course, to attribute TradeWeb and BondBook's respective rise and fall to evolutionary versus revolutionary trading model discrepancies, is to oversimplify a complex set of dynamics. The failure of another multi-bank site, BondClick, sheds some light on this. BondClick, backed by Deutsche Bank and JP

Morgan Chase among others, closed shop after only three months of trading. It died not for its lofty ideals and vision, but because it fell prey to petty infighting. The short tale of its downfall is a fable of management by committee and the dangers of consortia being destroyed by themselves. Decision-making was made unbearably slow by the 7-bank governance structure; rival banks brought all their enmity from Wall Street into the boardroom, and different investment strategies proved irreconcilable. Eventually, BondClick was bought out by MTS/BondVision in May 2001. Under the terms of the deal, the 7 banks in BondClick would join the 13 existing shareholders in BondVision on an equal basis, and MTS would hold 30% of the company's equity. Effectively, BondClick was taken over and taken apart – with the brand, technology and most of the staff unceremoniously ditched.

Politics aside, conflicts of multiple interests may sabotage many consortia-owned ventures. Many banks seem not to have reconciled the necessary trade-offs in their investment strategies. For example, it seems unclear whether banks intend their e-markets, particularly the inter-dealer kind, to become utilities (realising the simple economic objective of cutting out the brokers and their cut), or to be for-profit corporations (analogous to public exchanges). This confusion seems to reign most when both the private equity and securities trading divisions have made investments in competing systems with conflicting motives (strategic as opposed to ROI). Some banks seem not even to have reconciled their position with respect to e-exchanges at all, that is, whether they intend to sabotage exchanges in order to prolong the life of market-makers, or whether they are investing in e-exchanges in tandem with traditional models so that the e-exchange cannibalises, rather than preys on, market-making, and provides a substitute 'income' once that source dries up.

Ironically, from an individual multi-bank-owned e-market's perspective, it may find its competitiveness undermined by its own owners. The venture's ability to make unfettered decisions in its own best interests may be perverted and subverted by its bosses' conflicting vested interests. In the same way that mutually owned exchanges had their agility impaired, consortia-owned e-markets' ability to respond quickly to changing market conditions and to actively protect and expand their income sources may be hindered by competitors-cum-shareholders with their own agendas. TradeWeb and MarketAxess may provide a bellwether of who will give way to whom. TradeWeb intends to expand into forex, for example, but many of its investors also held or hold an equity interest in either Atriax or FXall. It also intends to expand into corporate debt, which would place it in direct competition with MarketAxess. Similarly, it is anticipated that MarketAxess will start offering Treasuries. Such a move would make sense for MarketAxess, as all corporate bonds are priced off Treasuries. However, there is an 80% ownership overlap between the two and no sign of a merger on the cards. Whether these markets, as independent businesses, prevail over their dependencies, will be an acid test of what happens when your competitors for market share own you.

Many consortia are equally vulnerable: their boards peopled by traders with barely any experience of running a business, who represent banks that can't agree on anything, in an intensely competitive market, with limited resources that are being eroded by the economic downturn and lack of demand. A general rationalisation is underway and many sites face a bald choice – merge or fold. Already the casualty list is growing. To cite but a few high-profile examples: in the European retail equities sector, Morgan Stanley pulled out of its joint venture with the OM Gruppen in the Jiway crossing system, which is now positioned for eventual closure, as trading volumes remain stagnant. In the derivatives sector, Cygnify, a multi-bank derivatives platform offering portfolio and risk management and pricing tools, backed by LabMorgan among others, filed for bankruptcy in September 2001. In the fixed-income markets, BondUSA, Intervest, VisibleMarkets, TruMarkets and State Street's BondConnect all went out of business, while LimiTrader began licensing its software, BondNexus was acquired by BondDesk, BondClick by BondVision and Trading Edge by MarketAxess. In all, there were 21 names listed in the Bond Market Association's (BMA) 2000 annual survey of electronic trading systems that had been dropped from the 2001 edition, which totalled 79. The death toll is set to grow.

However, this aggregated figure masks the variance in evolutionary cycle stage at the regional level. As of December 2001, there were at least 49 systems based in the US supporting trade in fixed-income securities and derivatives, compared to 68 in 2000, and 11 in 1997. In other words, the more advanced US market has accelerated through the propagation and proliferation stage and has entered the rationalisation period. By contrast, there were at least 24 mainly European fixed-income trading systems, versus 5 in 2000. Finally, in the 2001 report, the BMA, for the first time, identified 6 platforms for trading loans, including syndicated loans, loan pools and commercial mortgages.

If a site boasts high levels of liquidity, à la TradeWeb, the odds of continued success as a solo act are in its favour, while the weaker players may well find themselves swallowed up in the near future. Wall Street is rife with rumours about who is next. However, to the observer, the rationalisation process is an interesting one. In the creation of as wide and deep a pool of liquidity as possible, the pendulum is swinging toward those consortia-based models that rely on dealers to initially supply liquidity (to the buy-side).

However, the moral of the success story is not as simple as dealer ownership and pilot dealer-driven dealing. Very recent events in the forex market underscore this point. Atriax, whose dealer-dependent model was about as pedestrian as you can get, was the multi-dealer successor to independent Integral's CFOWeb. Integral conceded defeat to the liquidity superiority of

Atriax, who inherited its technology. That concession proved premature. Atriax was pitted against another contender-pretender; FXall. While there was little differentiation in what they purported to offer, with respect to liquidity, Atriax had a clear and present advantage. It had the three biggest boys in the playground as backers (Citibank, Deutsche and JP Morgan Chase), plus the major info-mediary (Reuters), while FXall had the also-rans, and Atriax also secured double the number of liquidity providers (70 compared with 32). Under the basic liquidity-ownership and evolution-not-revolution hypothesis, Atriax should have survived the battle for supremacy. It did not. Although the very recent death of Atriax makes post-mortem speculation imprudent and premature, nevertheless, it is speculatively possible that conflicts of political and business interests negated its advantages. For example, Reuters may harbour ambitions of extending its proprietary inter-dealer system to the buy-side segment of the market, or Atriax's overlapping bank backers may have opted to throw their lot in with a product expansion by the already successful TradeWeb. On the other hand, bad timing, bad management and a host of other devils may have beset the venture. The bottom line is that liquidity ownership and well-timed evolution are clear success factors, but they are necessary (or usually necessary) but insufficient preconditions. Politics can cloud these clear business rules.

IMPLICATIONS OF LIQUIDITY POWER MONGERING ON TRANSPARENCY AND EFFICIENCY

In the meantime, the rise of online consortia has raised some concerns about the amount of power that broker-dealers now have in the bond and forex trading arena. Board seats and votes, the equivalent of exchange seats, are now directly proportional to the actual cash investment. On an intra-consortium basis, any broker-dealer that owns more than 20% is likely to be calling all the shots. However, the compromised spirit of independence, and therefore investor acceptance, may constrain individual equity interests to between 5 and 15%. More broadly, however, this issue of power and control has some more sinister connotations.

So far the economics of markets or exchanges as businesses are poor. It is highly probable that banks are not investing capital in these ventures for the lucrative returns they might generate, but to protect their intermediary role and to access trade flow information. The Net's promise of liberating markets from the stranglehold of middlemen may be defeated by these equity structures.

In the first instance, as alluded to above, dealer-owned e-markets may retard the process of liberating markets from dealer dependency. Their trading systems are more likely to be structured so that either one nominated dealer or one of the limited number of owner-dealers acts as prescribed principal in all transactions with designated clients. This protects the credit risk premium attached to market or price-making capital commitment. Second, even if the model is not patently designed to preserve the intermediary function and prevent 'unnecessary' competition (between investing banks and/or between investing and non-investing banks), it may still be designed to provide an alternative source of price discovery information to that which acting as broker-dealer provided by default.

In general, whether electronic trading systems actually do raise transparency levels and disclose more information (including to whom they disclose it) depends on the design of the system and is primarily a business decision by the owner. These decisions reflect the needs and demands of the intended users of the systems, as well as the business interests of the owners of the system. Business interests are important in this respect, as the strategic non-disclosure of information can be an important element of the business model underlying the system that is provided. Better access to trade-related information is generally regarded as a valuable asset. Therefore, market participants that benefit from information asymmetries (such as dealers) may want to prevent these from disappearing. If network effects and first-mover advantages result in dealer-owned systems becoming dominant, then the participating dealers will still effectively be able to benefit from information asymmetries.

In fact, electronic trading systems may prove a better source of information than the telephonic price enquiry and trade system. Electronic networks capture all sorts of information on the various participants in the system. For instance, in multi-dealer systems, it is possible to record the search and trading activity of customers as well as the reactions of dealers (in terms of pricing speed and quality and 'hits and misses', that is, whether a quote request finally results in a trade). In principle, dealers only have information on their own business conducted via the system. System providers, however, have access to all the trade-related information, which can be highly valuable. Whether and how this information will be disseminated remains an open question. The watchdogs, however, are already looking for answers.

In a report commissioned by and for the BIS (2001), it was alleged that one of the reasons why dealers have been very active in promoting systems in which they, rather than third parties, are involved, is that these systems provide them with more exclusive access to trade-related information. And that this access to flow information is enough of an incentive for intermediaries to offer electronic trading to their customers, even if it results in declining profit margins for actual trading.

However, those profits might not be on such a decline. Despite the blurb on co-operation in the interests of enhanced transparency, heightened competition, and improved overall market efficiency, consortia also provide dealers with a mechanism to 'co-operate' in their own interests:

> Ever notice that all the New York to Chicago flights are the same price?

This is an anonymous quote by an anonymous insider at a bond trading platform excerpted from the January 2001 edition of the *Wall Street & Technology* journal (Schmerken, 2001). The none too subtle insinuation that consortia are cartels in disguise, designed to prevent spread compression, confirms a suspicion long held by outsiders. To lend more credence to this, in November 2000, the US Justice Department sent demands for information, dubbed 'civil investigative demands', to some of the dealers involved in consortia, such as FXall and Atriax. It was reportedly asking questions about competitiveness effects and possible price collusion, that is, the extent to which the information exchange process permits firms to co-ordinate their behaviour. So far, however, no formal allegations have been made.

CONCLUSION: OPEN MARKETS BOTH NEED AND ATTRACT LIQUIDITY

In the final analysis, however, the evidence is inconclusive. There has been too little history for any clear patterns to emerge. Perhaps single-dealer sites will continue to successfully serve a distinct market segment. Perhaps the independent portals, such as CFOWeb, died an untimely death merely because they were before their time. Perhaps MarketAxess has been relegated to the illiquid markets because TradeWeb's first-mover advantage is too strong, but then again, perhaps it will succeed in using technology to create liquid markets that didn't exist before. Perhaps many of the consortia will fail anyway because of management by committee and conflicting interests. Rumours are surfacing that suggest that at least some of them operate suspiciously like cartels, not consortia, and will fall victim to internal subversive elements and sabotage. Perhaps the cartel bosses have ulterior motives and hidden agendas in terms of protecting the status quo and access to inside flow information. On the other hand, it is also possible that there is a legitimate role for sell-side liquidity provision, that electronic markets are viable businesses in their own right, and that bank investments are also motivated by the simple need to cut costs and increase volume in low-margin commoditised products.

However, it is clear that, as electronic trading in certain product markets matures, there is a pronounced trend towards openness and liquidity.

DISINTERMEDIATION: PLAYS BY THE POWER PLAYERS

As we have alluded to previously, traditional brokers will become electronic fallout. First, in OTC markets, inter-dealer brokers are facing a dubious future. IDBs have always provided a service that met a fundamental need in the OTC trading arena. Dealers have traditionally relied on these brokers to work a trade so that competing dealers aren't privy to the identity of the off-loader, which at least partially prevents shorting. However, as dealers have acclimated to the ways in which the Web can create broader, deeper, more liquid markets, with enhanced transparency and secrecy, super-fast, low-cost execution and so on, many have begun to ask; 'who needs a broker, when a machine can do a better job more cheaply?'

In the fixed-income market, in particular, this has become a rhetorical question. Recent inter-bank dealing figures from the US indicate that in 1998 only 5% of bonds were traded electronically, by 2000 the proportion had grown to 25%, and, at current growth rates, as much as 40 to 50% were dealt electronically by the end of 2001.

The inter-dealer broker Cantor Fitzgerald, proving itself more prescient than its competitors, recognised this threat early on and converted it into an opportunity. In 1999, it launched a product and a division called eSpeed. Cantor reportedly spent over US$200 million over a three-year period on developing eSpeed and went so far as to roll it out as a direct public offering. eSpeed is ultimately an electronic alternative to the inter-dealer broker, as it offers Cantor's banking clients the option of off-loading large bond transactions online. Transparency and volume is the bait that lures dealers to any inter-dealer broker market, and that is exactly what eSpeed delivered to its clients via the World Wide Web. In February 2002, the two-and-a-half-year-old company reported its first profits, despite being one of the hardest hit by the events of September 11. After three years of multimillion dollar investments, eSpeed is the first of approximately 80 electronic bond trading companies that have started up in this time to report a profit. Whereas eSpeed designed an entirely new system for this new medium from scratch, competitors Garban and Tullet & Tokyo Liberty have essentially built Web-based front-ends onto their existing internal systems that their in-house brokers have used for years, creating ETC and LibertyDirect respectively, with LibertyDirect seeming even more like a quick-fix than ETC. ETC at least integrates voice and data technologies, enabling the electronic confirmation of voice trades. ETC is reportedly transacting over US$200 billion per month, representing 25% of Garban's Treasury business.

Jeopardising this survival strategy, however, is a monolith called BrokerTec – a huge consortium of 14 banks who collectively control about 85% of the global inter-dealer market – that is working to create its own online wholesale marketplace. BrokerTec is designed as an anonymous order-matching engine, which is quite distinct from the quote-driven IDB model, and provides central counterparty and settlement services, as well as repurchase trading. BrokerTec is backed by the very dealers that have fed Cantor, Garban and Liberty for years and threatens to cut the inter-dealer brokers completely out of the food chain. While the dealers accept the need for an anonymous intermediary, they no longer see the need to give margins away to some third party when they can own that intermediary themselves. Centralised liquidity is, as always, the key and ownership by the liquidity providers is one of the best means of securing it. Clearly, one assumes that the backers of the system will also back it in their order routing – although this is not guaranteed from board to desk level. However, BrokerTec is rumoured to have, somewhat unethically, twisted its umbilical cord to its dealer parents to ensure that this happens. The platform apparently gives preferential rates to its owners if they commit to using it for a large proportion of their US Treasury trades. But cheap pricing is only the carrot. The incentive programme has worked because traders were forced on pain of cut commission to use it by their managers. As one head-trader at a part-owner commented; 'unless you put a gun to their head they're not going to use it' (Sanders, 2001). As an at least partial result, BrokerTec almost doubled its market share to about 40% of the US$160 billion a day inter-dealer Treasury market by the end of 2001, at the expense of the eight other independent competitors. BrokerTec's jump in trading volume also coincided with the September 11 World Trade Center attacks, which destroyed the headquarters of its two biggest rivals, Garban-Intercapital and eSpeed. BrokerTec, with the aid of the OM Group, furthermore contends that it can provide a more efficient matching system for not only the US market but the European market too. BrokerTec is already generating over 20 billion euros of trade a day in Europe. Once again, the irony is that the Internet, the purported great leveller, has bred alliances of big boys, which are dominating the independents.

Chris Ferreri, head of IT strategy for Garban, acknowledges the fear gripping the broker community, and the sense of impending doom; 'we'll support voice broking as long as the commission structure supports it … [but] if clients are only looking for the cheapest way to transact, I'm not sure the broker will stay around' (Rafalaf, 2000). After September 11, Cantor shifted all trading of US Treasuries onto eSpeed and does not intend to replace the voice brokers. Ultimately, the industry economics may be destroyed by the positioning of BrokerTec by its backers as more of a utility than a profit-making or – seeking enterprise. Essentially it's a concerted effort on the part of the dealers to drive down cost structures in these very low-margin markets, including trade execution, settlement, risk capital and other costs.

The brokers are most definitely re-evaluating their value proposition; they need to demonstrate that they can provide more than these systems. Electronic systems naturally mean fewer brokers, and those few that survive will probably reposition themselves more as account managers. Just as the retail broker has morphed into an investment advisor, so the broker and salesman need to advance beyond transactional services and into the aggregation and distribution of data, helping their clients navigate the infinite amounts of data accessible on the Internet. In essence they become real-time electronic desktop editors and publishers.

Another interesting development is eSpeed's positioning as a technology vendor. More often the province of the true start-ups as a last resort strategy, eSpeed has capitalised on the infrastructure and competence it has acquired, by developing customised e-markets for clients in a multitude of industries.

There is one aspect of recent developments that does favour the broker, however. Collusion and cartels are difficult to sustain. The hidden agenda of each member eventually serves to sabotage the consortium as a whole. Even if it's nothing more sinister than the proverbial management by committee, consortia are often impeded by bureaucratic decision-making processes. Sluggishness – as an adverse side effect of their egalitarian structures and obligation to protect even minority interests – is one of the very reasons why exchanges are demutualising.

Furthermore, while the dealers are gleefully exploiting technology to eliminate the middlemen who exploited the previously fractured market structure, their own cannibalisation fears may paralyse them in the face of the inevitable future danger posed to their own customer dealing franchises. Some may even try to prevent the buy-side gaining access to these systems. Although broker-dealers' own intermediary business is not under any immediate threat (especially with OTC market segmentation still intact), parochial interests may serve to retard their ability to adapt to inexorable eventual changes. Despite the lip-service paid to 'eating your own cash cow before someone else does', when the time comes, many incumbents react to this threat by moving into defensive mode – deluding themselves into thinking that they can manipulate market forces to their own advantage. This opens a window of opportunity for the independents to encroach on their customer territory.

Finally, compared with the personal relationships formed in the current bilateral telephonic trading system, the nameless, faceless entity that is the multilateral electronic inter-dealer and multi-dealer system is not very engaging, which may well slow the adoption rate. Although the average dealer may be relieved at the respite from continuous broker harassment (in the process of trying to identify counterparties), nevertheless, the rounds of golf, liquid lunches and sheer feeling of being 'plugged in' are still considered fair compensation.

In the end, the wholesale fixed-income market will probably exhibit a hybrid structure for a while, supporting voice and data inter-dealer brokers with various bosses. However, there will unquestionably be fewer of them, and who will last is the million dollar question.

COMMODITISATION

Clearly, the essentially multilateral nature of electronic markets, and the relatively high degree of automation, does not lend itself to bilateral negotiation. Consequently, products traded in these markets need to be highly standardised, homogeneous, undifferentiated, in a word, commoditised. And as with liquidity, the need for commoditisation gives rise to it. Because they need commoditisation, e-markets tend to drive it – applying pressure to the accelerator if you will. The huge benefits derived from electronic trading, not least in terms of reduced costs, motivate market participants to promote the adoption of standards and standardisation measures. This is evident in the industry-wide search for technology protocols for communication. Examples include the FIX (Financial Information Exchange) protocol for the equities market, the FpML (financial products mark-up language), an XML-based (extensible mark-up language) meta-language, for derivatives application, sponsored by JP Morgan Chase and PWC, and the recent undertaking by the Bond Markets Association to develop an equivalent for fixed income.

A side effect of this trend is, of course, price compression and margin erosion. In any market, once competing products are differentiable only on price, downward pressure on price is inevitable, and survival hinges on operational efficiency. Accelerated product lifecycles is a much hyped, new economy trend, but there is some truth in it in the financial sector. Today's innovations are tomorrow's commodities and high-margin structured products rapidly migrate to low-margin commodities. Electronic markets, once the province of plain vanilla, have now started to sell more exotic flavours.

Tempering the Hype

Notwithstanding the above, the mega-trends and, it must be conceded, the hype, yet again, need to be tempered with reality. Even with the best will in the world, which is not itself a given, the existence of automated markets does not automatically reduce every instrument to a base commodity.

On balance, small or average-sized transactions in liquid, homogeneous products, with limited counterparty credit risk, are most likely to move online first. By contrast, the following types of products may continue to trade predominantly offline, at least until technology clears some hurdles:

- *If the product is relatively non-standardised.* Heterogeneous instruments require a more extensive pre-trade dialogue between counterparties about modalities.

However, this dialogue can be engaged on electronic media, such as chat boxes and messaging systems, although the interaction will still be bilateral.

- *If the market is relatively inactive or illiquid.* Thin markets may not be suitable for centralised electronic trading, because of insufficient liquidity on either side of the market.

  However, if there isn't a high demand for immediacy, periodic matching systems, where trades are batched and cleared at periodic intervals, may substitute. Alternatively, incorporating market-makers into an e-market may also overcome this problem.

- *If counterparty credit risk plays an important role.* The loss of control over the counterparty with which one trades may be a prohibitive factor in some markets. Examples include instruments that cannot be settled by some form of delivery-versus-payment (DVP), or those that entail large counterparty risks as a result of market movements (such as interest rate swaps).

  However, some systems (such as those in the inter-dealer foreign exchange market) have mitigated this by incorporating the system of credit lines that banks have on each other, while others have set up a central clearing party that stands between the counterparties and guarantees the performance of the trade.

- *If the trade size is relatively large.* Large trades in any instrument generally require intermediation. Due to high pre-trade transparency, the risk of moving the market when trading on an electronic order book is considerable. Customers may be more comfortable working with a dealer for large trades, either on the telephone or electronically. They may charge the dealer to 'work' the order on their behalf or have the dealer transact the block with them and take over the execution risk. Either way, the trader will split up the transaction into small portions and transact it through the 'machine'. The anonymity that electronic trading systems may offer may prove an advantage, since it may not be immediately clear to the market that all the trades are coming from the same address. Information about the trade size is therefore initially only known by the dealer involved. To the extent that automation leads to an improved audit trail, chances of detecting front-running activities by the dealer may be higher. In equity markets, crossing networks are used as a possible alternative venue for these large trades. To encourage large orders, some systems allow hidden or 'iceberg' orders that are not visible to other users but have lower price priority relative to visible orders.

In sum, and constraints aside, it is fairly inevitable that the electronic markets of the future will be characterised by commoditisation and will themselves propel the commoditisation of products.

CHAPTER 8

BALANCE OF POWER AND THE EFFICIENCY OF THE eXCHANGE

BUY-SIDE EMPOWERMENT

As should also be axiomatic by now, one of the biggest impacts of electronic trading is the empowerment of the buy-side of the market – an outcome common to almost every industry. This shift in the balance of power from the sell-side of the market to the buy-side is evident in several respects.

First, the shift from closed to open markets obviously favours the buy-side as it places sellers in direct competition with one another. Comparative pricing invariably induces spread compression. Thus, from a pure price efficiency perspective, the buy-side gains at the expense of sell-side margins.

However, the actual empowerment of the buy-side derived from the price formation process is more subtle. In RFQ systems, whereby investors can automatically dispatch an inquiry or a request for a quotation to multiple banks simultaneously, the investor obviously gains because he can compare the prices of competing banks virtually simultaneously, prompting them to price more competitively. However, in such systems, the banks generally still act as principal intermediaries. The investor is generally restricted to those banks with whom he has a credit limit, with the e-market merely acting as a conduit or switch. The system simply maintains a database of agreed transacting counterparties and routes accordingly. It does not act as principal to the transaction, commit its own capital, guarantee settlement, or in any way mitigate credit and settlement risk. Similarly, in systems based on the IDB quote-driven model, whereby displayed quotes can be hit, the investor still deals with a dealer, but his position is strengthened further since the IDB model elevates transparency and continuity. However, the central order-book/order-matching model, with an anonymous central counterparty, represents the highest degree of buy-side empowerment. This is because order-driven price formation is a subtle reversal in sequence. Instead of the sell-side quoting the prices at which they are willing to buy or sell, it allows the investor, in effect, to set the price at which he is willing to trade and then to wait for a counterparty to match that price. Furthermore, it potentially eliminates the middleman, his cut, and his informational privileges, that is, his being privy to valuable flow information. Finally, the fact that certain cross-matching systems, such as E-Crossnet, are owned entirely by the institutional investors is the culmination of this trend.

Moreover, as intermediaries try to justify their existence with new value propositions related to info-mediation, investors again benefit from the efforts of banks to offer them superior screened or filtered market data, research, portfolio and risk management and other forms of analytics.

As we have already conceded, there are many countervailing trends, such as the need for sell-side liquidity provision, sell-side dominance of the e-markets and so on; however, the underlying trend cannot be entirely obfuscated. Increasing transparency, disintermediation, spread compression and sell-side differentiation strategies, through the provision of cutting-edge value-added services, all serve to empower the buy-side of the market.

MARKET EFFICIENCY AND THE eXCHANGE[1]

In light of the preceding examination of the probable causes and effects of the trend towards virtual 'eXchanges' – in terms of increasing liquidity, commoditisation, disintermediation and buy-side empowerment – we can now examine the impact of electronic connectivity on the overall efficiency of markets. By textbook conditions, markets qualify as efficient if prices balance underlying supply and demand and adjust as smoothly as possible, without excessive volatility unrelated to changes in fundamentals. This is correlated with:

- liquidity, such that transactions are executed rapidly without unduly moving prices;
- orderliness, such that equivalent orders are executed at broadly equivalent prices; and

- stability and resilience, such that the above continues to hold at times of uncertainty and market stress.

As usual, a qualified yes is the answer to the question of whether electronic trading will lead to increased market efficiency. While it is almost axiomatic to state that electronic markets will enhance efficiency, certain obstructive forces may pervert the true course of market forces, at least in the short term. Much of the ensuing discussion has already taken place, but, by its nature, this synopsis or abstract on the subject of market efficiency is more abstract in style.

Effects in Principle on Liquidity and Efficient Price Formation

The BIS report (2001) on the implications of electronic trading from a systemic and structural perspective cast some light on this subject. Theoretically, as we have argued, electronic trading should facilitate the centralisation of markets. Technology makes remote access to multilateral trading centres[2] possible. Simply put, electronic markets are more open. More prospective market participants can gain direct (rather than indirect or intermediated) access. The ability to get connected should facilitate broader market participation (by, for example, retail investors). Electronic trading networks should also stimulate higher trading activity by existing investors. This trend will be reinforced by the lower cost of electronic trading. By widening access to markets (and market information) and by lowering trading costs, technology may – at least in theory – boost liquidity. Assuming that deeper liquidity in markets means more efficient price discovery, prices should better reflect aggregate levels of supply and demand. Furthermore, information (whether trade-related or not) will potentially be more easily and economically obtainable. Therefore, market prices should better reflect available information about fundamentals. Plus, since electronic trading should enable orders to reach the market far faster because of higher processing speeds compared to manual systems, prices should incorporate information more quickly, and therefore should adjust more quickly to (even small) changes in the fundamentals.

Potential Adverse Effects on Market Efficiency of Liquidity Fragmentation *and* Consolidation

Paradoxically to the overarching direction of change – convergence – the path to it seems to involve the reverse – proliferation. At present, many markets appear in a state of flux, with trading spread across several platforms supplied by competing providers. Fragmentation may have both benefits and costs.

The *benefits* include:

- *Benchmark pricing to improve efficiency*. Prices from the more transparent electronic order books can be used as benchmarks or reference points in existing markets.
- *Competitiveness effects in existing markets*. Competition with new, more transparent electronic markets may induce existing markets to lower costs and improve their own offering. For example, dealers may be obliged to offer greater transparency to their customers.
- *Easy access for end-users*. The strategy (and design) of certain systems is to attract new types of end-user, and ultimately benefit some markets through increased liquidity. In particular, retail customers may find it easier to participate in certain securities markets.

However, there are also potential *costs* of co-existence:

- *Fragmentation of order flow*. Liquidity may be adversely affected due to fragmentation of the order flow into multiple electronic and non-electronic markets. Of course, this is a potential problem whenever multiple market centres co-exist, irrespective of whether some of them are electronic or not. However, the relatively low entry barriers to setting up new electronic systems means that multiple systems are likely.
- *Costs from the duplication of systems*. These may arise from the cost of systems required to enable investors and intermediaries to track prices being quoted and traded in various market centres and from expenses arising from delivering an order from one market centre to another for possible execution.

In practice, however, most market participants do not see fragmentation as a major concern. First, OTC markets were formerly even more fragmented, so these markets are becoming more rather than less centralised. Second, open architecture allows different systems to interact simultaneously and on a common screen. The process can be facilitated by 'adapters' or middleware (software that aims to reduce the costs of investor access by providing a standardised interface across different networks). Taking the process a step further, traders may in the future use a 'smart agent' that searches among both markets and dealers for the best place to make a given trade, taking into account quotes, charges and liquidity. The low cost of arbitrage should therefore keep prices consistent across the market.

Furthermore, the fragmentation of systems is typical of the early stages of the product cycle. As a market matures, there will a period of rationalisation and a tendency to converge on systems with greater liquidity. This process is already underway. However, the five factors leading to consolidation – economies of scale, network effects, standard-setting, switching costs and tipping effects – may adversely effect efficiency.

Economies of scale arise because electronic trading systems, like most information goods, are characterised by low variable costs, the classic condition that tends towards monopoly. Network externalities arise because the benefit of participating in a network increases with the number of other participants. Since traders move to the system offering the most liquidity, the large systems become even larger. There is also the potential for first-mover advantages in being able to set standards. Switching costs then arise because users may have linked their internal operations systems to a given system, making them reluctant to change to a new system even if it is superior. Once a system becomes established, there may be 'tipping' effects: competition may be keen between rival trading systems when none accounts for a majority of transactions, but once one achieves a significant majority market share, it may then rapidly take over almost the whole market.

A system that becomes dominant due to such first-mover advantages may not necessarily be the most efficient. A technically better system arriving later may not attract individual traders to it even if it were optimal for all traders to switch. Once liquidity is concentrated on a certain platform, it will not easily migrate to another.

This raises the possibility of predatory pricing; a system being offered at below marginal cost to attract large numbers of subscribers who are then faced with higher fees once the system has an effective monopoly. Such predators need deep war chests, and it is the powerful incumbents, who intend to safeguard that power, who generally have such treasuries. There is also concern that dominant systems have little incentive to improve.

This relates to broader economic theory, which has undergone a fundamental change. Our knowledge of how macro-level markets and micro-level firms operate was passed down to us more than a century ago by the economist Alfred Marshall. It is based on the assumption of diminishing returns: products or firms that get ahead in a market eventually run into limitations, so that a predictable equilibrium of prices and market shares is reached. The theory was valid for the bulk-processing, smokestack economy of Marshall's day. But in the last century, developed economies have undergone a transformation from processing resources to processing information, from the application of raw energy to the application of ideas. As this shift has occurred, the mechanisms that determine economic behaviour have also shifted – from diminishing returns to ever-increasing returns (Arthur, 1996).

Perpetual increasing returns are the tendency for that which is ahead to get further ahead and for that which is losing advantage to lose further advantage. They are mechanisms of positive feedback that operate (within businesses, markets and industries) to reinforce that which gains success or suffers losses. Increasing returns generate not equilibrium but instability. If one competing product or technology gets ahead, increasing returns can magnify the advantage, and the product or technology can go on to lock in the market.

Mechanisms of increasing returns exist alongside those of diminishing returns in all industries. But in general, diminishing returns hold sway in the traditional, bulk resource-processing industries. Increasing returns reign in the newer, knowledge-based industries, where instead of bulk processing resources into goods or congealed resources, knowledge is processed into congealed knowledge. Modern economies have split into two interrelated worlds of business corresponding to the two types of returns. The two worlds have different economics. They call for different understandings.

Microsoft is the law of increasing returns incarnate: a living example of first-mover advantage that was converted into a reinforced lock-in network effect and, if you believe the vast numbers of their detractors, the devastation that this can wreak on competition and innovation. The law of increasing returns, however, is presumed to hold true *ceteris parabis*, that is, so long as all other things remain constant. Technology, of course, is not a constant. For example, the conquest of VHS over Betamax demonstrated this same effect, but VHS's dominance only held sway until videos were supplanted by DVDs. Whether Microsoft's far greater hegemony will ultimately be usurped by the next technology wave, will prove or disprove much about the apparent detrimental effect of network effects on market efficiency over the long term.

Potential Adverse Effects on Volatility

There is also some debate about the probable effect of electronic markets on volatility. Some market participants argue that the faster incorporation of news into prices will lead to higher price volatility in the short run. On the other hand, this argument can be countered by the fact that if prices were slower to react to news, they would have to make bigger moves to catch up. Also improved transparency may simply make volatility more visible, but not necessarily increase it. Another factor bearing on volatility in the very short term is the micro design of the trading system and the gap between human and computer computational speeds. For example, changes to the order-matching rule of the order book in the Japanese futures market have aggravated short-term price volatility. Traders need time to be acquainted with the current state of the order book. An imprecise perception of the state, due to the high frequency of order flows and high-speed execution by automated order-matching, prevents their order from executing at the intended price. The example suggests that the speed of the execution process must be in line with the speed at which traders react to price information and post new orders. Electronic connectivity means that orders can be executed in a fraction of a second. Unless market participants are able to respond over the same time frame, market prices may overshoot temporarily. The introduction of pricing engines (with automatic electronic order generation systems) by dealers may, however, bring the speed with which they can reprice and submit new orders into line with the speed of the order execution mechanism.

Finally, it also bears mentioning that the broader participation in markets by the retail investor may not necessarily benefit market efficiency and may have a detrimental effect on stability. Recalling the earlier hypothesis on the role of mass psychology in the causes of financial crises, direct participation by the less sophisticated investor may render markets far more vulnerable to these effects. Patronising as it may sound, retail investors may be more susceptible to panic attacks and the herding instinct. Boom or bust times may be amplified by the tendency of retail investors to react excessively to events.

Market Resilience Under Stress

Liquidity of Electronic Markets

When electronic systems were first introduced, trading tended to revert to the more familiar phone- or floor-based systems in volatile times. This no longer seems to be the case. There is no general tendency to desert electronic platforms when volatility rises. While liquidity in some e-markets may dry up in adverse market conditions, this was also true for traditional markets. It seems that in volatile circumstances trading moves towards the trading systems with the greatest market share, regardless of whether they are electronic, floor- or telephone-based.

An example was in early October 1998, when the dollar/yen rate fell from ¥133 to ¥112 in less than 48 hours. In several financial centres there was a marked migration *towards* electronic systems and away from voice brokers. Price action was continuous in these systems with little evidence of gapping (sudden jumps in prices). Dealers were able to use the system to track the market price without needing to transact to do so. So unwanted positions which would have unwound very quickly were not taken on in the first place. It may be that the yen appreciated faster because there was less 'shock absorption' by intermediating dealers but the return to orderly trading was also more rapid than in similar instances in the past.

Liquidity of Electronic Order Books

A particular concern for financial stability is that trading systems that function adequately in normal market conditions may cease to be effective in stressed market conditions. Order books may be more suited to markets where prices are more certain and information more uniform, and could function less well in stressed markets. Traders may become less willing to post limit orders, thereby reducing liquidity. Gapping might occur on order books if limit orders are withdrawn from the book because of increased uncertainty and/or an event causes a rush of market orders in one direction, which 'run through' the existing liquidity, executing against 'stale' orders away from the market price. It is not clear, a priori, whether gapping will be more frequent in an electronic order book than in traditional markets, although it may be more observable.

Some argue that market-making obligations (which are usually accompanied by corresponding privileges) smooth price adjustment and ensure a certain degree of liquidity in all market conditions. However, the extent to which market-makers carry out their obligations in very adverse conditions is often questioned. Market-makers are usually committed to quoting two-way prices in an instrument, either continuously or for certain periods within the day, within a predefined bid-ask spread and minimum trade size. Market-making obligations are less often a feature of order books than dealer markets. (An exception is represented by MTS markets, in which designated market-makers must usually maintain bid and ask limit orders of a certain size and within a certain spread for five out of the eight hours during the trading day.)

Electronic trading facilitates consolidation in the financial industry leading to a lower number of dealers, especially market-makers. The scalability made possible by technology means that more customers and transactions can be served by fewer intermediaries. The reduction in the number of market-makers could lead to a net withdrawal of risk capital from the markets. This could have implications for the ability of market-makers to provide liquidity, especially in times of stress, with risk for financial stability. However, it is not so obvious from previous examples of market turbulence that market-makers did provide liquidity when it was required. There have been cases in various volatile markets where market-makers simply stopped answering their phones. Ultimately liquidity may be provided by those end-users able to take a longer-term view because they are neither leveraged nor subject to daily marking to market.

Electronic order books may increase market liquidity in times of stress if these investors have greater direct access to the market. For example, they can post limit orders in order to look for bargains rather than requiring the intermediation of dealers. The visibility of these orders may then help price discovery in the remainder of the market: for example, by setting a floor to a price decline. Thus, the return to normal trading conditions may be accelerated.

Finally, the centralisation of clearing and settlement may eliminate concerns about counterparty credit risk, and thus may make electronic trading systems more resilient, because market participants would no longer be potentially deterred from trading by those concerns, which are likely to increase in times of stress. It should be noted that in stressful times, however, the robustness of the central clearer becomes a very important issue. Order books may suffer from reduced liquidity under stress if they involve a central counterparty whose creditworthiness comes under question in stressful times.

Operational Risk

Finally, electronic trading has also introduced a potentially significant risk to market stability: operational risk. On 15 April 2000, after a US court of law found Microsoft guilty of anti-competitive practices, high-tech stocks gyrated frantically. But investors were unable to trade a single stock on the LSE. Why? Because it was shut – for nearly eight hours – because its computers had gone down. And this incident is but a hint of the potential scale of the risk to come.

Causes of Outages and Delays

The growing use of electronic trading networks has been accompanied by a parallel increase in trading delays and outages on these systems. Most incidents, however, appear to have occurred on newer systems recently introduced by equity and derivatives exchanges. Well-established, dedicated systems, such as those used in the foreign exchange and fixed-income markets, seem to have experienced fewer problems.

A report prepared by the US General Accounting Office (2000) identified a number of factors responsible for delays and outages. Most of the outages did not result principally from the incapacity of the systems to handle large transaction volumes per se, that is, the inherent scalability and robustness, but rather from upgrades to expand capacity and enhance capability. The most common reason for system outages involved problems with vendor-supplied trading system software. Apparently, many online firms rely on vendor systems for major parts of order processing, and, when these systems experience problems, outages can result at more than one firm. Trading delays were primarily caused by heavy Internet traffic, particularly during periods of high market volatility. These problems were attributed to Internet service providers and the equipment of investors. Other reasons for delays and failures include hardware breakdowns, switches from automated to manual order processing in times of stress, breakdowns during the overnight updating of databases, and breakdowns in telecom equipment.

Implications of Trading Halts

Despite their frequency and, sometimes, length, so far outages and delays do not seem to have had systemic consequences. The apparent reasons for this are:

(i) they have not been too prolonged, so traders were able to delay trades;

(ii) in most cases there was no coincident big market news; and

(iii) other ways to trade were still available (competing electronic systems or telephones).

However, activity was generally lower than on normal trading days because some retail and institutional investors were reluctant to trade without the availability of centrally determined prices, particularly outside regular trading hours when liquidity is low.

In order to minimise the chance of trading halts occurring, system providers and users should make ample provision for contingency measures to be incorporated into the system. This is now definitely the case. In the wake of the September 11 attacks on the World Trade Centre, disaster recovery is being accorded huge attention. However, even if every precaution is taken, it is unlikely that the risk of failure can ever be completely negated.

Given this intrinsic vulnerability, one of the greatest sources of unease, from a systemic position, according to the BIS (2001) – an institute not prone to hyperbole – relates to what would happen if the infrastructure and very culture related to phone trading disappeared over time as a consequence of the colonisation of markets by electronic systems. So far, when outages have occurred, it has been possible to revert to earlier practices or alternative systems. However, as the reliance on electronic systems in general, and the degree of concentration, increases, this option may expire. It is conceivable that dealers would lose the ability to operate in a telephone-based dealer market if they became accustomed to trading on a central order book, in the foreign exchange market, for example. They may no longer have the essential contacts with dealers in a range of other banks to unwind positions. They may lack the skills to discover market prices in a phone-based dealer market, where the traditional voice broker has ceased to exist. Under stressed conditions, dealers may become disorientated and panicky by the lack of a central reference price and could either widen spreads considerably or resort to their favourite desperate measure of refusing to answer telephones.

Moreover, other questions remain. Would other trading channels be adequate to substitute in cases of system breakdowns? The sheer volume of trades militates against this possibility. For example, several exchanges have contingency plans for members to place orders by telephone if the electronic platform is unavailable for long periods. However, questions remain as to how telephone trading could cope with typical volumes in the contracts currently traded on those exchanges. Could a major operational failure in a large system lead to a loss of confidence in other systems, that is, would there be a risk of contagion? Are there enough private incentives for front-office traders, and their back offices, to undertake special training in order to cope with emergency situations?

Perhaps more alarming would be the prospect of a system continuing to operate but generating incorrect results. It may take a while for this to become apparent, by which time a large number of incorrectly processed transactions would have occurred, particularly in systems with complicated price determination algorithms. Recreating the transactions, even with electronic audit trails, would be an extremely onerous task and the potential for litigation and legal disputes about the status of such deals would be very high.

Another concern is adequacy of electronic control systems, which have yet to be subjected to stress testing or to have undergone a normal trial and error process. Safeguards have been incorporated into some systems, such as the automatic querying of orders well away from the last sale price or of unusually large size. This should guard against keystroke errors.[3] In fast moving markets there has been occasional confusion over the 'big figure' (that is, in foreign exchange quotes, the digit before the decimal point), although admittedly this is not likely to be a greater problem than under voice-based systems. Moreover, such an incident would have to achieve massive proportions before creating a systemic threat. Nonetheless, the issue of proper controls and safeguards becomes increasingly important as automated pricing engines are used for the generation of prices and orders, that is, as human intervention and judgement wanes and computers trade with computers. If this were to become a widespread phenomenon, small programming or pricing errors could have serious implications, as they could trigger a 'reaction' from another computer, amplifying the effect: all in all a process that may be difficult to control or reverse.

There are also concerns that operational risks may increase as more systems move onto the Internet, which may be more prone to delays and failures and less secure against hackers and viruses than are dedicated systems. So far, most system providers continue to use proprietary or private networks rather than the public network on grounds of security and reliability, but the trend seems to be towards increasing interoperability, open standards and, in due course, mainstream Internet access. In addition to the adequacy of encryption

Cause	Effect		
Technology	The Networked Economy		The Networked Markets
	From	*To*	*Impacts*
Connectivity on a Global Scale *Enables Communication/ Information Exchange*	Geopolitical Markets	Globalisation	Increasing: • Liquidity • Commoditisation ↓ • Buy-side Empowerment • Market Efficiency
	Divergent Industries	Convergence	
	Intermediated Markets	Disintermediation/ Reintermediation	
	Closed Markets *Pricing Info Distortions*	Open Markets *Transparent Pricing*	
	Fixed Pricing Catalogues	Dynamic Pricing Auctions	
Computational Power *Enables Advancement from Data to Intelligence*	Manual Processing	Automation	
	Dumb Data	*** Knowledge** *** Buyer Empowerment**	

Figure 8.1 Unprecedented change: part III

technology, systems should incorporate 'backups' in case key components break down. There is a danger that the current rush to get rival systems operating may mean that systems are not adequately tested before introduction.

The aggregate effects of technology on market structure and functioning or dynamics, and the ramifications thereof, are summarised in Figure 8.1.

Notes

1 Based on excerpts from the BIS (Bank for International Settlements), 2001, The Implications of Electronic Trading in Financial Markets, Committee on the Global Financial system, Basle.

2 If multi-dealer platforms supersede single-dealer systems, customers will have wider access to the markets and market information, although the market remains segmented. Moreover, if trading moves to order books, the segmentation will be eradicated, rendering the market interaction even more multilateral.

3 One incident in 1999 was reported involving a junior trader accidentally entering a $100 million instead of a $100,000 transaction into a system, which did not have controls or limits to prevent the immediate execution of this trade. Reversal of the trade is reported to have cost $50,000.

CHAPTER 9

AUCTION SYSTEMS

Continuing the theme of electronic exchanges, but on a slight tangent, the emergence of discrete or periodic, as opposed to continuous, live auction systems in the primary markets, whereby investors are able to bid for equity or debt offerings on the Net, is another interesting development.

Strictly speaking, this is once again a new form of distribution, however, e-auctioneers may eventually have a profound impact on the origination of debt and equity capital, by liberalising these markets and potentially reducing the very cost of capital for the issuers of these securities.

This phenomenon first occurred in the equity markets and of all the changes that the Internet may effect on the institutional side of Wall Street, the most fundamental may yet be the democratisation of equity underwriting.

EQUITY MARKETS

The Traditional System: Winners vs. Losers

Not long ago, e-evangelists were proclaiming that the Internet was poised to usurp the old-school-tie club of investment banking. Essentially this was because the process of capital underwriting and distributing initial and, to a lesser extent, secondary public offerings was, and still largely is, under the inequitable control of the heavyweight investment banks.

Under the traditional system, the bank dictates the price at which the shares will be issued or sold, to whom they will be sold, as well as the fee for its underwriting and distribution services. This, needless to say, puts the bank in a powerful position.

The Losers:
A. Issuers

■ *Explicit costs: extortionate fees*

Disempowered issuers are the first victims of this system. As a consequence of their dependency on banks as mediators, the privilege of selling equity in your business to the theoretical public does not come cheap. Banks' price tag for 'indispensable' new issue underwriting and distribution services is typically an extortionate 7% on deals of up to US$100 million.

■ *Implicit costs: underpricing and the cost of capital*

Furthermore, the costs to the issuer far exceed the fee levied. The banks almost always offer IPO shares for prices lower than they command on the open market, hence the stock price normally 'jumps' when it starts trading.

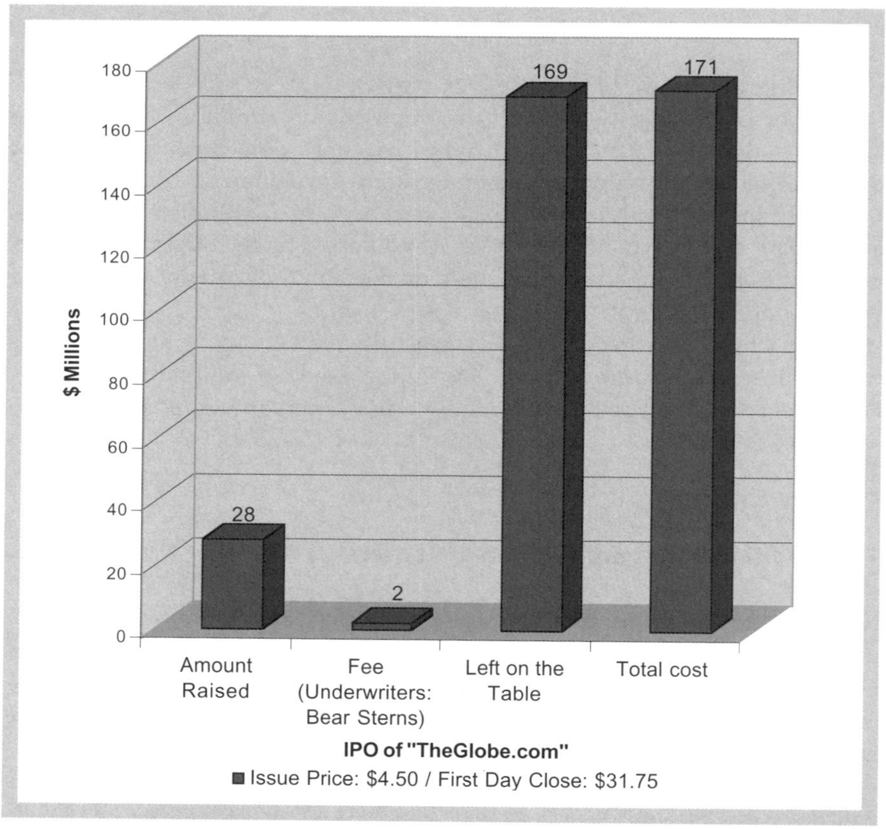

Figure 9.1 The real price of going public: a representative example

Source: Tully, 1999, *Fortune*, © 1999 Times Inc. All rights reserved.

It's not news that at the height of dot-com hype, the IPO market boomed, with prices rising up to 200% on the first day of trading, a phenomenon known as the IPO 'pop'. Were the shares priced at close to the market value, the issuer could have either diluted less equity or raised significantly more capital. New economy start-ups, green to Wall Street's ways, paid the highest opportunity cost. According to Hoover's IPO Central (Tully, 1999, pp. 112–18), start-ups paid (in addition to fees) an average of 40¢ in foregone capital for every dollar raised. While $25 billion was raised in the first half of the year, for example, had bankers' priced at the first day's closing price, the companies would have swelled their coffers by $10 billion more. A representative example of these explicit and implicit costs is presented in Figure 9.1.

B. Retail investors – creating the 'pop' but barred from partaking in it

The other losers in this game are the retail investors. Demand from retail investors is what, at least partially, drives prices up, but the right of admission to the IPO party is reserved for institutions – if you're an individual investor, your chances of getting shares in an IPO are virtually nil. In effect, there is much more demand than the lead bank takes into account when pricing a deal because the retail market is left out of the assessment process.

To make matters worse for individuals, many brokers carry stipulations stating that they have to hold onto the shares that they do procure for 60 days – basically until off-loading by institutions has already depressed prices. If an investor 'flips' the stock on the first day of trading, he will be frozen out of future deals.

The Winners:

A. Institutional investors – hot new issues at sweetheart prices

So who really stands to gain? The favoured few, normally the underwriting bank's preferred clientele of institutional investors, are able to buy the stock at the price set by the issuer's lead manager – previously at least 100% lower than the opening day's closing price on technology IPOs – and rake in windfall profits. The first day gains represent an opportunity to make a quick profit, and the majority of institutions flip the shares almost immediately (or in the grey market before official trading begins). In fact, institutions hold less than 25% of the securities in the secondary market, the balance is mostly in the hands of retail investors. And size, once again, does matter, as over 80% of IPO shares are allocated to the 100 biggest money mangers in the US.

B. The underwriter

- *Inflated margins*

But the biggest winners of all are, of course, the banks. At the height of the dot-com fervour, IPOs (and secondary offerings) proved extremely lucrative for firms, earning margins of up to 40%. In 1998, the three biggest Wall Street underwriters, Merrill Lynch, Morgan Stanley Dean Witter and Goldman Sachs, posted over US$1.2 billion in pre-tax profits from underwriting equities, which constituted a significant proportion of total profits in all three cases (20%, 10% and 12% respectively).

- *Institutional clients held hostage*

Furthermore, banks exploit their exclusive franchise to artificially protect other businesses. Funds receive shares on the basis of how much trading business they route to the firm. Thus, many institutional buyers also feel penalised by the current system, because not only can they not secure more than a nominal allocation of shares even if they are willing to pay a higher price, but it's not as if those shares are free. They know they must reciprocate by routing secondary trading through the bank's trading desks if they want a piece of IPO action at all, and trading conducted that way tends to be expensive. First, as we have covered, brokerage commissions are high, 5c a share on average, even though they could execute the same trade over an electronic trading system for 2–3c a share. Second, leakage and the market or price impact of big trades (their tendency to move the price against the institution placing the order) can amount to as much as 2%.

The Winds of Change

Even while Silicon Valley's fortunes were accruing in vast and disproportionate measure to Wall Street, the power players, predictably enough, vigorously defended the existing system, claiming that it helps to ensure responsible pricing in wild and irresponsible markets. They refused to adjust their pricing models to account for what they refer to as 'speculative excess'. Prices, according to them, must be consistent with fundamental value, and the new valuation methodologies (now largely discredited) never surfaced in primary markets. According to traditionalists, auctioning shares on the Net is abdicating the key role of pricing.

Nevertheless, most somewhat circumspect Internet entrepreneurs would have preferred at least half the shares to go to their customers, the retail investors. Similarly, the retail investors would have preferred a more equitable process – whereby the growing private investor base could get more equal access to IPOs, where deals were priced more accurately according to demand,

and where the same rules apply to all investors. The stage was set for the entrance of a new brand of electronic investment bank.

This expectation of imminent change was articulated in an article that appeared in the August 1999 edition of *Fortune* magazine:

> Thus, it is predicted that bidding for IPOs over the Web spells the beginning of the end of the quid pro quo culture on Wall Street. Critics of investment banking, primarily those customers in Silicon Valley, denounce the industry as 'legacy', an anachronism, sustained only by cartel-like alliances and a stranglehold on information. It is therefore exactly the sort of industry that the Internet was born to overturn. It is true that Web-based alternatives are still in their infancy and new models are still forming. Wall Street is not exactly quaking with fear. Then again, the thing that overtakes you always looks small when it's still in the distance. Ask the maker of any other legacy system. (Tully, 1999)

The Mavericks

At the end of the last century, a few mavericks emerged, including Wit Capital; E*Offering, backed by E*Trade and Sanford Robertson; and Epoch Partners, backed by Charles Schwab, Ameritrade and TD Waterhouse. The Epoch alliance's competitive advantage was the volume of retail investors that their group could access. In 1999, the three had 6.5 million accounts whose combined worth was $780 billion, which accounted for half of all online assets, and including day traders and active traders, this number rose to 80%. That's how they expected to convince companies to choose this new emerging bank to lead the deal, rather than a more traditional Merrill Lynch or Goldman Sachs. They also developed a platform to gather information and develop market intelligence.

Friedman Billings & Ramsey's online investment bank, FBR.com, took an equally controversial position. The basic stance was that a large part of the inequity lies in the failure to measure the demand from the retail segment of the market in the pricing process, when the institutional segment is only a fraction of the market today. FBR.com, which already acts as a lead manager, created its own solution in the form of a system that allows it to distribute issues to millions of investors in seconds. Their new order entry and management system allows the individual to enter the order directly into a secure area of the website, which goes directly into the database. Then the underwriter and the issuer can view the demand in an aggregated fashion at any time. The system also allows investors to enter the price that they would pay as a sublimit of the price range of the offering. This way the underwriter gets a better picture of demand at different price levels, which helps them price the offering more effectively. Their position is agnostic because FBR.com doesn't have the channel conflict that many traditional investment banks that are launching online ventures have. They have no army of brokers.

Finally, WR Hambrecht, another contender, has an even more novel model; a Dutch auction. Under this system, Hambrecht collects offers from both retail and institutional customers over the Web and then awards the shares to the highest bidders. An added benefit of this system is that full price investors don't tend to 'flip'. In a boost of confidence, Fidelity Investments acquired a big stake in Hambrecht, and now enables its retail customers, totalling 2.7 million Internet accounts, to bid for Hambrecht's IPOs over Fidelity's website. Moreover, the Reuters-owned ECN, Instinet, also owns a big stake in WR Hambrecht. Instinet will display Hambrecht's IPOs to its 11,000 institutional customers around the globe and collect their bids electronically. Now the funds, if they're willing to pay, can get all the shares that they need.

This relationship highlights one of the greatest threats to the distributional influence of traditional investment banks and their claim that only they can deliver those crucial institutional buyers. To continue to seize those high-priced orders from the institutions, firms need to keep bribing big investors with a stream of IPOs at sweetheart prices. If the Net siphons off some of that IPO business, funds will look for cheaper trading alternatives, such as ECNs. The ECNs allow institutions to trade directly with each other, and, with no middleman, there's minimal market impact and no commission other than the ECN's 2c a share. Wall Street firms' final defence of the status quo is the tailored research that they offer. However, if the Web is good at anything, it's the distribution of information such as stock research. So, the IPO pop looked set to fizzle, and in 1999 and 2000, six online investment banks managed 196 stock offerings, raising almost US$30 billion.

Revolution Interrupted

Then stock markets slumped and IPO activity ground to a near halt. IPO proceeds fell 59% in the first half of 2001 from the first half of 2000. Already struggling for deals or share allocation as distributors (averaging 1–2% of a deal), sadly, this proved a monumental setback for the e-upstarts. In 2001, three online investment banks issued a total of seven IPOs, raising just over US$1 billion.

Ironically, in the depressed M&A market, yet predictably enough, they've become the targets of the big banks themselves. Goldman Sachs Group recently announced its intention to acquire Epoch, and E*Offering was recently acquired by Wit Soundview, in turn formed from the merger of one of the pioneers; Wit Capital, and Soundview Financial, an investment bank. Banks, such as UBS

Warburg and Merill Lynch, with its Direct Markets (an in-house syndication and distribution application) have launched their own initiatives.

Future Prospects

Nevertheless, the technology is still relevant. It is simply more efficient (as evidenced by the average of 4% levied by online investment banks). Once capital markets recover and retail investors become more active again, there is bound to be a resurgence. According to a recent KPMG report (Kiley, 2001), for example, online investment banks may not experience super-growth rates in the immediate future, but they will; 'it's simply a question of when'. New entrants are already positioning for this. I-Deal, for example, formed by the quartet of Microsoft, Merrill Lynch, Salomon Smith Barney and Thomson Financial, plans to launch in the second half of 2002.

Another impetus to the growth of this electronic market may, once again, originate in regulation. If developments in the secondary markets for equity (with reference to the emergence of ECNs and the head start that they secured from the SEC) set a precedent, one can extrapolate some general evolutionary principals. Specifically, new technology's potential to liberalise may only actually be realised when regulators intervene to counteract the stranglehold of those who benefit from inequality.

Several leading investment banks have been assailed with regulatory probes by the SEC, the US Justice Department, the Attorney's Office and Congress into alleged malpractices or anti-competitive practices in underwriting and distributing IPOs, especially during the Silicon Valley boom, and have been hit with a barrage of private class action suits. At the root of the problem, of course, is the discretion that investment banks (as opposed to the market) have in pricing. First, it is alleged that the investment bank equity syndicate desks channelled generous IPO allocations to institutional investors in exchange for a proportionate amount of unrelated business, such as paying inflated commissions on other share transactions. Although this type of quid pro quo understanding is typically covert rather than overt, and therefore difficult to prove, already CSFB has been hit with a US$100 million settlement, one of the largest on record, by the SEC and the NASD for such practices. Second, it is alleged that the equity desks, who had an explicit motive to create IPO feeding frenzies, rigged the after market to create one, by channelling shares to specific investors in exchange for supporting the value of the stock in the after market. Such 'laddering' artificially inflates the share price, which, in turn, artificially inflates public demand. Third, it is alleged that banks won business by allocating popular IPO tranches to potential IPO candidates, including chief executives of start-ups in Silicon Valley. This mutual back-scratching is dubbed 'spinning'. The only losers were the small investors who ended up holding overvalued stock in overhyped companies. The outcome of these investigations may provide the breach for e-investment banks to gain a foothold.

One other unintended outcome of this is deserving of some speculative comment. This profitable 'pop' is, as we have said, a direct outcome of price misalignment with demand (such that underpricing produces shortfalls) and because market access is unequal. If potential buyers, who were previously discriminated against, are granted equal and indiscriminate access, and if price were set at market equilibrium, what will this do to the level of demand? Demand from discount brokers' day traders may be based not so much on investment fundamentals, but on greed and a desire to profit from a pricing distortion that may only be caused by their exclusion. Thus, the cost of capital may not lower in the aggregate. On the other hand, new issues have, until recently, been oversubscribed by multiples and thus, while the democratisation of distribution may reduce the pop, it will continue to occur.

DEBT CAPITAL MARKETS

Online issuance has more recently extended to debt capital instruments, although the dynamics have been somewhat different. Lagging far behind their equity equivalents in terms of secondary 'e-trading', the world bond markets now seem to be on the verge of an e-revolution. Secondary e-trading of bonds is also a forerunner to the electronically issued bond, or e-bond, where all steps in the issuance process are performed on the Web. Electronic issuing has only occurred at a sizeable level since the beginning of 2000. On 27 December 1999, Freddie Mac launched the first e-bond – a US$6 billion deal. Its precise timing was determined by Warburg Dillon Read's determination to be the first bank to use an Internet book-building system. A year later, e-bond issues are a daily event, with every major international bank scrambling to provide an Internet Web-based bond distribution mechanism. The Internet is now set to transform the primary debt markets.

The Winds of Change: Driving Forces

Two main causal factors can be distinguished in this process.

1. *Technology:* technological evolution increasingly delivers accessible product and service information, efficient distribution and secure transactions. The Internet offers a tool for broadening distribution and reducing costs, as developments in retail banking have shown. For bond issuers, the Internet

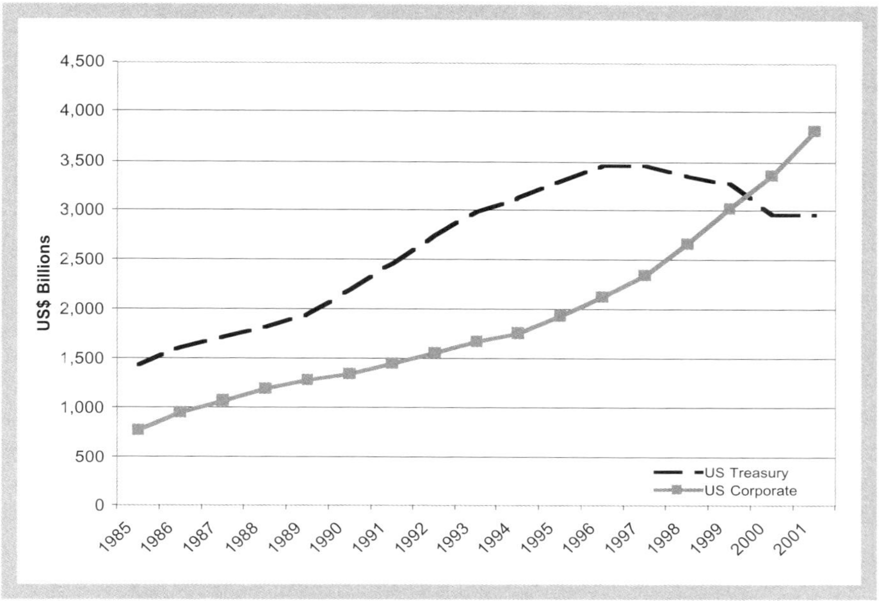

Figure 9.2 Corporate debt outstrips government: outstanding level of public and private debt (1985–2001)

Source: The Bond Market Association (BMA); Bond Market Statistics, www.bondmarkets.com, April 2002

allows the targeting of a much wider group of investors, including a range of medium-sized investors previously considered too small to participate in the primary markets, and the procurement of much more information about investor behaviour.

2. *Market conditions:* the nature of the bond markets themselves is changing. Globally, governments are borrowing less, and are changing the structure of their bond markets to create fewer, bigger issues, as Figure 9.2 shows. Corporate borrowers are stepping into the vacuum created by the relative withdrawal of governments. Industrial reorganisation and consolidation, via M&As, has led to rapid growth in the corporate bond markets, with the United States being slightly ahead of Europe in developments. In 2000, corporate bond issuance set a new record at a total of US$428.6 billion. Furthermore, the investor base is broadening as retail investors enter the market. At retail brokerage giant Charles Schwab & Co., an average of 2.7 bond trades are now conducted for every 10 equity trades, and 20% of all fixed income trades are conducted via the web site (Sanders, C., 2001). In order to adapt to this changing environment and broaden their investor base, issuers are turning to new measures to achieve their objectives.

Models

Issuers of securities through electronic syndication have two main formats from which to choose:

- They can bypass the investment banks totally with primary offerings, issuing directly to the investors via websites, either their own or a third-party site (so-called primary market bidding systems). This method contributes further to the trend towards disintermediation observed worldwide, which is probably the most fundamental structural impact of the e-bonds.
- Alternatively, they can use specialist third-party sites, mainly banks and other intermediary actors.

Advantages and Impact on the Structure and Dynamics of Origination

In general, online distribution of bonds allows investors to bid for paper online, moving issuance procedures away from closed auctions to primary dealers to more open auctions with a wider participation, also improving transparency, which allows borrowers more precision in sizing and pricing transactions. The derived related benefits include:

- *'A seat on the syndicate desk'*
  Electronic new issuance and trading provide transparency for issuers and investors. Electronic new issuance, especially, provides transparency for the issuer, in terms of the ability to see 'the book being built' online in real time. Issuers (and investors) can gauge demand for an issue directly as a deal progresses, without the information filters of the traditional syndication process. This enables the issuer to better size and price the transaction.

  This is obviously also to the investors' advantage. Online systems can display exact prices or orders submitted, just as real-time quotes with volume levels do for online equity traders. For example, Hambrecht's OpenBook tracks orders on a bar chart, which updates bid concentrations at various prices (however, bidders' identities are not disclosed). Intervest showed the bids in tabular and in graphical form (ranked in the issuer's favour, in and out of the money), with the individual bidder's bid highlighted relative to other anonymous bids, so that he can adjust his price and order quantity according to how comparatively aggressive his competition is.

- *Valuable information about market conditions*
  This increase in the transparency of the system in turn facilitates the analysis of investor behaviour. It provides issuers (and investment banks) with unique information about the historical supply and demand dynamics of the corporate bond marketplace. In certain instances, this information is made available to the investors as well.

  Unless this becomes standard practice, e-bonds may potentially exacerbate the information imbalance in the market. Measures from borrowers to make their actions more open and predictable, and, potentially, sharing of information, are necessary if investors are to, at least partially, give up the costly use of intermediaries as information providers.

- *Access to bonds*
  Successful bidders can buy the quantity of bonds that they want in a deal, avoiding the common situation of supply shortfall, which is attributable to underpricing and therefore, distorted demand.

- *Greater price stability in the secondary market*
  Investors awarded bonds in an auction get the quantity of bonds that they want, at the price that they bid. This produces greater price stability of an issue in the secondary market because securities are more likely to be placed with long-term investors.

- *Broader investor base*
  Sales of corporate bonds are inefficient, taking place over the telephone through investor networks – usually small ones. Online auction systems potentially offer a far wider distribution of securities than is available through existing channels. The e-bond empowers all current and potential bond investors to participate on the same financial conditions in a primary bond offering, whether they are small or large. This ‘democratisation’ of bond issuance meets these smaller investors’ needs for real-time information about new issues and fairness of access to purchase bonds in the primary market.

  By corollary, the use of the Internet enables borrowers to target directly a much wider group, including the range of medium-sized investors and asset or fund managers considered too small to have participated previously in the primary markets. In addition, the possibility of bonds being traded in small amounts may make them attractive to retail investors as well. The Fannie Mae deal with denominations of US$1000 showed that this is possible, as over 100 retail investors hit the company’s website. Another example was the World Bank issue, where US middle market accounts and US retail investors purchased 21% of the issue through more than 550 individual tickets.

e-Bonds can offer issuers more efficient access to a wide and diversified client base. In the long run, the role of investment banks, which traditionally 'find' the buyers for new issues, could be significantly reduced.

- *More economical*
  One of the main potential impacts of the Internet could be in cutting the cost of issuing and buying bonds. Commissions and other fees paid to intermediaries form a significant part of the cost base for borrowers and investors. In addition, online auctions significantly speed up transactions. Traditional bond auctions might take a day or two to complete, using armies of as many as 100 salespeople. By contrast, $300 million worth of Dow Chemical bonds sold out in Hambrecht's two-hour auction. Hambrecht also saved Dow Chemical cash, charging 30 basis points of the deal, whereas Wall Street would have charged at least 40 basis points.

Thus it seems likely that the dealer and broking community may be the losers in this equation, with part of their commissions and fees reverting to issuers and investors in the form of reduced costs. However, the banks themselves will also be able to reduce their own cost base, as Internet-based selling requires less salespeople, thus minimising a labour-intensive exercise.

The Mavericks and Pioneers

1. The first proper issuer on the Internet scene was Freddie Mac, the US mortgage credit agency, with its January 2000 launch of an e-bond, using the Internet as the main marketing platform. Fannie Mae, the US mortgage lender, followed shortly afterwards with two bonds issued in the same period. An estimated 10% of the combined US$10 billion deal was reportedly issued via the Internet.

2. Other frequent borrowers have quickly turned to the electronic distribution system to market their securities more widely. The World Bank has so far launched two e-bonds, with the pioneering launch being made later in January 2000, in which about one-third of orders totalling US$ 5 billion came through the Internet. That figure rose to about 50% of the second issue. There were five distinctive features of the bond which, combined, made this an innovative transaction:

   - *Electronic bond syndicate:* online offering of the securities by all nine financial houses in the syndicate. Goldman Sachs and Lehman Brothers were chosen as the two leading underwriters for the transaction, based on their technological expertise and top-management commitment to the concept of a fully integrated e-bond.

- *Electronic bond distribution:* using online brokerages to deliver greater reach and attract new investors.
- *Electronic order entry and allocation:* live, real-time book-building, allowing more precise bond pricing.
- *Electronic dissemination of all new bond information:* Web-based electronic roadshow and investor marketing.
- *Electronic secondary market trading:* Web-based trading immediately after the pricing of the new bond.

3. The European Investment Bank became the first borrower to sell sterling bonds via the Internet in early February 2000.
4. The first sovereign to launch an e-bond was Argentina with a €400 million, five-year issue in late January 2000. About 40% of orders came over the Internet.
5. The €3 billion, 11-year issue from the Finnish Treasury in February 2000 made Finland the first European sovereign to launch, price and distribute over the Internet. Nearly half the orders were taken online, reaching investors in ten European countries.
6. So far, e-bond markets have been dominated by agency, sovereign and supranational issuers. But it is not only governments that are latching on to the Net's potential power. Other issuers have also appeared, such as Ford (who became the first direct issuer of commercial paper on the Internet in early 2000) and the state-owned Greek telecom company OTE. Both allowed part of their recent currency offerings to be syndicated via an intermediary's website. Roughly two-thirds of orders for the Ford deal were placed and all the debt was allocated electronically. Telecom companies continued to be in the forefront, as Finland's Sonera launched its first e-bond in early March 2000.
7. Since then, Daimler-Chrysler has entered the fray with its June 2000 US$2 billion global electronic bond issue offered in two tranches. The first tranche was US$1 billion of five-year notes and the second was US$1 billion of ten-year notes. The sale was increased in size from US$1.5 billion to meet investor demand. It was the largest US corporate bond sale ever to use the Web.
8. Finally, Dow Chemical became the first industrial company to sell its bonds through an Internet Dutch auction in August, when it issued US$300 million of five-year paper using online investment bank WR Hambrecht's open auction platform, OpenBook. In a typical deal of this nature, you

Table 9.1 e-Investment banks

System	Ownership
OpenBook	WR Hambrecht
DealComposer	The Engine Room
American Express Credit Corporation	Amex
BondConnect	Bridge Information Systems; State Street; The Boston Stock Exchange; OM; NetExchange
MuniAuction	MuniAuction
Bloomberg Municipal System	Bloomberg
cpmarket.com	Prescient Markets
Ford Motor Credit Company	Ford Motor Credit Company
PARITY	Thomson Financial
Treasury Direct	US Treasury Department
Valubond	Valubond

would see the investment bank allocate bonds to 15 to 20 accounts. In this online deal, bonds were allocated to 57 accounts. Hambrecht's online auction for Dow followed two others a few days earlier. One was held by Bear Stearns, and the other by Deutsche Bank, but both auctioned their own bonds, not a third party's.

On the other side of the equation, a number of new electronic intermediaries or auctioneers are starting to make an impact. Some of the new players include those shown in Table 9.1.

WR Hambrecht is probably the most interesting as a start-up:

> Two years ago Wall Street was scornful as an upstart investment bank, WR Hambrecht + Co began holding Dutch auctions for initial public offerings, with the aim of eventually licensing the technology to other investment banks. Now, one major endorsement later, several investment banks and other players are seeking access to the firm's auction technology – and no one is laughing anymore.
>
> In a major coup WR Hambrecht developed a customised version of the firm's auction technology for Freddie Mac's reference note sales. Now a number of big Wall Street investment banks have approached WR Hambrecht with similar intentions. Wall Street players, once cool to the idea, confirmed Hambrecht's success at starting to convert its rivals. Any such alliances would go a long way to validating the brainchild of Bill

Hambrecht, who started WR Hambrecht in late 1997. Hambrecht has done several IPOs via the Dutch auction model. The firm has long hoped to license the product to others, but until the Freddie Mac breakthrough, few thought it would succeed.

The Dutch auction method often allows issuers to raise the maximum amount of capital possible at a lower cost, without the headaches of a first-day pop, leaving a fortune on the table, subsequent flipping and price decline. Hambrecht expanded its auction model in August, underwriting the first-ever online auction of corporate debt, a $300 million bond deal for the Dow Chemical Co. Hambrecht has been very public in its marketing of OpenBook (the debt auction model) and are willing to share the technology with other investment banks. The Dow Chemical offering validated the model by offering fair access to a good security.

After all the derision WR Hambrecht suffered for its Dutch auctions, it begs the question: why is Wall Street so eager to enlist now? Some of the pressure is coming from the client side, pushing to sell its securities via the auction system to maximise the capital raised; and it's the investment bank, reluctant to lose the client's business, that agrees to seek a working agreement with Hambrecht. The auction process used by Hambrecht combines proprietary software with a method of providing complete transparency for the underwriters, the issuer and the buyers of the securities. For that reason alone, investment bankers don't like it. (Wirth, 2000 (abridged))

Future Prospects and Impediments

In the World Bank's revolutionary vision of the future of bond markets, the Internet acts as a powerful catalyst to fundamental change, enabling real-time connectivity of demand and supply. But how far away are we from this kind of network?

Whether the Internet transforms the structure of primary markets depends on whether the ability to buy and sell on the Internet attracts new buyers to the fixed-income market and whether issuers are able to use the Internet to bypass traditional lead managers and sell directly to these investors. These questions remain unanswered.

Even less ambitious prospects for e-bond development hinge on technological readiness. Full-scale exploitation of the potential of the Internet cannot be achieved without issuers, e-enabled intermediaries or new e-intermediaries and investors all being ready to go online.

The experience to date is a reality check; indicating that the electronic distribution capabilities developed by banks have been front-end façades only, with no interface into central order book systems, necessitating manual order re-input, and no straight-through-transaction-processing capabilities in the back office. This has led to the Internet, the engine of efficiency, producing duplication of effort, waste and confusion.

It would seem that the lack of real progress at the coalface is attributable largely to the fact that these e-enablement investments were a panic reaction to major issuers, such as the World Bank, using Internet capability as a deciding factor in new issue mandates. Their weeding out and exclusion from the process of the technologically ill-prepared prospective lead managers sent shock waves through Wall Street. Consequently, without resolving channel conflict and cannibalisation issues, these banks prematurely embarked on e-primary issuance strategies.

Compounding this, the fixed-income investor base largely rejected the click-and-buy model. They proved reluctant to replace their well-functioning offline relationships with salesmen with online relationships with either borrowers or e-intermediaries. Even if STP economies were on offer, most of the buy-side were not operationally able to realise these economies either, and, over and above automated transaction execution, there was limited demand for more 'info-mediation' from institutional investors, already over-armed for battle. Finally, the much-hyped expansion of the customer base has been constrained by measures to counter security and credit risk, such as password-only accessible accounts with approved credit limits.

So far, no one seems able to quantify the precise benefits of Internet distribution and banks are now re-evaluating their strategies. However, going forward, most are likely to take the view that the risk of not pursuing Net strategies is too high. They are likely to continue on down the learning curve, but will adjust their position somewhat. Most now see the Internet as a complement rather than a substitute to traditional channels of issuance, supporting not overthrowing the existing market model. The pre-trade support in terms of research, advice, capital commitment, distribution systems and market-making abilities of intermediaries still adds a lot of value. However, the actual execution of the auction, the price–quantity bidding process, does lend itself to this medium.

Making online corporate bond auctions commonplace, however, will depend on (1) getting the systems workable (institutional investors have so far been reasonably forgiving of unstable systems, but will not continue to be so indefinitely) and (2) getting buyers off the telephone and onto the Web. Websites alone can't pull that off. So all those bond barkers at investment banks may find themselves redeployed. They won't be intermediaries in deals so much as customer-service representatives – this medium is new to investors and they want hand-holding to ease the transition. In the long term, though, clients will eventually bypass the phone. It is simply more time- and cost-efficient to buy and sell bonds with a well-functioning online system.

In terms of attracting new buyers from the retail market – the holy grail – most banks will make the bullish assumption that the bond markets will adopt the equity market model. Market conditions are favourable right now, with increasing demand for bonds as a safe, reasonable yielding investment alternative. However, in future, wholesale access to the retail markets is likely to be accomplished via retail e-intermediaries, evidenced by Goldman's recent link up with Schwab for this purpose as well as Ford's with Fidelity.

So far, e-bonds have mainly come from high-quality names with solid credit ratings. In the short term, it seems unlikely that electronic selling of less prominent actors will play an important role in the e-bond market, reflecting a strategic choice on the part of banks to introduce the new investor base to the fixed-income product using high-quality names. Thus it may take a while before retail investors get the opportunity to buy high-yield bonds online. Even in high-grade markets, investors will continue to require advice from salesmen and credit analysts, as the high-yield sector develops, and as investor protection mechanisms continue to advance. Banks thus seem unlikely to rush to target their new clients with high-yield bonds. Issues of technological readiness, credit-rating, credibility, name recognition, investor education, regulation, legislation and language need to be addressed first.

Another impediment is the lack of a common distribution platform. Clearly, each firm having its own unique platform is not a winning model. A common syndication platform would allow the competing banks in the underwriting syndicate to offer synchronised prices for all the trades an investor might want to make to facilitate the investment, including swaps, switches and repos. In addition, investors want only a few portals into the bond markets and a central clearing house, not multiple URLs and passwords. Unfortunately, market participants' attempts at 'co-optition' have tended to get bogged down in 'management by committee' quagmires. Even so, the Internet is not going to kill relationship banking. Bond issuers will continue to pay a premium for the swaps that underpin their capital market financings, a premium that ensures the deal as a whole is done smoothly. Just as an institutional equity investor is unlikely to use E*Trade or Charles Schwab for a $500 million order, the World Bank is unlikely to ask banks to compete on-screen down to the last basis point for a $500 million swap.

There is considerable potential for change in the coming years. As technological evolution and readiness to use technology develops, and as new players with low-cost infrastructure enter the market, these changes will be felt among dealers and brokers. In this new environment, those providing the infrastructure for trading bonds online and those providing the content, that is, new issues and new institutional clients, will be most likely to profit.

Competitive Landscape of the Future – New vs. Old

The race to sell corporate bonds over the Internet is clearly on. The investment-grade arena has been seeing spurts of new issuance online by the top established underwriters since the start of 2000, with heavyweight firms including Goldman Sachs, Merrill Lynch and Lehman Brothers unveiling Internet underwriting capabilities. Online competition entered a new level in mid-2000 when three firms – Bear Stearns, Deutsche Bank, and the upstart, WR Hambrecht – launched underwriting sites and completed new offerings in a Dutch auction process. Bear Stearns and Deutsche Bank brought deals for their respective firms.

However, as mentioned previously, investor reaction has so far been mixed. According to *Euromoney*, for certain key market participants – notably the large institutional bond investors – 'being able to deal on the Internet ranks somewhere between a non-event and a mild setback' (Lee, 2000). So, as they and other firms begin to explore the possibilities online, they could be facing not only a new technology but a disruptive one. A disruptive technology is a technology or a business model or product or service that isn't good enough at the outset to be embraced by the market. The disruptive technology theory predicts that the ability to complete corporate bond offerings via the Internet will take root first at the fringe and then at the core. As stated repeatedly, it is so much cheaper than through the traditional business model that it will take over the market eventually. However, it opens a gap that might enable new entrants, who cannot offer the same quality of service that top investment banks can provide, to secure an advantage over the large players in the battle for online underwriting.

In the corporate bond market, the MarketAxess consortium of big-name Wall Street dealers is poised to dominate secondary trading. As mentioned previously, MarketAxess is owned by such big-guns as ABN Amro, Bear Sterns, Credit Suisse First Boston, Deutsche Bank, JP Morgan Chase, Lehman Brothers, Salomon Smith Barney and UBS. And MarketAxess' corporate market dominance is threatened only be the equally powerful TradeWeb consortium. Platforms for underwriting new issues, however, remain fragmented.

The old-guard banks and dealers know that corporate bond underwriting online is a strong competitive threat. But they have such a vested interest in the old way that they're going to hang on to that as long as they possibly can. It's in their best interest to slow the process down. However, when change becomes inevitable, they'll be able to adjust. They will fire people if they have to and they have all the technology in place. Consequently, many analysts are sceptical over whether smaller firms could grab a substantial portion of the market for online bond underwriting.

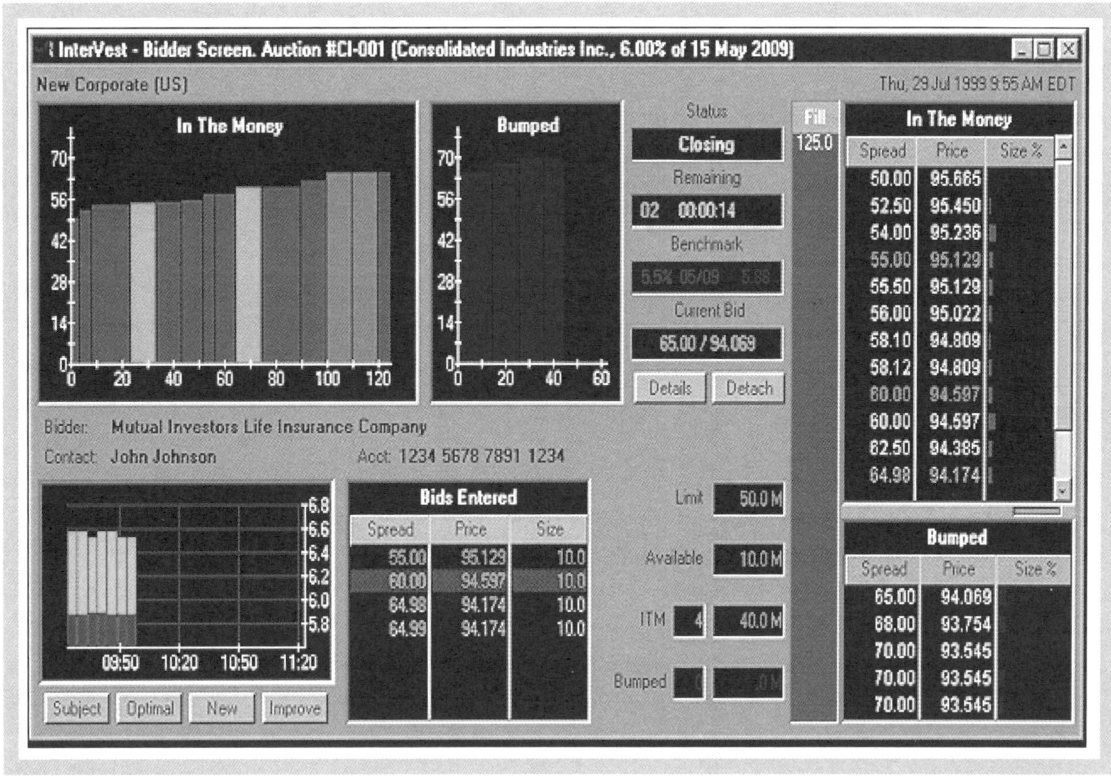

Figure 9.3 A model e-Bond auction system

And, while online underwriting may become an important part of the market, the traditional way of doing business will continue to be central for many participants. Bonds may have been relegated to commodity status, and people may potentially use the Internet to take orders, but this will continue to be a people-driven marketing process. Meanwhile investors maintain that the ideal securities to be sold over the Internet are those with critical attributes that are measurable. The kinds of bond that will trade over the Internet will be the most liquid. As the Internet becomes more pervasive, the most standard kinds of bond that don't have special features, and therefore have liquidity, are the ones that will benefit. As new issuers seek to tap the market, they will begin to consider why they should incorporate new features in it. They will begin to make their securities as standard as possible to maximise their liquidity. Moreover, the discrete auction model is viewed as the most appropriate for more heterogeneous, illiquid securities (see Figure 9.3).

ARCANE AND ILLIQUID MARKETS

The auction format has also proved to be the model of choice in some of the more obscure or esoteric e-markets that have emerged. First, other versions of primary markets have materialised. For example, the venture capitalist-backed Direct Stock Market uses this format to effect online private equity placement or distribution. Gaps in the corporate lending market, such as loans to SMEs and trade finance, are also being filled by website-based markets.

Second, this model is being used for the secondary trading of loans. DebtDomain, for example, links over 50 European banks. Even structured finance sites, like Visible Markets, have emerged, trading structured fixed-income products, including collateralised mortgages and asset-backed securities. Finally, a number of distressed debt (non-performing consumer or commercial loans, such as credit cards, student loans, utility debt, trade receivables and so on) exchanges have emerged. Examples include eDebt.com, DistressDebt.com, DebtForSale.com, AssetExchange.com, CollectionsX.com, DebtAuction.com, and TheDebtMarketplace.

Even failed independent e-markets who have repositioned themselves further down the food chain as technology vendors are driving innovation in this arena. For example, ePit Systems, has launched the ePit Interval Auction – a system designed to enable exchanges and institutions to conduct dynamic auctions that share the same price discovery techniques as continuous markets, in order to help newer markets to build and concentrate liquidity.

CHAPTER 10

STRATEGIC RESPONSE OF THE TRADITIONAL EXCHANGES: THE DEATH OF THE OPEN-OUTCRY PIT

As electronic trading networks gradually become indistinguishable from electronic exchanges, the impact on traditional exchanges and exchange-traded markets has been dramatic. In equity markets in particular, a power struggle of epic proportions is underway.

WAR GAMES: WARRING FACTIONS

The earth is quaking under global exchanges: a classic market share battle is being waged between the technologically advanced new entrants and established brands (with the ECNs pitted against the NYSE and the NASDAQ in the archetypal equity markets in the US). The outcome is likely to be what it usually is when competition intensifies: profit margins will shrink, rationalisation through M&As will ensue, and customers will benefit from wider choice and lower prices.

RELATIVE COMPETITIVE ADVANTAGES

As discussed previously, the technology harnessed by the ECNs has conferred on them significant competitive advantages in terms of *inter alia*:

- *speed* (real-time trading eliminates the time-lag between a pit trader receiving and executing an order)
- *access* (globally linked electronic markets give traders access to markets that may not have been available to them previously)
- *anonymity* (anonymous trading both levels the playing field and reduces market impact on prices)
- *cost* (the vastly lower transaction costs afforded by electronic trading platforms benefit all participants but especially private investors).

As a result, ECNs have hijacked a sizeable portion of the trading business from the markets in which they have been active, especially from the NASDAQ OTC market. Now, however, a number of developments, including SEC rules that came into effect in 1998, which permit the ECNs to secure exchange status, have all but revoked exchange protectionism. The new regulatory environment will enable ECNs to target the NYSE and other exchanges' products and customers more effectively, and so seize even more territory. Opening the gateway to exchange-listed equities should send tremors through the established exchanges' foundations. If events in the OTC market – where the nine ECNs (led by Instinet and Island) have commandeered almost 50% of NASDAQ's trade in four years – form a precedent, then the NYSE and other major exchanges are now literally threatened with extinction. They must adapt or die. Specifically, they must offer competitive execution, or superior liquidity – their sole advantage – will leak into cyberspace.

TURBULENCE IN THE WORLD'S EXCHANGES AFTER YEARS OF INERTIA

Ultimately what threatens the established exchanges, with their economic inefficiencies and poor manoeuvrability, is the sheer rate of technological change. The legacy of a non-profit mindset, they have been hindered by their slow and conservative decision-making structures and processes, exacerbated by the misaligned interests of members, or the vested interest that they have in preserving the status quo.

The exchanges should not be underestimated, however, as they have demonstrated an ability to ward off competition in the past, and they're not likely to just roll over and die now. Already they're taking action to defend their position.

Exchange Demutualisation and Technology Investment

To compete more nimbly, a number of the world's largest exchanges either have demutualised, or are in the process of demutualisation. In almost every instance, they have attributed their decision to competitive pressure from various forms of ECNs.

One of the advantages of public company status is a less cumbersome decision-making structure. Moreover, an IPO raises capital to (1) invest in technology (not only to fend off ECNs, but also to position in the burgeoning global market for electronic securities exchanges), and (2) to build up a war chest of currency for acquisitions. Certain exchanges have succeeded in the former campaign. The OM Gruppen (operator of the Stockholm Stock Exchange), LIFFE (with its Connect product), the Deutsche Börse (with its Xetra product), and the LSE (with its SETS product) have actually managed to position themselves as leading providers of electronic trading technology. However, OM has proved to be LIFFE's nemesis in this regard. In fact, the technological sophistication of European exchanges is one of the major reasons why ECNs have had less success in penetrating these markets.

A public flotation of an exchange is, however, fraught with difficulties, not least because of the novelty of valuing a securities exchange. This has proved an impediment to many such initiatives.

The following is a sample of major stock and commodity futures exchanges that have demutualised or stated their intention to demutualise:

- London Stock Exchange (LSE)
- NASDAQ
- Deutsche Börse
- Euronext
- London International Financial Futures and Options Exchange (LIFFE)
- Chicago Mercantile Exchange (CME)
- Chicago Board of Trade (CBOT)
- New York Mercantile Exchange (Nymex)
- The International Petroleum Exchange.

Many other exchanges have thus far resisted yielding to this pressure. The Big Daddy of them all – the NYSE – numbers among those. Significantly, it was the NYSE's powerful specialist member firms that defeated its own aim to demutualise.

Finally, it should be noted that, in the wake of demutualisation, exchanges expose themselves to the risk of a take-over by an investment bank, which has broader implications for markets.

Merges and Alliances

Another major strategy pursued by exchanges has been to strengthen their position through merges and alliances. Again, however, despite the obvious benefits (a broader range of lower cost products for a larger customer base), exchanges have been impeded by their politically contaminated decision-making processes.

The LSE–Deutsche Börse debacle ranks as one of the most high-profile failures. A 1998 proposed alliance between the two – which was extended to an ambitious eight-way link-up of exchanges – failed. It was resurrected in 2000 as a proposed merger to form a new e-exchange; iX. The parties even conscripted the NASDAQ into the venture to form a joint high-tech exchange. This too was eventually abandoned – over disputes about the technology (Xetra vs. SETS) and ownership of the new entity. This left the LSE, in particular, quite vulnerable, and in 2001 it became the target of a hostile take-over bid launched by the much smaller Swedish exchange, under the command of the OM Group (who had taken it over after the exchange went public). Although it successfully defended itself, in the final chapter of the saga, the LSE then tried and failed to take-over its own offspring, LIFFE.

Politicking and internal strife have sabotaged ventures in other markets too. In the derivatives markets, a set of simple cross-Atlantic partnerships were initially established. The US CBOT agreed to an alliance with the European Eurex, and their two biggest rivals, respectively the CME – through its Globex2 – and LIFFE – through its LIFFE Connect – also announced a link-up. However, things began to go awry when plans grew more expansionist. A plan to create a global derivatives trading platform through A/C/E (Alliance/CBOT/Eurex) has fallen apart, partly because of CBOT's minority stake in a CME–Chicago Board Options Exchange (CBOE) joint venture to form a single stock futures exchange. The parties have now resorted to arbitration to settle the dispute.

In fact there has been such a merry-go-round of tried-and-failed mergers and alliances among the world's stock and derivatives exchanges, rousing much animosity, that they're almost impossible to chronicle or chart. Nevertheless, a few merges have been successful. Some prominent examples are cited below.

In the US equity markets, NASDAQ successfully merged with the American Stock Exchange (Amex) in 1998. However, the merger only really exists on paper. In the European equity markets, Euronext is the product of a joint venture between the French, Dutch and Belgian stock exchanges. It was initially a defensive response by the snubbed exchanges to the LSE–Deutsche Börse proposal, but ironically, has since succeeded where they have failed. As of June 2001, 1588 companies were listed on Euronext, and trading volumes on its central electronic order book averaged €148 billion for the first six months of 2001. Euronext, however, is not yet fully integrated.

In European derivatives markets, Eurex was born of the merger between the Swiss and German derivatives exchanges (after a tenuous link between the Germans and the French was severed). As a screen-based trading system, Eurex demolished floor-based LIFFE's near monopoly in certain key instruments (for example, Eurex has secured almost 40% of total volume in long-term (10- and 30-year) German bund futures contracts).

There have even been attempts – one successful – at cross-market acquisitions. At the end of 2001, Euronext beat other bidders, which included the LSE and the Deutsche Börse, to acquire LIFFE. Once Euronext's derivatives business is migrated to LIFFE's Connect platform, it will probably become the largest European derivatives exchange by total number of contracts traded and represent a strong competitor to Eurex. On the cross-Atlantic front, Amex and Euronext are now in tentative alliance negotiations, while, rather incestuously, NASDAQ has entered into a joint venture with LIFFE.

In the newer commodity and commodity futures markets, a few recent developments in support of consolidation have also taken place. For example, Germany's two electricity exchanges, the Deutsche Börse-affiliated European Energy Exchange and the Leipzig Power Exchange (backed by power exchange Nord Pool) merged in 2001. The new exchange was christened EEX.

Finally, more recently, there have been a number of overtures by exchanges towards the ECNs themselves. For example, after NASDAQ's proposed alliances with the Deutsche Börse, the LSE and even the NYSE amounted to nothing, it eventually acquired a majority holding in the quote-driven European ECN, EASDAQ, which it has since renamed NASDAQ Europe. And the Swiss Stock Exchange has now formed a joint venture with the TradePoint ECN, christened Virt-X.

In European markets, the scope for further consolidation is high. The US has only 3 national and 5 regional exchanges (excluding NASDAQ and the ECNs) but Western Europe still has over 30 stock and futures exchanges.

THE MASTERS OF THE UNIVERSE

At the same time that European exchange convergence is gaining momentum, on the other side of the Atlantic, the market share battle between the technologically advanced upstarts and the exchanges is intensifying. And for the players on either side of this chess board, the stakes are mounting. This power struggle has been but a forerunner to a more fundamental one. The same forces that gave rise to the ECNs in the first place – regulation, technology and entrepreneurship – are slowly moving the very epicentre of the securities industry away from the floor of the NYSE to an as yet unformed marketplace in the ether. The prize is not just to be the leading US and European trading centre, but to be a key node in the global 24-hour market that many believe will one day emerge.

The idea of a global equity market – a single trading platform (or two or three linked platforms) on which all the world's blue-chip equities can be traded (with a similarly consolidated back office) – is a tantalising one, but one which is gaining real purchase. Exchanges around the world are starting to position for this reality. In 2001, the NYSE, Euronext and the Tokyo Stock Exchange announced the formation of a global equity market (GEM). Other exchanges, including Australia, Hong Kong, Mexico and Brazil, were quick to pledge their allegiance. Converts believe that within three to five years any investor will be able to trade in any market in the world (but be able to trade and settle where he lives). There are also some global alliance precedents in the equity and commodity derivatives markets. Globex, for example, tried to link up derivatives exchanges around the world to allow trading books to be passed around with the sun.

No one knows for certain what the future market topography will look like, but a few eventualities seem likely. Equity and equity futures, options and other derivatives exchanges are likely to converge. Euronext's acquisition of LIFFE and the tender by the Deutsche Börse (who maintain an interest in Eurex) and the LSE (for its own spawn) seem to support this trend in Europe at least. Through a series of intra-national mergers, regional trading will consolidate on one or two electronic central order books, which, through international alliances, will be passed from regional time zone to time zone, via electronic interfaces. It should be noted that cross-border alliance strategies, such as the GEM initiative, are already as important as acquisitions to secure regional dominance. The current major contenders in North America include the NYSE, NASDAQ and Instinet, while in Europe, the Euronext–LIFFE grouping and Deutsche Börse–Eurex grouping seem most strongly positioned. The commodities and commodities futures markets will follow a similar pattern. This future landscape will however still feature regional exchanges (for smaller cap stocks) and for niche players.

The North American equity market is arguably the nucleus of the global financial markets. Events there are pivotal, and the drama being staged by the three major competitors in this market is becoming riveting.

The NYSE is still the very hub of the market. However, even as it and the other regional exchanges are driven to overcome resistance to change, floatation to avoid sinking and alliance strategies – intended to raise capital, invest in technology and boost liquidity respectively – may not be enough. Similarly, for the ECNs, whose rise to power has been unprecedented, their fall could be just as fast as their ascent.

If we plot markets and exchanges in a two-dimensional matrix (Figure 10.1) and label the axes liquidity (low to high) and electronic connectivity (low to high), ECNs would occupy the high-tech/(relatively) low liquidity quadrant, while exchanges would be positioned in the (relatively) low-tech/high liquidity quadrant. Naturally there is convergence on the high-tech/high liquidity quadrant, with a virtual central limit-order book in the very apex. While both exchanges and electronic trading networks are aggressively pursuing strategies to get there first, it is an anomaly called the NASDAQ that has the edge.

The NASDAQ is a highly competitive electronic stock market. It lists nearly 5000 companies with a market capitalisation currently in the region of US$4.5 trillion. It trades more shares per day than any other US market and has the largest dollar volume of trades of any financial market. In 2000, the dollar value of trading on NASDAQ reached a record US$20.4 trillion, exceeding the

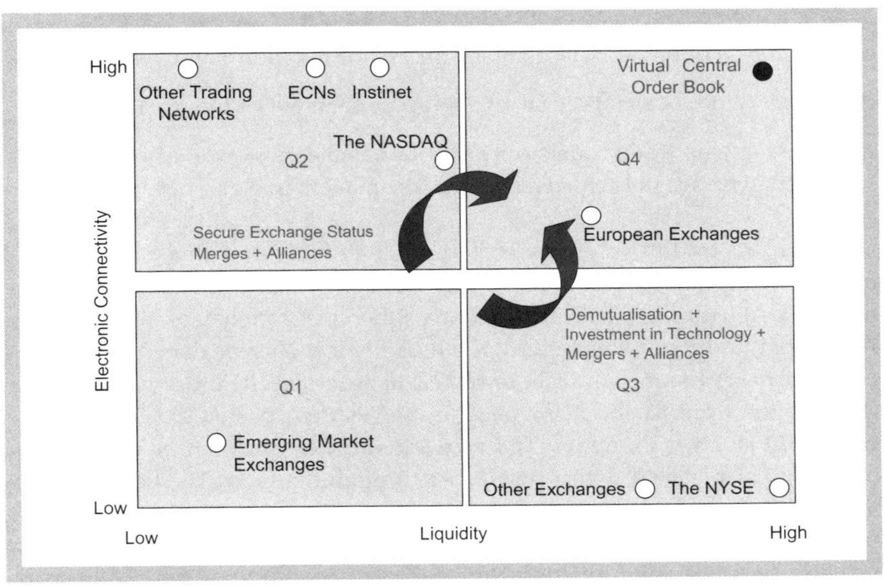

Figure 10.1 Competitive environment analysis: relative positioning perceptual map

previous record of $11.0 trillion set in 1999 by 85.2%. It has the capacity to trade 6 billion shares a day.

Its strengths are inherent in its hybrid structure. It is electronic, enabling multiple market participants to trade through a network linking buyers and sellers globally, is both quote- and order-driven, has capital commitment from multiple firms, facilitates both retail and institutional sales, is more transparent, highly liquid, has continuous order flow, and narrower spreads.

NASDAQ market participants, who openly compete for order flow, number approximately 1000, and comprise market-makers, order entry firms, and alternative trading systems (ATSs) that include ECNs and unlisted trading privileges (UTP) exchanges.

The 425 registered NASDAQ market-makers are independent dealers (for example Knight Securities; Spear, Leeds & Kellog; Herzog, Heine, Geduld) who compete for investor orders by displaying buy and sell interest (quotes and customer (market and limit) orders) in NASDAQ-listed securities. Market-makers are obligated to display two-sided firm quotes and commit capital in all securities in which they choose to make a market. On receipt of an order they either trade from own account inventory or seek a counterparty. They can also interact with market orders brought to NASDAQ via ECNs and broker-dealers. They provide immediate and continuous trading. There are four types of market-maker:

- *retail* (who have a retail brokerage network to serve retail investors);
- *institutional* (who work large block orders for institutional investors);
- *regional* (who focus rather on a geographic segment of the market);
- *wholesale* (who trade shares for institutional clients as well as other broker-dealers who are not registered as market-makers in a given stock).

ECNs are trading systems that display either one-sided or two-sided quotes, which reflect actual orders. Buy and sell orders which are represented in NASDAQ through ECN quotes are either institutional or public orders forwarded to the ECN by subscribing brokers or broker-dealers. When one of these participants uses an ECN to represent an order, the order is first routed through the ECN to check for matches and is then posted electronically on NASDAQ as an ECN quote. The forwarded order can then be executed on NASDAQ or matched with a new order through the ECN. The best ECN buy and sell orders, or 'top of book', will frequently drive the inside market, meaning they represent the best bid and ask prices for a security. ECNs provide order anonymity for institutions and market-makers. They foster competition among market participants and enhance market liquidity. As discussed previously, the nine licensed ECNs are Instinet; Island; Redi-Book; Archipelago; B-Trade; Brut; NexTrade; Attain; MarketXT; and GlobeNet.

A NASDAQ order-entry firm is a type of broker that enters customer orders into the NASDAQ system. Order-entry firms have the ability to access bid and ask quotes for market-makers and securities listed on NASDAQ. Order-entry firms add to the market's liquidity by bringing additional orders into NASDAQ. However, they differ from market-makers in that they do not commit capital or maintain price quotations in NASDAQ securities.

Recent Developments

The NASDAQ has taken full advantage of a number of regulatory developments that amount to the abolition of exchange protectionism and which have lowered entry barriers to new markets. The rescinding of the NYSE's Rule 390 (which prohibited NYSE members' routing order flow or market-making in stocks listed pre-1979 except on the NYSE or other registered exchanges) was a major coup for the NASDAQ. The repeal of the Buttonwood founding agreement rule authorises off-exchange trading of all listed stocks (thus boosting the market's efficiency and allowing market-makers to match orders internally and capture both sides of the spread). Even this will soon become extraneous, as in 2000, the NASDAQ submitted an application to be granted exchange status. The association has also demutualised.

On the technology front, the NASDAQ has also been enhancing its systems. In many instances, however, these system enhancements equate to fundamental structural changes. In January 2001, the SEC approved the NASDAQ's SuperMontage proposal, which will act as a central order book – displaying the best three quotes or orders for each stock traded. This will effectively link the nine disparate ECNs as well as the market-makers. The SEC overrode objections from the ECNs in the interests of enhanced transparency, liquidity and narrower spreads, all of which favour investors. It is intended to be launched in early 2002. At the same time, however, an alternative system will be launched, enabling the ECNs also to display their single best quotes on NASDAQ screens, not just when that quote is the best in the market. This will also create the potential for true competition to exist between marketplaces trading NASDAQ securities.

This development is probably the most crucial. NASDAQ has suffered cruelly at the hands of the technologically advanced race of ECNs. However, ECNs, as discussed, are essentially a product of the NASDAQ, and were born more of changes in the regulatory framework that surrounded NASDAQ than of market forces. The original objective was realised, NASDAQ dealers aren't dodgy dealing anymore, and the NASDAQ is now a super-competitive market. The subsequent changes in the regulatory framework could now destroy ECNs entirely. As alluded to, ECNs could form an evolutionary prelude to the creation of something more grandiose and more permanent – a global, electronic, order-driven stock exchange. Ultimately, if NASDAQ were to become a fully automated order-driven market based on a central order book – in essence operating like ECNs do at present – the need for ECNs would disappear. Such a NASDAQ 'superECN' would harness so much liquidity that other ECNs would find it impossible to compete. A NASDAQ virtual CLOB would afford a far greater level of transparency and create wider and deeper liquidity and narrower spreads. Investors entering either limit orders or market orders would be guaranteed that their order would be executed at the best possible price available on the market. Market-makers too would find themselves marginalised. Ultimately, with SuperMontage, NASDAQ is moving very definitely in this direction.

In addition to the replacement of the QuoteMontage with the SuperMontage, the OptiMark and Primex auction system have also been integrated into the NASDAQ market. OptiMark – essentially an electronic matching system for trading equities – was launched on San Francisco's Pacific Exchange in January 1999 and on the NASDAQ in October 1999, and is due to be rolled out to Japan's Osaka Stock Exchange shortly. The system is able to link markets and allow investors to trade baskets of securities across different exchanges in a single transaction, without the risk of partial execution. It has effectively created a hybrid market structure integrating the continuous market with periodic call auctions. In this model you have a continuous displayed order book, then every ten minutes, the orders are swept into the OptiMark engine. Any book orders which don't get filled are returned to the book.

Primex will provide investors and market-makers with a unique auction format for trading NASDAQ and exchange-listed stocks. It will give brokers and market-makers the means to expose their orders to the broadest possible audience – an electronic 'crowd' of competing broker/dealers, proprietary traders, institutions, ECNs and even the orders of other customers – who will bid anonymously for the execution. The system is designed to provide best execution and, in particular, opportunities for price improvement – that is, opportunities for orders to receive prices that improve upon the best quotes. By auctioning securities, the system ensures that orders are fairly priced based on market forces. Electronic connections encourage broad participation, enhancing system liquidity. The system is capable of conducting instantaneous auctions for market orders and immediately executable limit orders in both NASDAQ and NYSE-listed stocks. Participants can participate anonymously, acting as agent or principal. NASDAQ has licensed Primex to be its exclusive operator for all US securities and the system will be offered to all member broker-dealers as an optional service. This creates a truly hybrid market, electronically offering listed companies and investors the best aspects of both the dealer-based and exchange or auction securities markets. Primex's investors include Merrill Lynch, MSDW, Goldman Sachs and Bernard L Madoff Securities. This will co-exist with the NASDAQ InterMarket – an electronic, quotation-driven marketplace that links the OTC market and exchanges, enabling NASDAQ market participants to trade all exchange-listed securities, including those listed on the NYSE and Amex.

Decimalisation, which was recently introduced on the NYSE, is now being launched in OTC stocks, and should also stimulate demand, because spreads will narrow, thereby reducing the cost to trade.

NASDAQ's stated vision is to ultimately become a global market of markets, built on a global network of networks, which link pools of liquidity, assuring the best possible price at the lowest possible cost. However, international expansion is one area in which NASDAQ's success has been less than spectacular. In fact, it has suffered several setbacks, especially in Europe, where it has repeatedly been either spurned by prospective partners or caught in the crossfire of multi-pronged alliance hostilities. However, it has now secured an alliance with LIFFE and has acquired a stake in the floundering EASDAQ ECN.

So, where in the war does this leave the NYSE? Although, with its antiquated open-outcry trading floor, the NYSE is nothing less than archaic in both form and function, its supremacy in world markets remains unchallenged. However, its hegemony may not be forever. In certain respects, the exchange is showing signs of yielding to technological pressures by, for example, recently initiating a similar display of its specialists' order books. Nevertheless, a degree of destructive, even futile, self-protection is still evident. Some time ago, the SEC, to advance the cause of the National Market System – an ill-defined Platonic ideal of the marketplace in which information flows freely, markets compete and investors invest without a middleman – began promoting the idea of automated execution, which would cut out the middleman. The NYSE and its specialists greeted that idea as enthusiastically as the NRA embraces One World Government (Vinzant, 1999). Their resistance is explainable given that NYSE specialists control exclusive franchises on stocks, and hence command operating margins of over 55%. By contrast, there is an average of 11 dealers making markets in each NASDAQ stock and, as a result of this healthier dose of competition, NASDAQ market-makers earn margins of less than 25%. Furthermore, more recent proposals by, for example, former SEC chairman, Arthur Levitt, to centralise stock trading by electronically linking all markets were thwarted by opposition from the NYSE and some sympathetic politicians. The NYSE's own motion to demutualise was vetoed by its members. However, market forces cannot be obstructed or diverted in perpetuity, and the ultimate mega-trend is undeniably that of convergence.

CONCLUSION

At the moment, the new electronic environment is characterised by schizophrenic trends:

- ECNs are gaining market share at the expense of brokers, market-makers, NASDAQ and established exchanges
- The exchanges propose to demutualise and go high-tech
- NASDAQ and the ECNs intend to become exchanges
- Consolidation among the ECNs and exchanges is evidenced by a spate of alliances, merges and acquisitions.
- Liquidity, already spread thin geographically, qualitatively and quantitatively, is actually fragmenting even more dangerously, even as convergence remains the overriding tendency.

However, a few long-term trends are clear. Execution on physically distinct trading floors appears increasingly anachronistic, given the ubiquity of the Net. Electronic trading has already virtually destroyed open-outcry trading on futures exchanges in Europe and in Asia. And while some exchanges, notably in the US, have resisted so far, the death of the trading pit is unlikely to be far away. Exchanges are ultimately legacies from the pre-telephone era, and have only clung on through protection. Once that goes, the open-outcry ring will be relegated to history.

Second, the traditional exchange structures, created by and for middlemen, are being ruptured. Personal relationships and a local presence in the market are no longer important factors in a system where orders are anonymous and execution is based purely on price and volume.

Finally, the electronic trading networks, led by the ECNs, the exchanges, led by the NYSE, and the NASDAQ, by all accounts, at the forefront, are already converging on a virtual central order book. However, the road to this Eldorado may take many different paths. Perhaps a literal monolithic CLOB will be rejected as anti-competitive and monopolistic, and a 'virtual' (in every sense of the word) single market may metamorphose out of multiple interconnected electronic exchanges. While the landscape of the future is as yet uncharted, one thing is certain: 'we will have one global exchange, and it will be in the ether' (*The Economist*, 1999).

DOWN THE FOOD CHAIN: THE SUPER-CLEARERS

This convergence trend is evident further down the value chain as well. In tandem with front-office operations (order-matching or trade execution), back-office operations, including clearing (scrip registration) and settlement (when money changes hands), are also centralising to optimise efficiency.

Initially, trade processing initiatives focused on the efficacy of domestic clearing and settlement systems. In this respect, at least, it is the Americans who have forged the way. Their exchanges may still be stuck in the Dark Ages (or so say the Europeans), but their clearing and settlement systems are state of the art. In the late 1970s, America had as many as seven separate clearing and settlement organisations. New York was notorious for its 'paper blockages', and the markets would periodically have to close in order to catch up on the paperwork. To resolve these problems, the various groups were amalgamated into one body. First, regional depositories merged into the Depository Trust Company, which then became the largest depository in the world. It then merged with the National Securities Clearing Corporation, the largest clearing operation in the US, to form the Depository Trust and Clearing Corporation (DTCC). The DTCC, which is mutually owned by its member banks, now handles the clearing and settlement of almost all American security trades. It acts, in effect, as the central counterparty (CCP) for all shares traded on both the NYSE and the NASDAQ, and registers changes of ownership. As the DTCC has dematerialised scrip, share certificates no longer physically change hands and registrars have been made redundant. Costs are low, at five cents for an average equity trade, relative to the European average of nearly ten times as much. This clearing and settlement consolidation was critical to the success of the National Market System.

Despite this impressive operation, the DTCC is continuously tested merely to keep up with volumes. Thus far, it has been able to cope with the peaks in business, but those peaks are becoming ever-more vertiginous. On its heaviest day in 1998, it handled some 6.3 million securities trades, but only three years later, trading volumes on the heaviest day had risen to over 18 million, worth a gross total of US$722 billion. However, the volume of actual settlements is minimised through 'netting'. Of that US$722 billion, for example, only US$22 billion had to be settled, after offsetting debits and credits. Nevertheless, capacity constraints are pending.

The processing efficiency focus has since broadened to cross-border clearing and settlement. With the demand for international investment tripling every three years, and the emergence of electronic multinational market structures, improving cross-border trade processing has become one of the industry's top priorities (since back-office functions are key to the success of any front-office trading system). In the US, for example, interest in foreign investment has surged (over US$4 trillion is currently invested in foreign securities, which is three times the amount invested in 1990), but investors are still predominantly dependent on woefully inadequate traditional cross-border clearing and settlement channels.

In a cross-border environment, the performance of all the trade processing functions – confirmation, clearing, novation (where applicable), settlement and custody – spans nations and may be facilitated by one or more intermediaries. The status quo is far from optimal. Currently cross-border trades can be settled by multiple routes, such as participation of a global custodian and/or network of local sub-custodians, direct membership in a foreign CSD or in an ICSD. These traditional channels are described briefly below.

❑ *CSD to CSD (Central Securities Depositories)*

It is relatively common for domestic CSDs to establish bilateral links to facilitate settlement between two markets. In such cases, trading counterparties, provided that they hold membership, can settle without the involvement of external intermediaries.

❑ *Local agent*

Non-resident counterparties will often employ a local agent or custodian bank with membership in the local CSD to settle on their behalf.

❑ *Global custodian*

Alternatively, non-resident counterparties trading in multiple locales will employ a global custodian bank with membership in multiple CSDs worldwide. Global custodian networks consist of local branches and sub-custodians.

❑ *International Central Securities Depositories (ICSDs)*

The ICSDs (Euroclear and Clearstream), originally developed for the settlement of Eurobonds, have developed linkages with CSDs all over Europe. They have effectively built an infrastructure for cross-border settlement in Europe and act as a single point of entry for their participants in all eligible securities. Trades submitted by a member or a domestic clearing house acting on behalf of a member will settle via:

- Book-entry transfer if both counterparties are ICSD members
- Linkage to the CSD in which the counterparty is a member
- Across the ICSD bridge if the counterparty is a member of the other ICSD.

Alternatively, a trading entity may hold direct *membership in a foreign CSD.*

Source: Rosberg, 2001

Impediments to cross-border trading, borne of the deficiencies in the current complex trade processing system, include the following:

- Clearing and settling a cross-border trade costs upwards of ten times the cost of domestic clearing and settlement.
- Foreign exchange and legal risks, arising from discordant legal practices, are significant.
- Counterparty risk increases appreciably, due to the presence of intermediaries and discrepancies in regulatory frameworks.
- The lack of global conventions in settlement cycles and messaging protocols cause complications and the risk of failure:
  - Cross-border settlement is based on settlement date (as opposed to trade date) and since settlement cycles vary across orders, there is no predictable schedule for the process.
  - Messaging protocols have yet to be rationalised. Although widely used protocols such as SWIFT (Society for Worldwide Interbank Financial Telecommunication), FIX (Financial Information eXchange), and ISTIC (Industry Standardisation for Institutional Trade Communication) have begun to gain dominance, there is no single convention for global connectivity.

As a result of these shortcomings, it is estimated that 15–16% of all cross-border trades fail.

Thus, there is a growing demand for innovation on the cross-border front, which is particularly acute in Europe. The existence of more than 30 clearing and settlement organisations on the continent with poor or non-existent links between them, and incompatible settlement dates (which range from one or two days after trades (known as T+1 or T+2) to T+ four weeks), makes the clearing and settlement of intra-European trades – at an estimated €28 (US$24.90) – prohibitively expensive. Worse still, efforts to improve the system have so far failed to produce results.

Reformation is being retarded by a number of factors. The first is simply that the legacy systems were designed for national, not international, use. The second is that clearing and settlement, like much of the equity business, are havens of vested interests and anti-competitive practices. And the third is that, because clearing and settlement is frankly so mind-numbingly boring, the business has been largely neglected, not only by investors but also by traders, bankers and regulators. They have tended to focus instead on the wrong end of the business: the stock exchanges' trading platforms, which are, in fact, quite efficient in Europe.

By way of example, the LSE, shortly after the Big Bang, embarked on a process to speed up settlement (then done on a rolling fortnightly basis). It launched operation Taurus to dematerialise share certificates and implement wholly electronic settlement. But the project's cost ran out of control, and there was resistance to change from bank registrars, whose livelihoods were under threat. In true City tradition, the outcome was a highly public divorce of the chief executive from the exchange, followed by the settlement function altogether, which was ceded to a new organisation called Crest. Ironically, in Continental Europe, the bourses retained ownership of their domestic clearing and settlement organisations, while the banks owned the two international bodies that handled cross-border business, Euroclear and Clearstream. This ownership structure is now one of the biggest impediments to change.

Now, however, as cross-border trading in Europe grows exponentially – a function of the growing but still nascent equity culture, the emergence of pan-European trading platforms, and the conversion to the euro – overcoming capacity constraints is becoming critical. Local systems and bilateral links are not likely to withstand the types of volume increases currently being projected. And, ironically, the absence of good infrastructure may also be deterring even stronger growth rates. The European market's first priority is now the development of a cross-border clearing and settlement infrastructure. This development is expected to encompass:

- automation of trade management
- development of a regional central counterparty
- consolidation or harmonisation of linked settlement infrastructures
- synchronisation of cycles
- rationalised regulations.

At the post-trade, pre-settlement stage of the process, in which the matching, trade confirmation and instruction functions are performed, proposed solutions seek to address the lack of automation and convention in information exchange. Currently, disconnected bilateral dialogues, manual handling and multiple messaging protocols impinge on risks and costs. This is exacerbated by different settlement cycles, which cause bottlenecks. The main thrust is thus in facilitating interoperability between protocols and proprietary messaging languages – eliminating time-consuming translation procedures.

With respect to clearing, the ultimate goal is widely agreed upon: a single central counterparty serving all of Europe (and, some would advocate, the entire world). With respect to settlement, two alternative pan-European settlement structures have been proposed, based on two market models: the 'hub' model which translates as a central settlement agency, and the 'network' model which translates as multilaterally linked settlement agencies.

Current consolidation efforts reflect these end goals to some extent, but only provide the benefits associated with back-office alignment in very limited contexts. For instance, following the 1997 formation of the European CSD Association to foster CSD-to-CSD linkages based on a common model, a multitude of linkages between CSDs has been established, which facilitate direct channel settlement and minimise intermediaries. The most notable settlement efforts have been expended on establishing two ICSDs:

- Euroclear (formerly a leading eurobond marker clearer) acquired the French settlement system, Sicovam (after being rejected by Cedel), to forge one of only two ICSDs. The merger of the Paris, Amsterdam and Brussels exchanges in late 2000 into Euronext was followed up by consolidation of the exchanges' clearing operations in the French system Clearnet, which acts as the CCP, and which then feeds into Euroclear. Euroclear is now the primary CSD for all three markets as well as an ICSD. Its strategy is based on the 'hub and spoke model' (cross-border hub/domestic CSD spokes) for European settlement and it is attempting to merge with other domestic CSDs.
- In 1999, the Deutsche Börse's clearing operation ClearStream merged with Cedel (also traditionally a major eurobond market clearer), which is owned by a consortium of more than 90 banks and securities houses, to form the other ICSD. Clearstream is now poised for a take-over battle, having received offers to become a wholly owned subsidiary of the Deutsche Börse, or, the industry's preferred outcome, to merge with Euroclear. Settlement is currently done on a trade by trade basis, with plans in place for the implementation of netting and delivery-versus-payment (DVP) settlement. Its strategy is based on a network approach, with individual CSDs operating on a common system and standards.

Both Euroclear and Clearstream are, through merger and alliances, expanding their range of instruments and markets and beginning to live up to their potential for effective international settlement service.

The Settlement Network – a 2000 innovation of the UK's CSD Crest (and the largest in Europe) and Swiss CSD SIS – represents a new model to compete with ICSDs for the elusive goal of pan-European settlement. The two CSDs have agreed to act as conduits to each other's markets and use Intersettle, the network of global custodians created by Swiss banks.

There has been less co-operation in clearance, however. One of the first priorities is to develop netting functions – as it is estimated that full-scale netting of cross-border European trades would reduce settlement instructions by one-half to one-third – and establish domestic CCPs. There are currently only two such examples:

- Clearnet, owned by the Paris Bourse, acts as CCP and clearer for the three Euronext members.
- The London Clearing House (LCH) acts as the CCP and clearer for the LSE, LIFFE and the TradePoint/Virt-X exchange.

With the acquisition of LIFFE by Euronext, the LCH and Clearnet may mimic their respective exchanges and merge. Already they have conducted inconclusive merger talks, and have formed a joint venture in the interim. The Deutsche Börse has plans to use Clearstream, in which it has a 50% interest, as its CCP. Finally, in this vein of CSD-CCP integration, the London Clearing House is expected to merge with Crest, and the Norex alliance between Scandinavian exchanges was recently set up to found a CCP and centralise clearing and settlement.

Virt-X (the recent joint venture between the Swiss Stock Exchange and the TradePoint Consortium) will eventually use the LCH as a CCP and Euroclear, Crest and SIS for settlement. NASDAQ Europe intends to establish its own clearing and settlement operation. These consolidation developments are presented diagrammatically in Figure 10.2.

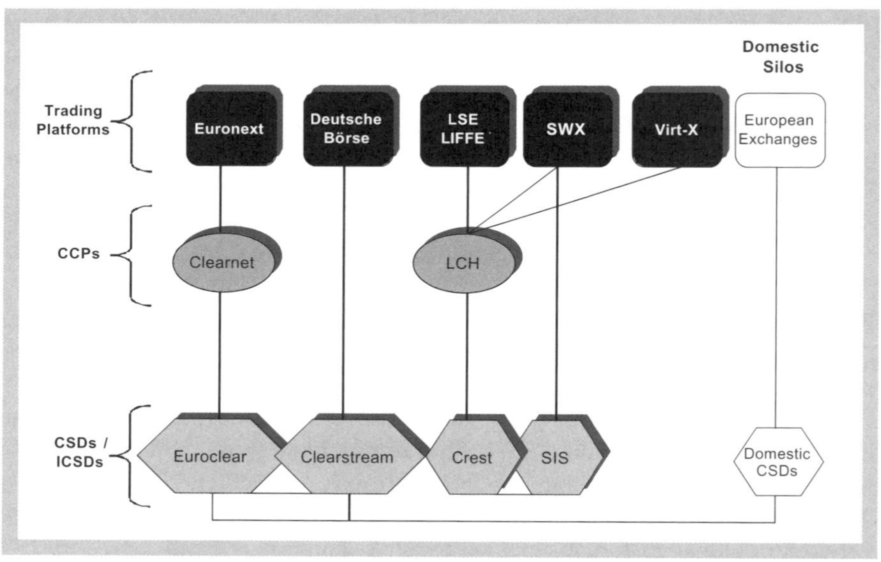

Figure 10.2 Sample of European clearing and settlement consolidation developments

Source: Rosberg, M., 2001: Achieving cross-border trade processing goals, Securities Industry Association, research reports, Vol II, No 3, p. 9, New York

Current consolidation activity is still deficient however. It represents small to mid-scale clustering and does not resolve the long-term problems inherent in a decentralised structure. Even interconnected vertical domestic silos will necessitate multiple intermediaries and concomitantly high costs and risks. Neither the most urgent need for a pan-European CCP, nor the lesser one for a single CSD, is being met. None of these three clearing and settlement groupings relates all that easily to any of the others. It would be preferable to have a single public entity in Europe to act as a CCP and manage trade clearing, even if there were more than one settlement organisation. This is known as the 'hourglass' model, in contrast to the Continent's silos. It would have competing trading platforms at the top, a single CCP in the middle to maximise the scope for netting, and possibly two or three settlement bodies at the bottom.

The European Securities Forum, a body set up by the big banks to campaign for a European CCP that would maximise the scope for netting, looks to the DTCC as a model of what Europe needs. It cannot be replicated exactly, if only because Europe has neither a single regulator nor a unified regulatory system. However, in theory at least, it should be possible to synthesise Clearnet, the LCH, Clearstream, Crest and Euroclear, either through a formal merger or by rendering them 'interoperable'.

The difficulty lies in subduing those vested interests. Now that Europe's stock exchanges are becoming publicly traded companies, they treasure the revenue streams generated by their clearing and settlement arms. The relatively higher cost of clearing and settlement in Europe translates into higher income for those operating the system. The upshot is that Europe's exchanges are now more reluctant than ever to shed their clearing and settlement arms. An exchange owning its settlement arm is akin to a vertically integrated value chain structure, whereas a CCP equates to a utility model.

In other regions, centralisation of clearance and settlement is also coming to pass. In Asia, Japan has sensibly adopted a model similar to the US one, with a single clearing and settlement organisation, albeit one that is owned by the Tokyo Stock Exchange, and more recently the concept of an Asian regional CCP and settlement hub has been gaining credence. In the Americas, the major development is the incorporation of the Emerging Markets Clearing Corporation and Government Securities Clearing Corporation into the DTCC.

Finally, if there is a case for one CCP in Europe, or at the very least for a system of interoperability, there is one on a global scale too. In support thereof, the DTCC recently hosted the first ever international conference for CCPs. A DTCC White Paper presented at the conference emphasises the benefits of netting and novation services and advocates the creation of a global CCP solution to be promulgated alongside national and regional initiatives. Right on cue, the Group of 30, a high-level industry think tank, has set up a committee to look into clearing and settlement on a global level. The initial inclination is to shun a monopolistic global CCP model in favour of a system based on the three natural time zones, in order to spread the volumes, and thereby provide, if not competition, then at least some scope for benchmarking. The committee may also delve into such matters as accelerating trade settlement to T+1 everywhere – in tandem with the Global Straight Through Processing Association and the Omega joint venture between the DTCC and Thomson Financial – and even ultimately to DVP, the model towards which the forex market is moving. (The Continuous Linked Settlement (CLS) Bank, for example, was recently established to mitigate credit and, specifically, settlement risk in the forex market and intends to launch in 2002.)

Finally, it is also worth noting that this whole consolidation trend may also be a partial response to the threat posed by new entrants. Efficient clearing and settlement confers on a prospective e-market a powerful competitive advantage. European exchanges' state-of-the-art trading systems (including Deutsche Börse's Xetra; LSE's SETS; OM Gruppen; and LIFFE's Connect) have made it difficult for young ECNs to penetrate the market. However, their advantage may reside in lower clearing and settlement costs – these costs vary on average between €10 and €80, while Virt-X, for example, claims that it will charge only €2 per trade. It purportedly effects these cost savings through its multi-CSD settlement system which increases price competition between Euroclear, Crest and SIS, the three biggest settlement agencies in Europe.

In general, these operations – whether married to or divorced from a given e-market – are also positioning themselves for the demand for centralised credit and settlement risk mitigation. This may take the form of acting as the central counterparty, managing a centralised database of bilateral counterparty credit limits and limit utilisation, or otherwise guaranteeing the trade, and accommodating varying degrees of anonymity. In the future, the full provision of counterparty credit risk hedging, clearing and settlement services to centralised e-markets may be one of the most lucrative and powerful businesses in which to be.

CHAPTER 11

THE EMERGENCE OF NEW FORMS OF COMMODITIES AND RISK

Up until now, most of our discussion has revolved around the threats that technology represents to the survival of traditional markets and market players. It almost seems as if the super-efficient machine's irreverent encroachment on man's previously hallowed ground has thrust these players into a desperate fight for survival. Yet, at the same time, technology *is* creating new forms of life. In fact, this new electronic environment is as fertile as it hostile. However, to truly begin to perceive the possibilities, we need to take a step back again to view the markets for money from an historical perspective.

THE HISTORY AND FUTURE OF MONEY

What is money? And more importantly, what is capital? The answer to these questions opens a window that affords a glimpse into the future of money and capital, and the markets in which they are traded. In economic terms, money acts as a medium of exchange, a unit of account and a store of value. So, it's defined by function, not form. Yet, since its inception almost three thousand years ago, money has appeared in a myriad of forms, and it is this myriad that tells the story of money.

The story of money, as told by Weatherford (1997) and Vartanian and Ledig (1999), starts with the essential nature of money. In essence, money is a kind of *information*. In fact, all its functions involve the resolution of informational problems. Prior to the development of money as a social institution – that is, in a state of society known as barter – the prerequisite for a trade of goods to occur was the establishment of a 'mutual coincidence of wants' between the trading parties. Furthermore, since all goods were exchanged directly for one another, each good was priced in terms of every other, and expressed as ratios of exchange, such as eight bananas per chicken, or one ounce of salt per chicken. As a consequence, for any one good, there was not just one price, but as many prices as there were other goods for which it might be traded, and hence an almost infinite number of prices.

Eventually, however, certain commodity goods came to be used in *mediating* trades to help solve this informational problem. That is, certain goods began to be commonly traded for all other goods. These goods effectively acquired a purpose that transcended their original one. They were employed not as originally intended, but as a medium of exchange to facilitate a final trade. Thus, in its most primitive forms, money materialised as cattle, grain and other commodities that possessed a high utility value. Later, it materialised as salt, cowrie shells, decorative beads and other goods with a high perceived value, and/or those which possessed better properties for the very purpose of exchange, such as durability, transportability and so on. Eventually, it evolved into 'precious' metals, including gold, silver, copper, bronze, nickel, aluminium and iron. It is this exchange status possessed by a good that we refer to as 'money'.

These goods, which could be exchanged for any other good, massively simplified the price system. Since the price of all or most goods was expressed in terms of units of one other good, uniformity was established. In this capacity money had become a universal measure of value, which yielded enormous socio-economic benefits through the drastic simplification of commercial relations and the stabilisation of relative values.

Finally, money's origin in barter also exposes its social role as a general clearing and storage house for value. In contrast to barter, money expands market possibilities across time and space, by allowing trading parties to separate the point at which they add value to the stream of commerce from the point at which they withdraw it. That is, it frees trading counterparties from having to directly exchange that which they have produced for that which they need or want to consume, and instead allows them to sell, store the money and buy any good independently. Thus, money breaks the simultaneity of contribution and consumption imposed by barter and, in doing so, takes on the function of a store of value, and as a store of value, 'accounts' for value added and value subtracted from the stream of commerce.

After assuming a metallic guise, money began to dematerialise. However, in the first instance, dematerialisation is a psychologically induced process, rather than a material one. Once a particular money form evolves – as a medium of exchange, store and measure of value – its status becomes self-reinforcing. That is, it becomes generally accepted precisely because it is generally accepted or the acceptability of the money provides sufficient grounds for accepting it. Perhaps paradoxically, confidence in the mediating good's acceptance as payment for other goods is initially established on the basis of the good's utility, however, once that confidence is established, utility or commodity backing is rendered obsolete. Money's value as money does not derive from its intrinsic usefulness or value per se, but rather from the confidence among those accepting it that others will accept it. People do not care why the commodity will prove to be generally accepted, just that it will be. Once the general acceptability of a currency is established, it becomes 'backed', not by some commodity, but directly by the products and services that can be purchased with it. Contemplation of money's origin reveals its most essential component – confidence. From the first instant that this psychological shift occurred – when a hypothetical sack of salt was accepted as payment for goods or debt by a payee who had no need or heed for curing meat, but because he was confident that others would accept it – notionally, money had already de-materialised.

Money's ability to store value, however, forms the next chapter in the dematerialisation tale, and the discovery of money creation or money supply. For simplicity's sake, it is related anecdotally. Assume that a commodity has been established as an accepted means of payment, and that this commodity is gold. Because it acts as a store of value, individuals accumulate gold over time. They eventually need a safe place to store the gold, and identify the goldsmith as an appropriate storage place. The goldsmith accepts the gold from a depositor and issues the depositor a note. Eventually the paper notes issued by the goldsmith begin to circulate as money themselves. This is a critical turning point in the evolution of money, for it is at this point that money is transformed into true information, namely a claim, and is based on confidence in the issuer.

The goldsmith eventually discovers that only a small proportion of the gold is ever redeemed, since most people consummate exchange using the issued notes. This enables the goldsmith to earn additional interest income either by loaning some of the gold or by printing and loaning additional notes. This means that the gold reserves are not equivalent to the notes in issue, but simply sufficient to meet the expected but fluctuating demand for redemption. In the aggregate, the claims on the gold exceed the actual gold reserves by some multiple, for example gold reserves of 20% mean that five times that amount can be issued as notes. This represents another critical step in the dematerialisation of money. The money supply has expanded, in the form of paper currency, beyond the physical supply of the money commodity. Thus, in a sense, many of the notes represent a claim to something that does not exist. But, of course, it is not the gold per se that supports the value of the notes, but the general confidence in the money form as a viable medium of exchange.

This renders it 'backed' by the goods and services that one can buy with it. Eventually, it was in this vein that money was consigned to fiat money; paper notes issued by the government or central bank's mint – legal tender by statute representing a claim to nothing at all.

Ultimately, the history of money is the history of man, as money symbolises mankind's most basic desires and fears. Monetary forms have evolved constantly in tandem with changes in the economy, society, civilisation itself and with emerging technological advances. As each transformation occurred, the agents of change found themselves in a powerful position in being able to create money. The first major banking institution arose during the Crusades in the Dark Ages from within the Order of the Knights Templar. The Knights eventually came to act as the treasurer for the papacy in Rome and as financiers to the great monarchs of Europe. After the financial power of the Church in Europe waned, it was conferred on the great northern Italian merchant banking families. The city-states of Pisa, Florence, Venice, Genoa and Verona financed trading missions from China to the Sudan and from India to Scandinavia. However, as the Church forbade usury, the banks evaded the practice through the issue of bills of exchange, which began to circulate widely as a new form of money. Throughout medieval times, the merchant banking families prospered and, through the Medici family, gave rise to the Renaissance. Eventually, their power was superseded by that of the European monarchs, who lined their coffers with plunder from the New World. The Spanish conquistadors, returning from the Americas, funded the opulence of the Baroque and Rococo eras. Eventually their extravagance led to their demise and they were replaced by other reigning monarchs. Finally, with the spate of civil wars that ravaged Europe in the 18th century, and the rise of republicanism, the state wrested control of the issuance of money from the sovereigns and has dominated it ever since. Ultimately, the great struggle of history has been for the control over money; for to control the production and distribution of money is to control the wealth, resources and people of the world.

However, at the dawn of the 21st century, with the emergence of the information economy, money, *as a form of information itself*, has come of age. Monetary prices or price signals act as a dynamic neural network that balances the economic forces of supply and demand, and through which decentralised systems of production and consumption efficiently allocate our scarce resources. This homeostatic monetary mechanism – Adam Smith's 'invisible hand' – represents money's most fundamental link to liberty itself. The economic prosperity of free societies was historically possible only because of the decentralisation inherent in the institution of money. Now, with the birth of the Internet, as a decentralised, interactive, informational system, the electronic economy now possesses, in both form and function, the properties that define the very nature of money.

In this digital age, money is becoming nothing more than an assemblage of ones and zeros, bits and bytes, the fundamental units of accounting and computing, that are streamed over fibreoptic highways, transmitted from satellites, and relayed from one microwave station to another. This new money can be seen but not touched. It has no tactile dimension, no corporal existence, no height, no weight. We are witnessing the final phase in money's dematerialisation and the genesis of its new abstract state: money as energy that can transmute from one currency to another at the flick of an electronic switch.

The revolution in information and communications technology, which has heralded the death of time and distance barriers, and the accompanying diffusion of the ideology of liberalism, has given rise to the phenomenon of globalisation. As the markets for capital have globalised, their regulators have remained localised. Money now knows no national borders, or any border controls. By 1998, this nomadic electronic money had exceeded $1.5[1] trillion a day in transactions. The currency market is now the largest market in the world. The value exchanged in one year at a single hub exceeds that of the combined gross national product for the whole world. This is because currency trading no longer serves merely to facilitate trade in commodities; currencies are now exchanged for currencies in the purest market of all. These great capital flows have presaged the demise of state supremacy: governments are no longer able to dictate to the markets; instead the markets, which wield far greater collective power, are now able to sanction governments. Money flows are now as far beyond any one entity's control as the tides. In an era defined by global electronic connectivity, money has indeed become its own sovereign.

Yet, at a supranational macro-economic level, the implications may be profound. Weatherford, in *The History of Money* (1997), contends that:

> In the global economy that is still emerging, the power of money, and the institutions built on it, will supersede that of any nation, combination of nations, or international organisation now in existence.

Thus, after a prelude of almost three millennia, world history has indeed entered the cyber age – the age of money.

THE 4TH DIMENSION

In the context of dematerialised money, we can explore the broader concept of capital. Money itself, in this sense, is only one dimension of capital and, ironically, a materialisation of capital (whether it takes the form of physical notes and coins or a computer byte).

Hernando de Soto, in *The Mystery of Capital* (2000), delves into the source and the origin of capital by going beyond physics into the realm of metaphysics. De Soto noticed that the great economists of the past three centuries all perceived, if dimly, this other dimension of capital. Marx said that you needed to *go beyond physics* to touch 'the hen that lays the golden eggs', while Adam Smith said that you had to create 'a sort of wagon-way through the air' to reach that same hen. Yet, in the past, human beings have succeeded in conceiving of something that is physically imperceptible, and then of finding *indirect* ways to *perceive* it. De Soto avows that our ability to grasp and use those things we know exist but cannot see or touch is one of the greatest feats of the human mind. He cites several examples that exhibit this ability: we are continually surrounded by radio waves that are transmitted from all over the world, but can only physically sense them when we use a radio or television decoder to convert them to audio-visual energy. Similarly, latent or potential energy is inherent in water but only a man-made process can convert it to hydroelectric power. And throughout history, human beings have invented symbolic or representational systems – mathematical and musical notation, writing, double-entry bookkeeping and so on – to grasp with the mind what human hands could never touch.

In the same way, we are surrounded by assets that posses latent capital, which can be yielded by *representing* the assets with legal titles. Legal title does not merely protect the rights of the owners of assets with utility value, such as a building that provides shelter, but allows the asset to live a 'parallel' life. The symbolism or representation of property, such as a title deed, enables the asset to generate capital, such as leverage (by, for example, being ceded as collateral to secure the interests of banks or other third parties).

Thus, money and, more importantly, property title are to capital what a clock is to time. They are our mechanisms for perceiving and accessing something immensely powerful, literally, a form of energy. De Soto states that we have lost all awareness of the existence of this powerful capital transformation process, that its origins are obscure and its significance is buried deep within the economic subconscious of western capitalist nations. However, through De Soto and others, we are once again becoming aware of this fourth dimension of capital.

THE MULTIPLES AND DERIVATIVES EFFECT

So what is the relevance of this conceptual and abstract notion? In the context of the synthesis of money as ones and zeros and bits and bytes, and cognisant of the latent capital potential in assets that is realised or released by things such as stock shares, we can introduce the mathematical notion of multiples and derivatives. Kenichi Ohmae introduces 'The Dimension of High Multiples' in *The Invisible Continent* (2000). Ohmae perceived how multiples – essentially mathematical constructs – can be used to amass power.

He states that the most significant aspect of this new dimension is the application of unprecedented leverage. Multiples – whether they take the form of hedge funds' leverage ratios, or the P:E ratios of equities – can be exploited to artificially gain power. Speculators can attack virtually defenceless central banks (who lack this modern artillery) and devalue currencies. And because of their colossal market capitalisations, a profitless dot.com can make acquisitions with an equity swap. AOL used this to take over telecommunications and media giants such as Time Warner. Qwest, with almost no history, acquired a regional Bell telephone operating company, US West. The power of multiples is not fictitious.

In the go-go years of the 1980s, the American stock market averaged P:E ratios of 25, the European markets averaged ratios of 8. At the high point of the Japanese bubble, the Japanese equity market averaged multiples of 75. At the peak of Internet mania, some of the NASDAQ heroes had multiples approaching 1000 (or, since earnings were negative, multiples of infinity). The danger inherent in this is axiomatic, yet understandable in Ohmae's new continent. Viewed from the physical dimension, companies are worth an amount based on net present value. But for a company claiming a presence in the invisible continent, the expectations of the territory that the company might stake could lead to a market value anywhere from zero to close to infinity. Ohmae's allegory is simple: What was the value of a land claim in California in 1848? (Ohmae, 2000).

Allied to this is the derivatives effect. In this digital age, it is possible to commoditise and disaggregate anything. If something – or a representation of something and, therefore, anything – can be digitised, that is, reduced to ones and zeros, bit and bytes, it can be rendered tradable over this electronic medium or in this electronic market. Furthermore, such a tradable financial instrument is almost infinitely divisible.

Hence, in recent times we have witnessed the emergence of new forms of commodities markets – incorporating both a spot market and market risk derivatives market, such as futures. One of the most interesting examples is the emerging market for bandwidth. The concept has some interesting dualities, that is, space for bits and bytes on the network is being traded on the network and in the process is optimising the space or capacity utilisation of the grid or network. Other interesting examples include the new electronic markets for power or energy, including electricity. Moreover, we have also witnessed the emergence of new forms of risk, including credit risk and weather risk. Risk and risk aversion have always existed, and for some time there has been some mechanism for the risk averse to transfer or hedge that risk, such as insurance. Now, however, in the era of digital commodities and globally connected electronic markets, it is possible to desegregate and commoditise any form of risk and sell it to risk buyers in a virtual market.

Credit risk can be defined as the exposure to loss relating to a change in the creditworthiness of a counterparty which may impact the counterparty's ability to fulfil its obligations under a contractual agreement. Changes in creditworthiness can be due to changes in credit rating or due to a default. It can be divided into pre-settlement and settlement risk (which exists during the period from trade execution to settlement, when there is a risk that the counterparty may not make good its obligations under the transaction). A credit derivative is an insurance-like tool that involves a credit protection 'buyer' paying an annual premium in return for the protection 'seller' undertaking to pay out if there is a default by the underlying entity. It is essentially a financial transaction whose payoff depends on whether or not a credit event (such as a bankruptcy, default, upgrade or downgrade) occurs. (Another variation is a credit basket, whereby, for example, if one of five companies defaults, it is considered a credit event.) Banks generally sell this protection, repackage it and on-sell it to institutional investors, who then become the end-sellers. Bond buyers are the main target market for these instruments since buying a credit derivative is technically the same as 'going long' credit risk, but with higher yield. These instruments are particularly well suited to hedge emerging market exposure incurred in foreign direct investment (FDI). After stripping out credit risk, residual market risk (price sensitivity to changes in market conditions) and market liquidity risk (the risk that a position cannot be easily unwound or offset at the price quoted in the market due to lack of market depth or market disruption) remains. It is anticipated that current credit derivatives will, in turn, form the forerunners to further disaggregated credit risk – that is, credit risk that has been broken down into its fundamental components or causes (such as industrial action, land invasion and so on). Such credit events – which *fundamentally* jeopardise a borrower's ability to repay its debt to a lender – may, in the future, be stripped out and hedged (by being sold to risk buyers, that is, speculators).

Already, one can now 'go short' or 'long' interest rate, exchange rate, volatility risk, liquidity risk and other market risk, credit risk, weather risk, disaster risk, and any as yet inconceivable derivatives through a plethora of innovative new instruments. Furthermore, since these products and markets are still in their infancy, they are typified by illiquidity and scarce information (simply because the relevant risk pricing *knowledge* doesn't yet exist), and consequently arbitrage opportunities abound. While the territory is still virgin, and fundamentals and technicals have yet to be charted, technology can help traders, by, for example, exploiting linkages with underlying or allied markets that are not yet explicit, modelling probabilities and so on.

The evolutionary path from infancy to maturity of the emerging commodity markets is shown diagrammatically in Figure 11.1.

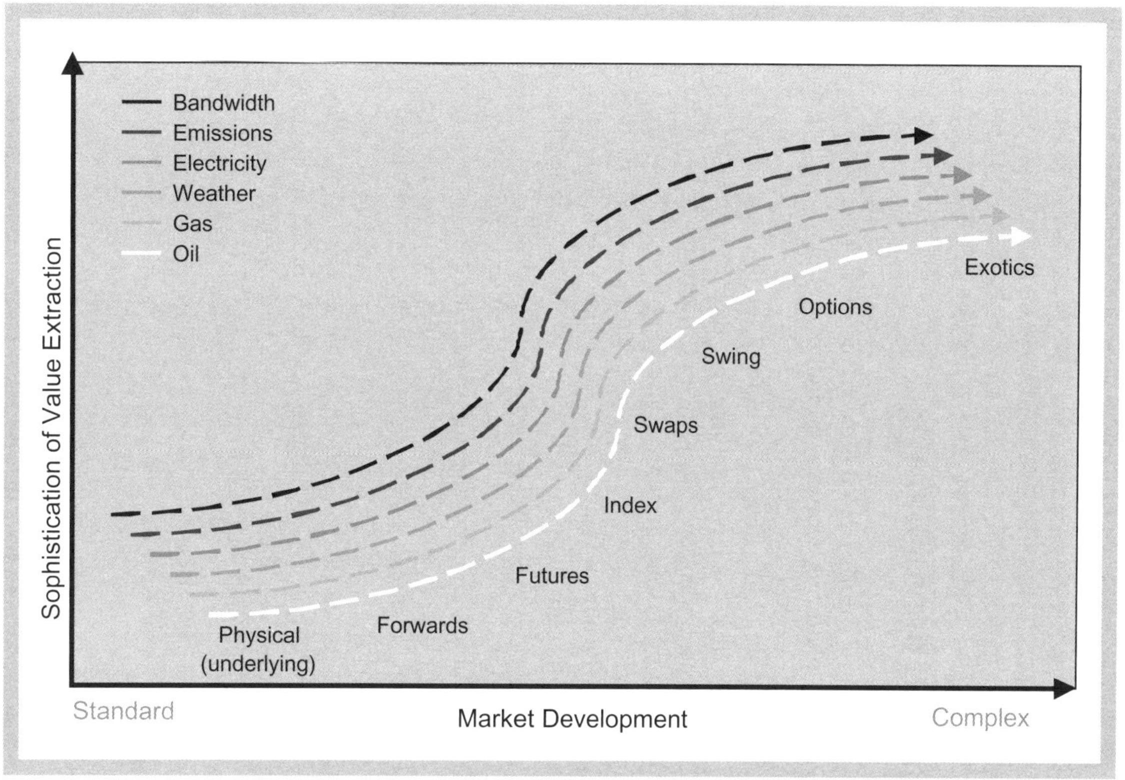

Figure 11.1 Product development cycle in commodities markets

Source: Arthur Andersen/Risk Publications, 2000

Moreover, the evolution of commodity markets in oil, gas and electricity has followed a continually shortening time period from inception to full liquidity. Within the global oil markets, traded markets evolved over a 15-year period, UK gas over a 10-year period, UK electricity over less than 7 years, and in Scandinavia, the development of a liquid power market took less than 3 years to develop.

EXAMPLES

Credit and Other OTC Derivatives

Obviously, the most futuristic of the electronic derivatives markets are the credit derivatives platforms. However, in the interest of a complete directory, the new platforms exclusively trading other OTC derivatives are presented below, although it should be noted that most of the relevant sites cited in the preceding tour of e-markets have ventured into their respective derivatives.

Although increasing demand, liquidity and transparency in credit derivatives are likely to push trading online, the reality is that the current market sites are not actively trading in any real sense. Only 2% of all credit derivative trading volume, which itself is quite low, was transacted electronically. Nevertheless, growth rates are high. According to Greenwich Associates (Wright, 2001), the average volume of trading in credit derivatives by European institutional investors tripled in 2000, while the total number of product users in the market almost doubled, and liquidity improved. This is a classic virtuous cycle case – as more users use them, the more useful they become, and credit derivatives are following a similar but accelerated growth pattern to interest rate derivatives in the early 1990s. Creditex is the most prominent of the e-markets. It is owned by a powerful consortium of banks and is modelled on an exchange basis. In 2001, in its first full year, Creditex traded approximately 200 names on the platform. As the market becomes more standardised and liquid, Creditex is well positioned for the future (see Table 11.1).

Commodities

In the nascent commodities markets, there are as yet few true examples of electronic markets. Most of the trading takes place on either established commodities exchanges, notwithstanding that they may be electronic exchanges, which have expanded into the newer products, or on an OTC basis, again albeit via single-dealer electronic channels.

Table 11.1 Sample of OTC derivative electronic trading networks

System	Instruments	Type	Ownership	Ownership Composition
Crossing				
Creditex	Credit derivatives	Cross-matching; Anon	Consortium	Deutsche Bank; JP Morgan Chase; CSFB; BoA; MSDW; Soc Gen; UBS Warburg; Dresdner KW
CreditTrade	Credit derivatives	Cross-matching	Independent	CreditTrade Limited, minority shareholders include JPMC, Internet Capital Group, Prebon Yamane
Inter-dealer				
Volbroker	FX derivatives (options)	Inter-dealer	Consortium	Citibank; Deutsche; Goldman Sachs; JP Morgan Chase; UBS Warburg. All designated market-makers/ liquidity providers
Blackbird	FX + interest rate derivatives	Inter-dealer	Independent	Derivatives Net (DNI); Minorities: Reuters and Garban
EBS	FX derivatives	Inter-dealer	Independent IDB	EBS
ICOR – not yet live	FX, interest rate and equity derivatives	Inter-dealer	JV	Reuters; Icor Brokerage
Swapswire – not yet live	Interest rate derivatives (primarily swaps)	Inter-dealer/ multi-dealer	Consortium	Citigroup; Deutsche Bank; Goldman Sachs; JP Morgan Chase; UBS Warburg; MSDW; CSFB; BNP Paribas; Merrill Lynch

Bandwidth Trading

In an age of accelerated industry lifecycles, telecommunications has rapidly proceeded to the mature commodity phase, defined by plummeting tariff structures and consequently high volume–low margin economics. In classic business school models, operational efficiency is a critical success factor in such environments. Since 1998, annual price erosion of 60% has become the norm. According to Forrester Research (Arthur Andersen/*Risk*, 2000), while network demand is expected to double annually from 1998 to 2004, network capacity is expected to grow 100 times during the same period.

Demand is rising as a result of deregulation, industry convergence (such as cable and satellite television, cellular telephony and so on) and, most significantly, the growth of the Internet. By 2004, 99% of transoceanic demand is expected to be generated by Internet and corporate data users. Switched voice traffic will represent only 1% of total demand. However, while capacity demand is expected to increase, the reality is that no precedent exists to accurately predict the scale thereof.

Supply – the availability of bandwidth – continues to increase due to advances in technologies. The most important advances include the general move towards digital technology, fibreoptic deployment, new satellite technologies, and the replacement of physical hardwired switches with software. A key advantage of digital systems is their greater immunity to electrical noise, which causes analogue or wave signals to deteriorate en route. Optical fibres enable light signals carrying information to travel at, well, the speed of light. Furthermore, for both copper and fibre, new technologies enable higher bandwidths to be squeezed into the same cables or fibres. A technology called Digital Subscriber Line (DSL), for example, uses techniques from computer networking (compression algorithms) to get more bandwidth out of copper phone lines. In the optical fibre sphere, a recent technology called dense wavelength division multiplexing (WDM) is having a dramatic effect on the medium's already enormous bandwidth. By using the colours within light waves, WDM increases the capacity of existing links more than a hundredfold, enabling over 1.5 million phone calls to be transmitted simultaneously over a single fibre. The network expansion is uneven, however, producing bottlenecks. One of the current bottlenecks is the interface between fibre and copper systems. Data that has been travelling on the fibre superhighway (that can carry a two-hour digital movie in half a second) has to gear down dramatically as it hits the intersection with copper. The problem is that, even with high bandwidth copper technology, the current generation of switches just cannot convert the data quickly enough to maintain high bandwidth rates. Recently, however, a device has been developed that can switch signals at 100 gigabytes a second and at a fraction of a volt. The bandwidth of the optoelectronic device is large enough for a single tiny chip to handle all the digital traffic of a large corporation. Also, the use of software instead of hardwired switches means they can be upgraded simply by installing a new program, rather than replacing the hardware in every exchange. This consequent exponential growth in global telecommunications infrastructure is evidenced by the growth in installed capacity of long-distance telephone lines. In 1996, the four dominant providers in the US (AT&T, WorldCom, MCI and Sprint) had a total bandwidth of 1 terabit and could handle 15 million simultaneous calls. By

1999, this had grown to 22 terabits, and by the end of 2001 to over 100 terabits, with many more telecoms suppliers and significantly lower costs.

As was the case with other utility industries, the deregulation of the telecommunications sector has led to a fragmentation of the industry value chain with premiums retained only in the areas of content and access. Bandwidth is the key commodity in this industry, and is rapidly assuming the characteristics of commodity in terms of fungibility, liquidity, ease of pricing, access and availability of information. Accompanying this commoditisation of capacity is the need for risk management on the supply-side. Hedging the fundamental uncertainties surrounding market supply and demand, the risk associated with current and future investment in building capacity, and regional pricing disparities, is becoming critical. In an environment of falling prices, carriers, in particular, face high exposures.

The use-or-lose nature of capacity precipitates prices that are both cyclical and volatile. Thus, for both suppliers and buyers – from incumbent carriers, new hybrid consortia, to fragmented ISPs or ASPs – bandwidth market centres increasingly represent a key channel. They are crucial to smoothing cyclical demand, optimising network capacity utilisation, operational efficiency, reducing cost of sales and, therefore, increasing profit margin.

Currently, the major electronic markets for bandwidth include RateXchange, Band-X, Arbinet, The Global TeleExchange, CommerEX.com, Bandwidth.com and whatever becomes of the bankrupted Enron Broadband. Approximately US$25 billion of international capacity of 'circuits' is traded annually. In addition, US$600 billion of available domestic and international fixed and wireless minutes are traded. By 2002, it is estimated that the volume value of minutes traded will reach at least US$4.6 billion.

In terms of the typical evolution of commodity markets, the ability to trade the physical commodity at neutral hubs will be essential to the actual delivery of capacity, the development of a benchmark pricing point, and the building of confidence in counterparty and technical reliability, which will pave the wave for the financial derivatives.

Energy Trading

Energy trading, including electricity, gas and oil, is truly at the forefront of new commodities and commodity derivatives trading. According to Forrester Research (*Risk*, 2001), online energy trading will continue its rapid growth from US$400 billion in 2000 to US$3.6 trillion in 2005, although it is a highly volatile market. Despite turbulence, energy companies, in particular, have invested heavily in electronic trading sites – either on a proprietary basis or as part of consortia. While Enron dominated initially, new industry consortia, such as TradeSpark and ICE, are posing threats. Trading styles are also changing – from art to science – with the art of the person-to-person deal now being supplemented by large-scale programme trading.

In time, the majority of trading will probably converge on only a few key sites, differentiated on the basis of value chain position. The three key positions will be (1) *liquidity hubs* (designed to exchange price risk on pure commodities), (2) *merchant platforms* (offering industry market-makers a venue for trading products to maximise margins on their own long-term assets and customer contracts), and (3) *solution sites* (proprietary or branded sites of energy companies designed to structure special deals and provide customised services for their wholesale customers). It should be obvious that this is a modified version of the crossing, inter-dealer, multi-dealer and proprietary trading structure.

MAJOR ENERGY INDUSTRY INITIATIVES

- *Intercontinental Exchange (ICE):* Launched in August 2000, this electronic trading platform was founded by oil giants BP-Amoco, Royal Dutch/Shell, and TotalFina-Elf, together with Deutsche Bank, Goldman Sachs, MSDW and Soc Gen. The consortium has now been joined by six major US power companies. The platform currently trades OTC energy and precious metals products, but this could be expanded if, as intended, it acquires the International Petroleum Exchange (see Screen Shot 11.1). At the end of the first quarter 2001, ICE's total notional volume traded reached US$70 billion since its inception and it now routinely trades more than US$1 billion a day.
- *TradeSpark:* TradeSpark was established in September 2000 by eSpeed (the electronic marketplace engine), Cantor Fitzgerald and five of the largest US energy producers/distributors (Coral Energy, Dominion, Axia Energy, Koch Energy Trading, TXU Energy Trading and Williams Energy Marketing and Trading Company). It began live trading in October 2000 in North American natural gas and electricity products. By the end of the first quarter 2001, its total notional trading volume had reached $30 billion.
- A partnership between the *Chicago Mercantile Exchange (CME)* and *CheMatch* (the B2B chemicals market) intends to provide the derivatives counterpart for bulk buyers and sellers of fuel, as well as chemicals and plastics products.
- *Enymex* is the proposed new electronic platform from the New York Mercantile Exchange (and will be dominated by the institutional trading community).
- Two new electricity exchanges have been launched in Europe – the UK Power Exchange (*UKPE*); a division of Sweden's OM Gruppen and Germany's European Energy Exchange (*EEX*), a joint venture between the Deutsche Börse and Eurex.

Screen Shot 11.1 Electronic energy markets

Sources: www.intcx.com; www.ipe.uk.com; www.tradespark.com

Weather Risk Trading

Since the first weather derivative transaction was concluded in late 1997, the market has grown exponentially. In terms of value, a total of $7.5 billion worth of deals have been concluded, representing over 3000% growth in just four years, and from 82 trades in 1997, volume has risen to 2750 trades in 2000. However, in 2000, the fledgling market was subject to a 14.8% decline in the overall value of contracts. However, despite birthing pain, considering that at least 10% of the US economy is weather sensitive, the nascent market is poised for future growth. In fact, the weather risk market (including catastrophe bonds – CATs) has become one of the most dynamic sectors of the financial risk transfer arena, attracting participation from industries as diverse as banking, insurance, energy, agriculture and travel. LIFFE, the Deutsche Börse (on its Internet portal Xelsius), Eurex and the CME are in the process of calculating weather indexes as well as trading, which should give the market some impetus. In the meantime, most trading takes place offline, although many participants offer a single-dealer transacting channel, including energy participants such as Koch (see Screen Shot 11.2).

Trading Pollution and the Markets for Air

Environmentalism has gained enormous credence worldwide in recent years, and has been accompanied by a slight tactical shift on the part of regulators. There has been a growing realisation among regulators globally that incentive is more effective than the threat of sanction, and that instead of enacting straight penalty-based regulations, market forces can be exploited to better effect to minimise industrial pollution. Various market mechanisms have recently been introduced that serve to incentivise industries through price signals to reduce pollution by investing in innovative technologies. Tradable emissions credits become valuable assets for those that cut pollution at the lowest costs because excess credits can be sold at a premium to those with high abatement costs. Successes to date include the trading of chlorofluorocarbons under the international Montreal Protocol (designed to save the ozone layer) and the use of particles trading in Chile. In the future, the market for greenhouse gases, and carbon dioxide credits in particular, may burgeon under the emissions quota-and-tax system born of the United Nations' Kyotyo Protocol.

EnronOnline

Finally, no discussion about the emerging commodity and risk markets would be complete without paying 'respect' to the late Enron and EnronOnline.

Screen Shot 11.2 Electronic weather risk trading sites

Sources: www.ektweather.com; www.globalweatherexchange.com; www.sgweather.com; www.globalmarkets.socgen.com/weather/pages/cover

It would seem that the remarkable rise and fall of Enron was marked by audacity and rampant ambition. Enron, which was forged by the merger of two ailing gas pipeliners in the late 1980s, grew its revenues from a mere US$7.6 billion in 1986 to US$101 billion in 2000, and became the darling of Wall Street and the NASDAQ. Initially capitalising on the deregulation of the energy sector, Enron started exploring the potential of innovative financial structures and transactions but, with each new trade, it had less and less to do with energy, and more and more to do with making markets. It virtually single-handedly created and spurred the growth of sophisticated spot and derivatives markets in energy and a wealth of other industries. But Enron's reputation for financial alchemy turned from asset into liability after its third quarter results were released in October 2001, disclosing a US$1.2 billion reduction in capital or balance sheet stemming from a hedging deal with a related private equity fund called LJM. That reluctant disclosure from the opacity that always shrouded Enron HQ exposed the LTCM-style[2] financial house of cards that Enron had built of its balance sheet, plunging the company into a financial quagmire that rapidly led to its failure. While analysts have been scrambling for front-row seats at the autopsy performed by a veritable legion of apparently not very watchful watchdogs, the point of this discussion is not the dissection of Enron's imprudently structured balance sheet, but rather about the possibilities that EnronOnline created, which are still possible.

Before its spectacular implosion, Enron operated one of the most astonishingly successful online trading platforms in the world, EnronOnline. The energy business seems an unlikely place to look for a good Internet strategy. Most of the sleeping giants in this venerable industry have failed to come up with any such strategy at all. Yet Enron created what may be the most successful Internet venture of any company in any industry anywhere. EnronOnline, operational since November 1999, was, by the end of 2001, the dominant force in online energy trading. It provided spot and derivatives markets – in which Enron acted as principal intermediary – in commodity products throughout the world. These included gas, electricity power, oil and refined products, petrochemicals, liquid petroleum gases, natural gas liquids, and coal. Its reach also extended to non-energy products, such as emission credits, bandwidth, risk derivatives, such as credit derivatives, weather derivatives, as well as swaps, options, futures and other derivatives for hedging the cash flows in industries as diverse as shipping, plastics, pulp, paper, steel and metals. In fact, by 2001 its product range had expanded to over 1500 offerings. At the end of the first quarter of 2001, the platform had traded a notional volume of US$650 billion since its inception, and the daily volume had soared to about 5000 trades, with a notional value of around US$3 billion. Moreover, online trades made up over two-thirds of the company's trading business.

Internally, many experienced traders initially argued that by making pricing transparent, the Web-based trading platform would undermine the fundamental economics of Enron's wholesale business. The traders were right in a limited sense. EnronOnline indeed squeezed trading margins. However, this was more than offset by the gains. Transaction costs, for example, were slashed, as the entire trading process was automated. Automation also compressed the time between the placement of an order and its execution (from as much as two hours before the online operation's launch to a split-second), which greatly reduced the exposure of the firm to price fluctuations. Most significantly, the electronic platform led to a dramatic expansion in trading volumes. Following the introduction of EnronOnline, the firm saw a surge of 60% over the previous year in the physical volumes that it traded. Since volumes had grown by only 30% a year in recent prior years and since none of its competitors saw a similar spike, the extra growth is plausibly attributed to EnronOnline.

In the end, however, Enron failed because it got greedy. In the pursuit of its stated 'commoditisation of everything' mission, it established markets in an impressive array of industries. Although it asserted that the critical success factors for an 'open commodity exchange' to work were 'a truly fungible commodity and liquidity', instead it devised a 'principal-intermediated' model, which flouts conventional wisdom vis-à-vis exchange neutrality anyway. Specifically, however, in terms of this model, Enron acted as sole counterparty in every trade, which necessitated massive leverage that eventually proved unsustainable. Nevertheless, its failure was not, by all accounts, because of some dot-bomb-style overestimation of market demand for a new product. By contrast, its product innovation, and exploitation of the Net to bring those product markets into existence, was astonishingly successful. And the future potential of these new product markets is unlimited. Despite the shock waves that Enron's collapse triggered throughout the financial markets and the heavy losses sustained by many banks through their exposure to Enron, swarms of them have been picking over the carcass, which suggests that they agree. Ultimately what may emerge from the carnage is a series of more prudent single-dealer, followed by multi-dealer and exchange-based markets for these products in the future. While the original pioneer destroyed itself and forfeited its claim, a new land has nevertheless been discovered and Enron's legacy will live on.

Notes

1 Currently US$1.1 trillion per day (due to EMU).

2 Long Term Capital Management (LTCM) is the now notorious hedge fund, founded by two Nobel laureaes in economics and a former vice chairman of the US Federal Reserve,

that went insolvent in September 1998. At the time of its failure, it had liabilities valued at 50 times its equity. It was rescued by the US Federal Reserve because, as Alan Greenspan confirmed in his testimony to Congress, had this fund gone bankrupt, and liquidated its positions, at the height of the emerging market crisis it would have exacerbated the affected banks' losses and rendered many of them technically insolvent. This, he stated, would certainly have inflicted serious damage on the market and could potentially have impaired the economies of many nations.

Following the Fed's sponsored bail-out of LTCM on the grounds of systemic risk, the Basle Committee on Banking Supervision commissioned a study into so-called High Leveraged Institutions (HLIs). Among the resultant recommendations (in terms of banks' own credit risk management) were:

- Stricter credit limits and higher collateralisation for HLIs.
- Higher disclosure standards and transparency in reports by HLIs to banks, sound internal data generations systems, accurate credit analyses, and more rigorous due diligence practices to account for the specific risks associated with HLIs.
- More rigorous measures of exposure resulting from trading and derivatives transactions.
- Close monitoring of exposures to HLIs, taking into account their trading activities, risk concentration, leverage and risk management processes.

It is ironic that almost exactly the same thing happened with respect to Enron: Enron simply slipped through the net because it *ostensibly* wasn't a financial institution, but an energy company.

PART III

THE RESPONSE
Survival Strategies

CHAPTER 12

STRATEGIC RESPONSE OF THE BROKER-DEALERS

Having broadly reviewed the emerging macro-environment and the sometimes schizophrenic mega-trends sweeping the wholesale financial markets, we can now descend to the micro-level, to review the strategic response of the broker-dealers to this force that is wreaking change of epic proportions.

Of course, to use the term in the singular, as if there were a strategic blueprint for an archetypal bank, is a misnomer. Nevertheless, we can identify three generic strategic thrusts in the industry, derived from our simple causal model. Given that our primary technological drivers of change in the markets were connectivity and computational power – in turn, driving automation and artificial or man-*made* intelligence – the three simple strategic responses can be reduced to (1) automate, (2) connect, and (3) exploit data. This extension of the model is presented in Figure 12.1, and an elaboration on the rather more complicated application of these principles follows.

FIRST PRINCIPLES

These three core strategies – (1) automate, (2) connect, and (3) exploit data – are interdependent and are aligned with the interdependent businesses of securities dealers. Essentially, there are two distinct businesses and hence two distinct types of trading activity.

The Broker-dealer Function

The first is the broker-dealer function, whereby the bank earns the bid-offer

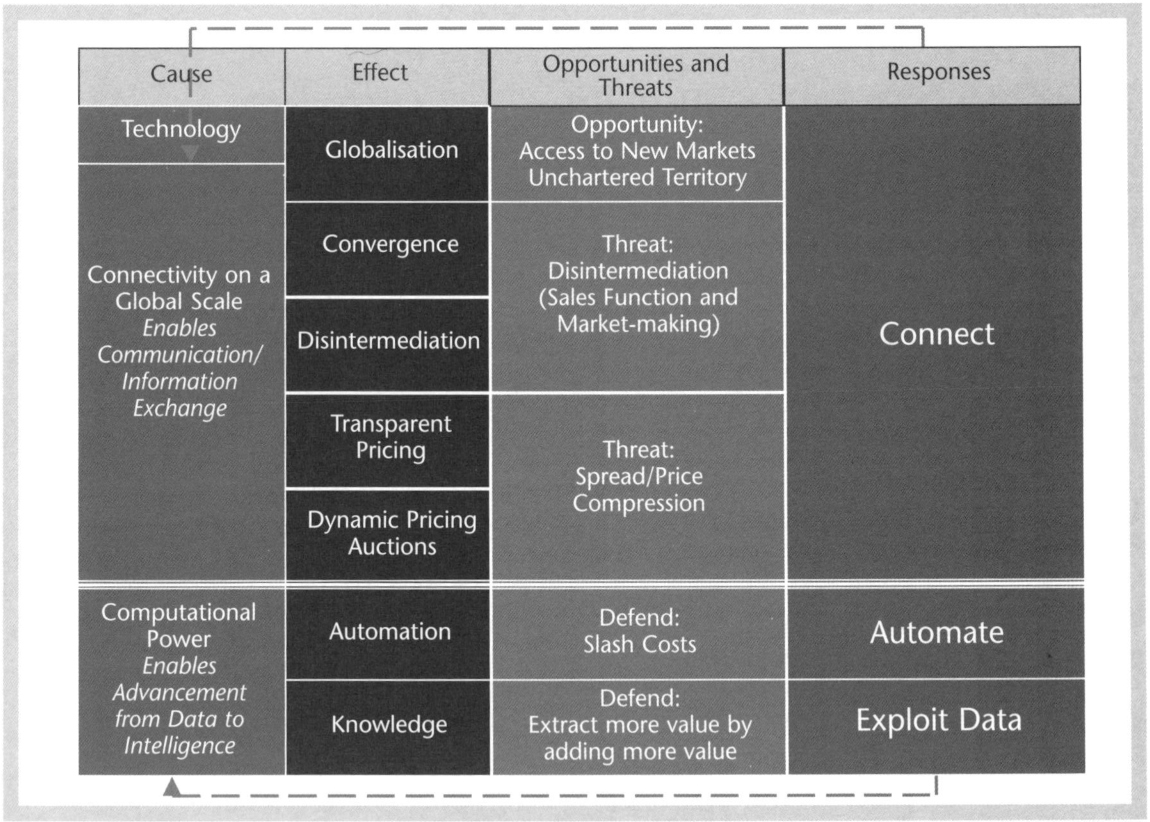

Figure 12.1 The response

spread by executing trades with customers at favourable prices. Customers range from private traders or investors, to institutional investors, brokerages, large corporations' treasuries, smaller corporate treasury outsourcing companies, dealers' proprietary trading desks, and so on. Customers seeking to enter into a transaction normally transact with the securities dealer through its sales function staff, who then intermediates with the relevant market- or price-making trader. Traders indicate prices at which they are willing to bid from sellers, or offer to buyers, with the spread to be crossed being the distance below mid-market when they bid, or the distance above it when they offer.

The pricing decision – how aggressively or conservatively the trader bids or offers for customer business – depends on the trader's assessment of (a) the expected credit costs associated with doing the particular transaction with that customer, and (b) the effectiveness of potential hedging opportunities (assuming the trader doesn't want the exposure). Perceived credit risk always serves to make dealer prices more conservative (although this can be mitigated by measures that improve the customer's creditworthiness, such as collateralisation or netting agreements). However, the impact of the residual market risk on price depends on the degree to which the hedging strategy is likely to be effective (again assuming the dealer does not want to keep the acquired position).

Traders can price most aggressively when the new trade reduces the exposure already in their portfolio, less so when they must hedge with available liquid instruments that expose them to basis risk, and less again when they must lay the risk off with brokers or other dealers. The trader optimises the trade-off between the need to execute transactions and the need to avoid credit and trading losses by steering a middle course between excessively aggressive and excessively conservative prices.

Apart from providing price discovery and execution of transactions (provision of liquidity and immediacy), dealers provide other services to their customers, such as research (economic, fundamental, technical), trading expertise, information about the current state of the market, and clearing and settlement services. Alternatively, banks can also provide pure brokerage or agency-style order-matching services in certain markets.

Proprietary Trading Function

In their other activity, which in some ways conflicts with their role in facilitating customer trades, traders take proprietary positions, either by paying the bid-offer spread to a broker or another dealer to create an unhedged exposure, or by not hedging a position acquired from a customer. He minimises the cost of these trades by implementing them in liquid markets, where bid-offer spreads are small. Positions are based on the trader's perception of whether current market prices adequately reflect the underlying value of a market instrument, and his derived expectations about future market price movements.

Proprietary trading profitability depends on the predictive content of the conditioning information on which trades are based:

- At one extreme is *arbitrage*, where traders are almost certain that any available trades will be profitable, since contracts of equivalent economic value must ultimately have the same market price.
- At the other extreme is *speculation*, where the rationale for the trade (for example the opinions contained in economists macro-economic forecasts, or the patterns detected in historical market prices by technical analysts) generally lacks the influence of self-equilibrating market forces to ensure its own accuracy.

Most proprietary trades fall in between arbitrage and speculation. They generally consist of relative value trades, where a combination of economic theory and empirical evidence (such as information garnered by salespeople from their customers' current trades or enquiries) implies circumstances where price movements may not be entirely random.

In sum, dealers take positions and trade for their own account as their primary business, and usually make markets for their customers by providing bid and ask quotes. In the process of seeking to profit from a bid-ask spread and in exploiting pricing anomalies, they add liquidity to markets and thereby assist their customers in trading and hedging.

Overall, market-making is a volatile and capital-intensive component of the income sources at securities firms. It is also highly profitable. This is expanded on in Chapter 13, but by way of interim corroboration, according to Moody's (2000), principal transaction revenues account for roughly one-third of the pre-tax profits earned by the securities firms that it rates. Anecdotally, it's a particularly lucrative line of business in the more traditional market structures. NYSE specialists, for example, who reportedly command margins of up to 55%, act as principal in up to 30% of their trades, but those trades account for up to 75% of total revenue. Furthermore, proprietary position-taking on the back of market-making has a far higher probability of success. Firms that are more dependent on 'pure' proprietary trading tend to carry lower credit ratings from Moody's.

The Impact of the Internet

The Internet has made all types of information, including financial prices, far more widely accessible, threatening the natural informational monopolies enjoyed by large financial institutions. By increasing transparency and strengthening the bargaining power of the buy-side, new trading technologies threaten the market-making businesses of securities firms and, therefore, the stronger basis for proprietary trading. According to the ultra conservative Moody's (2000) for example, complete disintermediation of traditional broker-dealers is occurring in some plain-vanilla products. Thus, the Internet either has, or potentially will have, a rather adverse effect on this fruitful line of business. Consequently, securities firms are fighting the onslaught of disintermediation and price compression by literally playing the trading networks at their own game.

Essentially, all e-strategies can be reduced to one of three types: applications that aim to increase revenues by adding new channels to access customers; those whose aim is to reduce operating costs by augmenting those channels with efforts to increase efficiency through automation; and those that try to secure a competitive advantage through data analytics.

AUTOMATION

In the first instance, firms can use technology to reduce operating costs by automating pricing, trade execution and transaction processing.

While back-office automation is obviously more of an internal measure (the external linkages in the settlement chain notwithstanding), one cannot really separate internal and external measures in a mature industry. Price erosion dictates simultaneous internally focused strategies to lower cost structures (and thereby raise margins) and externally focused strategies to increase transaction volume.

CONNECTIVITY

As alluded to above, firms can then use the network to increase revenue by adding new channels to expand customer contact. Specifically, dealers can invest in developing proprietary offerings and invest in or simply connect (as liquidity providers) to multi-dealer pricing and trading systems in a variety of product markets. This will serve to leverage their pricing capability to a wider market more cost effectively.

THE CRYSTAL BALL

Thus, banks can equally play the new entrants at their own game by using technology to reduce costs and increase volumes. The basic model diminishes the role played by the salesforce (by enabling the customer to contact the price-making trader directly) and, if the pricing engine is automated, it also diminishes the role of the trader (since live trader intervention will not be necessary) and of course it diminishes the back office. This is, however, fundamentally a tactical modification of the existing business structure and pays scant attention to the needs of proprietary traders.

Securities firms can then advance to the next level by exploiting the power of data analytics in order to add both internal and external value, to use a cliché. What is meant by this in practice will become explicit in the next section. However, suffice it to say that value originates from predictive capacity. Essentially, a significant portion of business and indeed life's activities revolve around trying to forecast the future. Whether it be trying to anticipate client needs or trying to anticipate market price movements, banks, as with any other entity, spend much of their time, energy and money in trying to crystal ball gaze. Computational power can be exploited to produce a better crystal ball.

INTERLINKAGES – KNOWLEDGE IS POWER

Data and data analytics is the adhesive between interdependent businesses (or e-nabled businesses) that produces a 'compound' effect. Basically, connectivity to electronic trading networks for customer dealing on single-dealer, multi-dealer or crossing platforms and proprietary dealing on inter-dealer or crossing platforms generates a flow of information that can be analysed for the purposes of portfolio optimisation.

Customer Dealing: The Big Brother Effect

The basic proposition is that customer deal flow is not just a source of revenue, but a source of information, which can then be exploited to generate more deals! The derived strategy is therefore to:

1. acquire access to deal flow (real time or historical). This is achieved by owning a stake in multiple single, multi and other trading networks 'co-optitively' (in order to hedge bets), and to then
2. exploit it.

In today's operating environment, no one values execution alone. Deals will only flow in return for adding more value than deal execution. In order to come up with a superior value proposition to customers, you need to 'know the customer's needs so that you can better meet the customer's needs'. The ultimate need is portfolio optimisation. Simplistically then, analysing customers' historical transaction data enables a bank to offer a customer portfolio optimisation service – essentially a type of value-added service for customers designed to meet a core need, that is, the optimisation of their unique risk-return profile in hedging and other activities. Enter sophisticated CRM and ERM systems (customer relationship management and enterprise risk management) that incorporate an array of features from predictive profiling algorithms to portfolio event alert mechanisms. This type of offering serves to generate more deals – the most valuable information for proprietary trading.

Proprietary Dealing: The Crystal Ball Effect

Of course, the bank's ultimate need is to optimise the proprietary portfolio. Technology can once again aid and abet in this pursuit. Multiple sources of market data, including deal flow, can be aggregated and integrated into a sophisticated artificial intelligence (AI – using the term generically) probability modelling system to produce the ultimate risk management and decision-making support tool for optimising the upside potential and downside risk of:

- position taking (identifying 'arbitrage' opportunities) in proprietary dealing,

and *back to the starting blocks*,

- market-making (pricing and hedging) in customer dealing.

The feedback mechanism and implicit interrelationships – made explicit by technology – should be patent. Figure 12.2 diagrammatically represents these interrelationships.

The Interlinkages in Motion

Firms that implement this electronic trading strategy successfully will function in an environment where – notionally – customers, promoted by the bank's remote portfolio optimisation system, will transact electronically with the bank through a single- or multi-bank channel, on a either a quote- or order-driven basis. In a simple quote-driven system, the customer will indicate interest by designating such key items as the transaction type, notional size, tenor, and whether they are bidding or offering. The information contained in this RFQ, together with the identified customer's credit rating and market data will then be sufficient for the dealer's AI program to return a quote or price, to which the customer will either respond favourably and accept, triggering the issuance of an electronic deal ticket, or not. The executed trades will then be sorted into portfolios, whose risks will be measured and managed electroni-

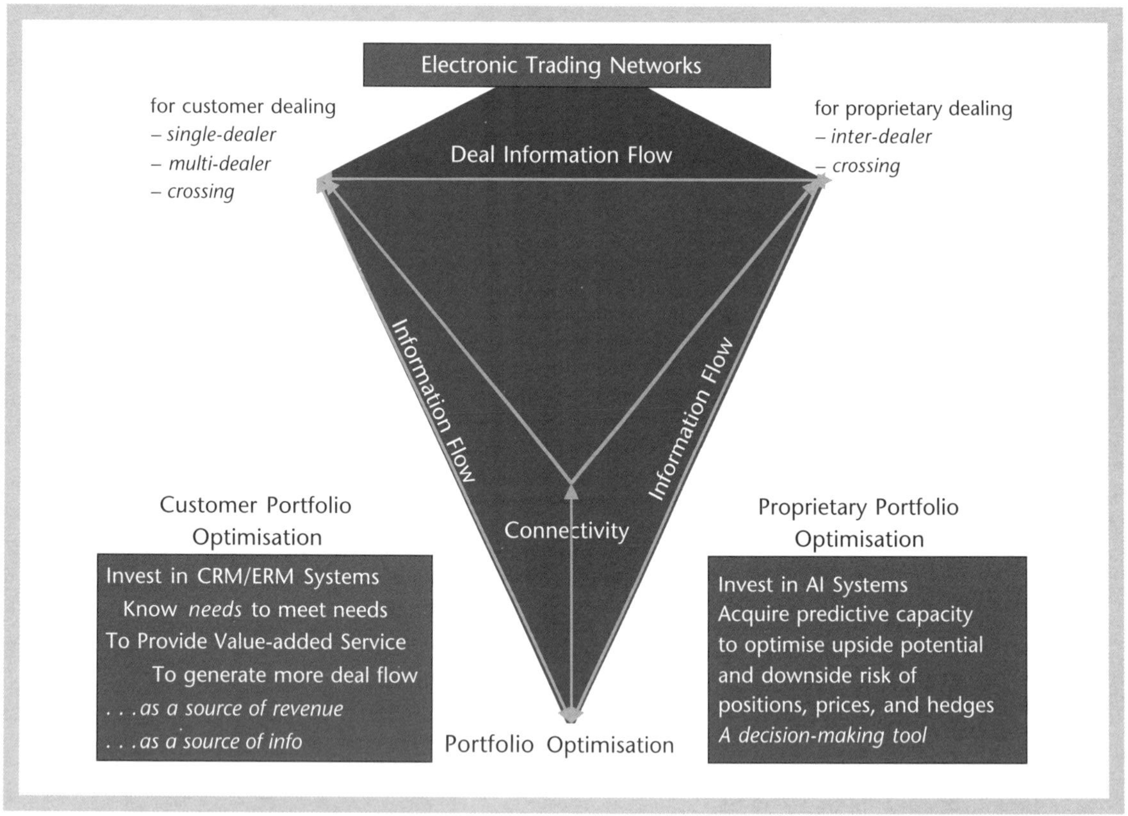

Figure 12.2 The feedback mechanism between customer and proprietary dealing strategies

cally. The executed trade or rejected price will also be factored into the customer's portfolio model. A database of customer indications and executed trades, together with a vast amount of current and historical market data, will then be analysed by a different AI program to identify and recommend or even execute proprietary trading opportunities. The transactions generated will be sorted and added to these same electronic risk management portfolios. The order model would operate similarly. Finally, the executed transactions will be processed to settlement automatically at optimal speed and cost.

The development of this capability – in which customers are prompted by their remote electronic risk and portfolio management system to enter into transactions with their dealer electronically, either through the channel site or through a market site, using its AI program, which is also able to evaluate proprietary trading opportunities – goes beyond current tactical approaches to technology. It will enable large trading operations to do significantly higher volumes of business, using a fraction of the current number of traders, and significantly lower the risk on positions. Moreover, because a single electronic deal ticket will be issued and used for all middle- and back-office functions whenever a transaction is executed, the extent of operational risk – perhaps the most important challenge to the success of a high-volume trading business – will be substantially reduced.

THE DISCIPLINE OF ARTIFICIAL INTELLIGENCE

The basis of this strategy is the observation that the two main activities that characterise the economic function performed by traders are completely specifiable as analytical problems with deterministic solutions. Accordingly, a computer program that solves these problems through the application of algorithms can, in theory, be at least as effective in executing and processing trades, with the obvious advantages of significantly reduced direct expenses and the elimination of transaction data recording errors.

The analytical foundation of this strategy is the discipline of AI, which is a set of rules for decision making under a completely specified set of contingencies, codified into a computer program (see box below).

Artificial intelligence currently comprises three distinct fields:

- *Expert systems:* These take the behavioural approach of devising decision rules from interviews with existing decision-makers in the organisation.

- *Fuzzy logic:* A mathematical extension of Boolean logic incorporating the concept of the degree to which a statement is true or an element belongs to a set (although similar, is distinct from probability theory).
- *Neural networks:* Computing structures that process large quantities of data for pattern recognition, classification and prediction, based on the structure of the human brain, permitting the relevant co-efficients to change in response to earlier errors in the same way that human beings learn to solve problems. Neural networks can almost be deemed to be learning systems, and are taught rather than programmed – a major distinction.

In the case of expert systems, the methodology is probably not flexible enough to solve problems as complex as the key trading decisions of customer transaction pricing, portfolio risk management and proprietary trade selection. Fuzzy logic is ideally suited for modelling the pricing decision, where the solution depends on the extent to which an effective hedging strategy is available, and the evaluation of proprietary trading strategies, which depends on the degree of predictive content in a prospective trade's conditioning information. In addition, neural networks, which form the basis of many of the price matching systems developed by electronic brokers, excel at risk managing large portfolios of transactions. Accomplished by recognising exposure imbalances beyond a specified tolerance, and by selecting proprietary trades by deriving logical rules, they screen large market databases in search of trades that meet the criteria. They then modify the rules as the market processes that created the trading opportunities in the first place change.

The world watched with considerable amazement in May 1997 as IBM's chess computer, Deep Blue, beat Garry Kasparov, the world champion, in a six-game match. With a machine's victory in this most cerebral of games, it seemed that a line had been crossed. Today, AI programs increasingly pass the oft-cited Turing test, such that human users cannot discern whether they are interacting with another human via an electronic interface or with a machine. However, in reality, the Turing test is only a measure of simulated intelligence and computer programs still rely heavily on their superior processing power to imitate it. Their problem-solving abilities remain largely linear, rather than lateral and the brute-force calculation capacity of machines is still only a poor substitute for the often intuitive, pattern-recognition abilities of humans. Computers still lack the defining characteristics of intelligence. Nevertheless, in the field of data analytics or informatics, the huge advances in data processing speed – especially through new technologies such as holographic data storage – continue to enhance the computational capacity of computers, their modelling, data mining and analysis, and problem-solving ability. Irrespective of whether the intelligence is simulated or not, financial market participants will increasingly substitute the artificial for the human variety.

CHAPTER 13

THE QUANTUM LEAP IN ACTION

We have already covered much of this in the preceding chapters, since the business of markets and the business of trading are becoming increasingly indistinguishable. Nevertheless, in refocusing through this strategic lens, we can indeed distil these three strategies in action from all the 'e-nitiative' commotion and deduce some key learnings apropos the implementation thereof.

FRONT-OFFICE AUTOMATION AND CONNECTIVITY

Pricing

Moore's Law, stating that the capacity of computer chips for a given cost doubles every 18 months, has so far provided a good proxy for the explosive growth in computational speed over the last decade. This increase has made the automation of data- and computation-intensive markets possible but, in so doing, has made the automation of trading a necessity for market participants. This has imposed some heavy demands on market participants, in terms of acquiring this technological capability and integrating it into the existing organisation, which as a result also has to have the ability to handle high speed and convolution.

Developments in the bond market illustrate this cause and effect dynamic. With the proliferation of electronic markets across the time zones, bond market traders now have to quote prices continuously in a multitude of systems.

Because the intermediary can be hit or lifted at these prices instantaneously in a rapidly moving market, prices are usually good only momentarily and are updated continuously. Depending on what systems are used, intermediaries in the bond market may have to post a couple of thousand prices each second on various systems. Consequently, according to the BIS (2001), the daily number of quotes on a single bond in a single system can be in excess of a million.

In response to this, many banks have now implemented so-called pricing engines for the high-frequency pricing of liquid and simple instruments, such as government bonds, that function with minimal human intervention. The previous example of the volatility on the electronic futures exchanges in Japan also highlights the pressure that traders are under to match their pricing speed with the speed of trading and their automated pricing response.

The trends depicted above notwithstanding, the scenario sketched in Chapter 12 is, of course, artificial and, in reality, the degree of front-office automation varies considerably. The unilateral statement that a computer program can produce superior pricing to that of human beings challenges credulity, so the key to the success of this endeavour lies in the choice of the types of product, the way the strategy is best applied to these, and to which customers.

Capital markets products range from simple instruments that trade in high volume at low margins in liquid markets (for example spot forex and government bonds) to complex structures that are either multidimensional, non-linear functions of market variables, or dependent on market parameters whose values must be estimated rather than observed (for example exotic options). As for customers, an important distinction separates less frequent end-users, such as corporate treasurers and pension funds, from other professional dealers who enter the market regularly to hedge their inventories. It is self-evident that artificial intelligence is most effective as a substitute for live traders when it is applied to simple products that are traded with professional dealers and, to a lesser extent, large institutional investors. For virtually all major financial institutions, however, this subset of their business does represent a significant proportion of the transactions that they do and the trading revenues that they generate. Thus, automated pricing engines have generally been developed by banks for their high-volume, low-margin trading activities, the conditions exemplified in the above examples, such as in forex, government bonds and sometimes equities.

Such pricing engines typically use the realised prices of a limited number of characteristic instruments as a basis. The methodology underlying pricing engines may also be used for arbitrage purposes if other market participants do not update their prices quickly enough. Although pricing engines automate much of the human mediation in trading simple liquid instruments, these systems will usually automatically alert their users in case human intervention is required. This can be triggered by a certain event, such as trade enquiries of a certain size, by a certain client, or in case of volatility spiking up. Most systems are equipped with a 'panic button' to suspend the automatic generation of quotes in volatile periods, such as prior to the release of important macro-economic data or in case of major moves in other markets.

Trading

In the trade execution zone, firms face some of the most difficult options and a complex set of cost/gain trade-offs. Essentially, as firms weigh up the prospects for proprietary or closed or single-dealer trading systems, and the prospects for the proliferation of open, multi-dealer, inter-dealer and crossing systems across their product range, they try to hedge their bets as far as resources permit.

The decision-making process effectively encompasses the *what*, *when* and *who* of trading in the electronic medium.

What: To Connect or Not to Connect?

Frankly, firms do not have a choice of *what* they do at the macro-level. There is no more question of 'whether' to migrate to the electronic medium. However, assuming that *what* is a given, *when* may not be.

When: Now or Later?

The electronic trading market is still in a very immature stage of development and hence is still set to undergo an intense restructuring period before it stabilises. Firms cognisant of this may prefer to avoid the risks and costs associated with this instability and delay market entry until after rationalisation. Unfortunately, from a timing perspective, the option of delaying entry is generally deemed too risky, given the potential competitive advantages that could accrue to first or early entrants. Thus, banks are now in the process of deciding between proprietary and non-proprietary trading solutions.

Who: Proprietary or Non-proprietary Systems

In the first instance, the proprietary channel versus non-proprietory marketplace decision should be based on an analysis of customer needs and preferences. Clearly, a multi-bank trading site does not serve an individual bank's immediate interests. Even if the initial model is based on limited transparency and a static or fixed-pricing RFQ system, over time it will invariably migrate to higher transparency and a dynamic pricing model, that is, auctioning. Comparative pricing on a pure trading engine will inevitably cause price-based competition and hence price compression. In the already commoditised product markets, bases for competition are weak, margins are razor thin, and provoking a price war is to be avoided at all costs. Moreover, in reality, the potential offsetting access to mouth-watering new markets and higher volumes may or may not materialise. Counterparty credit risk may continue to prohibit entry by smaller buy-side participants, leaving participating banks on the platform to fight for share in the existing market. The ultimate shift to an exchange model with a central counterparty is highly detrimental to a bank's ability to take and charge for credit as well as market risk. And finally, in the short term at least, the new channel will simply add to the existing cost structure. Thus, the overall impact on margin will be negative and on volume unknown. By contrast, a proprietary channel at least avoids the competitive pricing effect, although the cost and volume dynamics are similar. Thus the decision depends on the level of demand and whether or not the bank needs to respond to such a demand from its customers. Fortunately, among the existing customer base and potential new target market segments, customers have varying needs and levels of sophistication or 'techno-savvyness'. While the shift to open markets may be inevitable in the long term, the time-lag in certain market segments (size, type or geographic, such as medium-sized corporates, mid-tier institutions, and regional players) may be significant. This allows a bank to prudently avoid pre-empting competitive pricing while designing their proprietary systems to quickly adapt to its inevitability, that is, to link to open market structures. Thus, in the e-channel arena, firms' decisions to invest in developing a 'transactionally functional' proprietary offering for their clients are based on market segmentation and timing factors. Although prospects for the viability and sustainability of proprietary offerings will continue to wane over time, such an investment will not be a waste if the capex can be recouped (which depends on judicious targeting of market segments and re-deployable technology), and if valuable brand kudos and experience is acquired in the process.

Who: Non-proprietary Systems

Once e-trading in a given product market segment has matured to the point where the independent multi-price-maker sites are yielding to sell-side-owned ones, an individual bank has little choice but to enter the fray. In the open e-market arena, 'co-opetition' is becoming increasingly common as a means of diversifying investments and risk. However, in selecting which type of system, and which of a specific type, to connect to and/or invest in, banks still face a number of trade-offs, given resource constraints.

First of all, a bank needs to decide whether it intends to simply connect to a trading site or whether it needs to acquire equity in it. Clearly a stake in the market yields some significant benefits. The stakeholders will hold more sway over the shift from blind static pricing to transparent and dynamic price discovery, and over the shift from bilateral credit limits to central credit facilities. Moreover, when the shift does occur, stakeholders will be partially compensated for the loss in both instances. First, a bank may gain access to aggregate flow data and be privy to other information which would offset the attrition of informational asymmetries, Chinese walls notwithstanding. Second, the replacement of bilateral with central credit limits is less of a loss if the affected bank owns a stake in the CCP. Basically, ownership of the e-intermediary affords some protection and compensation to the banks threatened with disintermediation.

An interim strategy adopted by many joint ventures, for example, is to structure the market as a hybrid of the one-to-one and many-to-many model, such that the group of banks in the venture targets their cumulative client base (particularly corporate) without alienating the original relationship bank's clients or margins. The respective nominated 'house bank' always acts as the customer's counterpart, even though the customer may trade on the best price of all the banks. This type of e-market creates a unique selling proposition. Banks can increase customer *retention* through offering a range of competitive prices. The customer can compare the prices of the participating banks and trade on the best price regardless of the relationship with the bank. There is no need for the client to have a relationship with the bank offering the best price as his house bank will settle the trade with him, making a back-to-back trade with the relevant bank. At the same time, the customer's house bank retains the transaction margin. Thus, even smaller customers can secure the advantages over the single-dealer model. Furthermore, the participating banks may be able to obtain increasing order flows through the platform, which allows them to offer their products to the pooled clients of the banks and expand regionally. In addition, harmonisation with the partner banks is possible through a common understanding of the defined objective: create an environment which offers clients all the benefits of new online trading models, while strengthening the retention of the combined customer base. With respect to costs, partner banks have the advantage of being able to spread and reduce their development costs. However, in this model, banks concentrate on the retention of their existing customer base, at the expense of reaching additional clients beyond the pooled customer base. In addition, harmonisation may be time consuming and incurs the risk of agreement only on the lowest common denominator.

This example underscores some of the potential benefits that accrue to investing banks. On the other hand, the initial and recurring costs incurred in securing stakeholder status, relative to participant status, are significant, as are the risks. Allied to this, a bank needs to make some basic portfolio decisions with respect to risk diversification, given these costs and risks and resource constraints. Specifically, in hedging, a bank needs to place its hedging bets very carefully. It needs to decide, for example, on the number of markets per product, position with respect to simple or advanced models, and so on. And ultimately, an individual bank needs to assess the competing systems' relative probabilities of success. An individual market's sustainability in the end depends on securing a critical mass of volume. To this end, a bank needs to compare the competing systems from the end-users' perspective, before deciding with whom to align.

Who: Ask the Customer – Factors Bearing on End-users' Choice of Trading Systems

Explicit and Implicit Costs of Trading

In theory, end-users will choose the system with the lowest explicit and implicit costs of trading. And, by corollary, this is also the system in which an individual bank ought to invest. Unfortunately, it's not as simple as this. The factors bearing on cost depend on other factors that provoke a circular cause and effect argument that provides no simple basis for an investment decision.

For example, in most wholesale markets, the explicit costs of trading include market access fees, commissions, tax, clearing and settlement costs, and staff and technology overheads. While fixed technology costs may currently be higher for electronic markets than in traditional markets, electronic trading has the potential to significantly reduce many of the variable cost components of processing trades, and thus lower the average cost per trade over time. Moreover, the scalability of electronic platforms enables them to exploit economies of scale to a far greater extent than was possible in traditional markets. However, the proviso is sufficiently large trading volume. Thus, individual users will have a direct cost incentive to plug into the electronic system that has attracted the maximum number of other end-users. Of course the corollary is that an individual bank needs to be wired to the same market.

The implicit costs of trading include the price impact of the trade (that is, the extent to which the trade price deviates from the current market price as a result of the trade) or the bid-ask spread paid to a liquidity provider. In order-book markets, the investor may incur the cost of a potentially greater price impact. The investor has to pay either the cost of a potential price impact in the order-book market or the compensation for immediacy of large-order execution in the dealer market. In the former it is determined by the order-book conditions and in the latter by the dealer. The choice depends on the investor's preference.

In the world of institutional trading, minimising market impact is of paramount importance to investors. The data in the table below, which is derived from a much cited study (Plexus, 1998) by the Plexus Group – an expert firm in transaction cost analysis – clearly demonstrates the importance of confidentiality in avoiding market impact in institutional trading. In this study, the average large cap order comprised 120,000 shares of a $20 billion company, representing about one day of volume. The average small cap order comprised 50,000 shares of a $450 million company, representing about three days of volume. Delay measures trades that the buy-side firm wishes to release to the broker, but held back for fear of triggering further adverse moves. Missed trades result from delays and represent unfilled orders that are rescinded as a result of adverse price moves. Thus delay and missed trades represent another form of market impact.

Market impact dwarfs commission costs in institutional equity trading

Transaction Cost	**Larger Cap Stock**	**Smaller Cap Stock**
Commissions	0.12%	0.22%
Impact	0.20%	0.33%
Delay	0.53%	1.72%
Missed Trades	0.16%	2.22%
Total	**1.01%**	**4.49%**

Information leakage may reduce returns on big trades by as much as 3% – and that's a big number when expected returns on equities are in the range of 10% per year. Accordingly, for large transactions, investors have traditionally placed a high value on the advice, confidentiality and capital commitment of dealers. Such trades represent a majority of the trading profits at individual dealer firms.

However, as emphasised repeatedly, one of the primary advantages of electronic trading networks, such as the ECNs and especially electronic order books, is their high degree of anonymity and hence the potential to reduce leakage, front-running and thus market impact costs. Moreover, new order-management software is strengthening this advantage. The newest generations, for example, can automatically break up and manage large block trades to minimise their impact on market prices. This is particularly useful in portfolio reallocations, which entail the trading of large blocks of many different securities. Using new electronic trading algorithms, trades of 100,000 (or even a million) shares may soon be executed electronically. Although the need for manual order working of large block trades still exists, the minimum size that qualifies as 'upstairs' is increasing immeasurably. Thus, electronic order books, supplemented by order-management software, may offer end-users a lower (implicit) cost substitute for dealers in avoiding market impact effects on price.

On the other hand, electronic trading systems are also shrinking dealers' bid-ask spreads anyway. The dealer's spread, charged to investors as compensation for supplying liquidity and immediacy of execution, must cover his explicit trading costs, his profit margin and an execution or liquidity risk premium (that is, the risk of being unable to unwind the transaction at a predictable cost). Electronic markets potentially reduce all these components of the dealer's bid-ask spread.

Dealers' own explicit costs are diminishing through automation. However, profit margins are declining as electronic trading intensifies price competition between intermediaries by making price comparison easier and cheaper, especially in more commoditised markets, such as government bond and foreign exchange. This is aggravated by the presence of some intermediaries who only remain active in these markets in order to have access to flow information that can be used for proprietary trading, and for whom negative margins may not then matter. Liquidity risk premia may also decline if electronic trading increases market transparency and so enables dealers to better assess market liquidity depth in relation to the transaction size (that is, the volume that can be expected at each of a range of prices). Most systems that are currently in use, however, do not provide full transparency. Liquidity premia will also be reduced if electronic trading systems provide greater anonymity than traditional trading methods. Greater anonymity may enable dealers to gradually unwind large positions in smaller lots without having to expose their position to other market participants. In other words, expected price impact plays an equally important role for the dealer when setting the premium for which he is prepared to take over the execution risk, and he too will have price impact risk mitigated by the relative anonymity of electronic systems, especially compared to traditional inter-dealer markets.

However, while investors thirst for liquidity, whether they'll continue to pay for it at all is another matter. Many investors are not satisfied with the price or the supply of liquidity provided by broker-dealers. The performance of investment managers is closely scrutinised, and market impact costs often account for a great deal of a manager's underperformance, relative to benchmarks. Institutional investors will continue to take advantage of the reduced searching costs afforded by technology and will strive to cut out the middleman in an ever-increasing array of products.

Thus, in evaluating its connectivity and equity options, an individual bank needs to take account of the newer and better alternatives (in terms of lowering implicit costs) that are available to end-users, as well as the options available for bettering its own performance as one of the traditional alternatives. In general, banks need to find ways of working with rather than against the new structures, for example by entering into joint ventures with technology providers. This is elaborated on in Chapter 15.

Historical and Institutional Factors

Although the rational end-user will attempt to seek out the lowest cost per trade, which will tend to be found on the newer electronic exchanges, historical factors, and, allied to this, entry barriers erected by first-mover advantages and network effects, also affect the choice of end-users. As a result, the system with the least cost for end-users may not actually be chosen by the end-users. Thus, before casting its lot, an individual bank needs to assess the thwarting influence of such political rather than economic factors on the potential evolution of market structure.

Users' choice of trading systems will partially depend on the historical evolution of that market and its existing structure (usually referred to as 'path dependency'), vested interests and the relative market power of the various institutions, which may limit the scope for market evolution. An example of the role of historical factors is provided by the fixed-income markets, which have historically been dependent on dealers, and so any evolution to electronic order books may be delayed. Customers are apt to be involved in long-term relationships with their dealers, for whom they demonstrate a preference, and are comfortable leaving the minutiae of trade execution to them. Moreover, dealers have historically vested interests, which may provide an incentive for them to preserve the status quo. Thus, in the more liquid bond issues, the essential structure remains intact, with a schism between the inter-dealer and dealer-to-customer markets. For an individual dealer, therefore, investments in separate electronic inter-dealer systems and simple, blind, static RFQ-based multi-dealer systems that do not really optimise efficiencies for the buy-side are nevertheless safe(ish). By contrast, the traditionally highly centralised markets for European and Australian bond futures moved very quickly from floor-based trading to an electronic order book, as only the existing features of the market had to be automated.

First-mover Advantages and Network Effects

Users' choice of trading systems may also be limited by various externalities arising from the nature of technology-driven industries. So-called first movers may be able to set the standard or protocol for a particular type of trading system, after which users can be 'locked in' because the cost of switching to another system with a different standard is prohibitive. Another important issue governing the dynamics of market access, related to first-mover advantages in standardisation, is that of network effects. The value of a trading system will depend on the number of people using it, that is, the liquidity. Once a system reaches 'critical mass', it tends to attract more mass or liquidity, erecting high entry barriers in the process – not least through scale economies. On the other hand, competition may unexpectedly emerge from rival systems with sufficient critical mass in related fields that are able to provide network externalities similar to existing systems. Information companies, for example, such as Reuters or Bloomberg, have successfully used their dominant position in the provision of market information to enter the trading market.

In conclusion, in order to make sound electronic market trading decisions, individual banks need to take account of a multitude of variables in predicting the outcome of a buy-side versus sell-side-driven evolution. On the other hand, as the rationalisation phase advances, trading will tend to concentrate on only a few platforms, through a process of both organic customer acquisition and volume growth as well as mergers and acquisitions. Consequently, backing the proverbial wrong horse may not be too costly, irrespective of whether the horse acts as acquirer or acquiree. The only irrecoverable loss is in pure failure and exit by the market in which a given bank has invested.

Finally, in making their electronic platform decisions, banks need to look beyond front-end pricing and trading dynamics. First, it is critical that banks equip themselves with the right internal operational capabilities before they connect to a front-end façade. Excluding the true electronic exchanges (with central clearing operations), the panacea of STP – automated end-to-end transaction processing and the associated operational efficiency gains and economies – purportedly offered by most hubs, is a fallacy. In reality, they offer front-end transactional functionality only, not back-end transaction processing, the onus of which falls on the transacting counterparties. In fact, the functionality is not even true *transactional* functionality, which implies a transfer of funds. These are message-routing switches that facilitate an exchange of information only. Even to the extent that these systems provide 'seamless' interfaces into pricing, credit and back-office systems, the effectiveness thereof is still dependent on the relevant bank's internal system capabilities. In the absence of a high degree of back-office automation, automating the front office can have very detrimental effects on overall efficiency. Moreover, in an environment defined by price competition and low margins, a high-cost structure may be fatal.

Second, before entering any price-driven market where things such as brand loyalty and quality count for nothing, a bank needs to be in a position to price very competitively for execution *and* source new higher margin income from higher value new services. Even if the two become unbundled, clients will demonstrate a preference and lower price sensitivity for value added in terms of pre-trade data and reference pricing, depth of understanding of the market, settlement and so on. These matters are expanded on below.

Value-added Services

In the first instance, firms are using the Internet to distribute research more efficiently and to a broader base of customers. Once again, they are supplying their research on both closed, proprietary, single-dealer channels as well as on open, non-proprietary, multi-dealer channels. Securities.Hub, for example, is a prominent research portal sponsored by the largest broker-dealers in the US. From the portal, investors can recall specific research, market commentary, or product offerings from any dealer, but each dealer remains 'blind' to the activity of the customers of the other participant dealers. Securities.Hub is a scalable platform that allows the major dealers to deliver research inexpensively to a wider set of investors, which may attract more order flow.

Beyond generic and static research, firms are also investing in developing customised, or personalised, interactive 'info-mediation' services, which add substantially more value and can therefore be unbundled and premium priced or bundled and compensated for with trade flow. In order to provide such value-added services, however, firms first need to develop appropriate competencies.

Many traditional firms are slowly beginning to realise that the key to avoiding disintermediation is through a better understanding of their customers' needs. By having a more integrated view of its dealings with its customers, a firm can maximise the profit potential of these customers. Furthermore, if a firm understands the total risk associated with a given customer, it will be better able to allocate capital for risk associated with the customer's positions. Only now is the potential of technology to help firms manage their relationships at this level coming to the fore. According to the highly prominent journal, *Risk*, true 'customer relationship management (CRM) systems' will prove highly profitable for those with the foresight to build them (Davidson, 2000).

Financial institutions are not the first to realise the potential of technology to foster relationships with customers, and companies in sectors such as retail and the utilities have pioneered approaches from which financial institutions are now seeking to benefit. Like many of today's technology buzzwords, CRM is a new term for an old idea, or collection of ideas, with an inevitable e-commerce angle. What differentiates today's products is the way in which they are able to integrate various information sources on customers, and the new ways they are able to exploit aggregated information (Davidson, 2000).

Modern CRM systems embrace a number of technologies, such as contact databases and warehouses, middleware (for integrating systems), groupware (for sharing information between systems), customer profiling algorithms, event alert mechanisms at the front-end, and IP (Internet protocol) communications. Some of the dedicated financial CRM suppliers who have emerged have optimised their systems for the e-commerce environment, and have coined the term e-CRM to describe them. Institutions are starting to install these systems on their sales and trading desks, and to explore how they might be used in conjunction with risk management systems to provide a more full and balanced picture of the value and risks of customers.

Furthermore, institutions are using these systems as the basis for providing interactive risk and portfolio optimisation tools and toolboxes for the more self-empowered client. Essentially, in terms of portfolio optimisation, since the client's needs cannot be substantively differentiated from the bank's own, banks are leveraging their traditional internal competence to provide outward-facing *customer-centric* applications.

The best-of-breed developers, for whom this is core competence and for whom innovation is a competitive imperative, provide a source of inspiration:

1. Both Boston-based WorldStreet's and Toronto-based Janna's CRM technology have mechanisms to track and integrate customer information from across an organisation's systems, distribute it to people who interact with customers, and enable salespeople, traders and managers to collaborate on customer accounts. Janna includes a wireless interface for accessing the information from mobile phones or handheld devices. WorldStreet is available either on an application service provision (ASP) basis or for on-site installation. WorldStreet's customers include Deutsche Bank and ING Barings and JP Morgan advisory service. Janna's clients include Merrill Lynch's corporate and institutional client group, Lehman Brothers' institutional sales and research operations, and Donaldson, Lufkin & Jenrette Securities' money management division.

2. New York-based Axiom Software Laboratories, traditionally a risk management system supplier, has recently enhanced its systems integration and messaging technology to make it suitable for CRM in an e-commerce environment. The 'e-Business Command Centre' is able to monitor customer traffic on a firm's website, tracking what attracts customers' attention and where they spend time. It is then able to feed this information to the sales or trading desks or to management, linking it in with customer profiling databases, and sending alerts where appropriate. Similarly, WorldStreet's

system connects to real-time market data feeds and filters out information relevant to individual customers based on their profiles, including buying opportunities.

3. California-based Siebel's system is premised more on the notion that brokers can no longer maintain a competitive advantage based on execution services alone, and supports the provision of personalised, one-to-one advisory services, via multiple distribution channels from Web to Web-enabled wireless. Their CRM system is used by Chase Manhattan, Bank of America Securities, Dresdner Bank and a number of other financial institutions, and the company is now one of the fastest growing companies in the US.

4. Finally, in terms of linking the proprietary trading business to the client trading facilitation business, Intelligent Markets purports to offer an intelligent trading platform (for single-dealer, multi-dealer and exchange based models) which ostensibly incorporates a learning technology, utilising information on orders, trades, market environment and client behaviour to proactively notify salespeople *and* traders of transaction opportunities.

The Link between CRM and ERM

Because it attempts to integrate information across an organisation and provides a layer of analytical technology, CRM resembles enterprise risk management (ERM). The overlap is most clear in the area of credit, where the setting of credit limits and other internal policies is dependent on a knowledge of the customer. ERM systems have been notoriously bad at defining 'who the customer is', because most systems are based on market risk where 'who the customer is' is irrelevant. It's only in respect of credit risk that the customer matters, and 'who the customer is' is really quite complex. Thus, CRM systems could potentially enhance ERM.

Large organisations such as major banks and corporates often comprise multiple entities with complicated interrelationships. In risk technology, only a few credit limit management systems have attempted to address this complexity and for the most part such systems have not had the flexibility to also manage customer relationships. As indicated above, a relationship manager in an institution needs to understand not only risk, but the whole potential profitability of the relationship with the customer. CRM systems try to capture all the data associated with a relationship across the organisation and combine it with techniques for estimating the potential value and risk of the customer to the institution.

While there are clearly benefits to be had from integrating ERM and CRM systems – for improving both credit risk management and customer service, by, for example, using the sophisticated analysis of dedicated risk management systems to trigger alerts on customer portfolios – few firms are attempting this as yet. In the meantime, there is the potential to at least share some technological components, such as middleware for gathering, transporting and standardising customer information, and data warehousing for aggregating and storing the data. In the interim, vendors' actions endorse the likelihood of a long-term trend. Financial risk software specialists have begun forming alliances with CRM suppliers such as Massachusetts-based Satuit Technologies to interface with its Profile 2000 CRM system. Satuit's customers include Rothschild Asset Management and BNP Paribas.

In addition to integrating CRM with ERM to improve credit risk management through credit extension, and thus better servicing the customers, not least through a better upside-downside evaluation, internal risk management systems can also be rendered outward facing to provide clients with another value-added service, that of 'outsourced' risk management. This is expanded upon below.

MIDDLE-OFFICE AUTOMATION AND INTELLIGENCE

Although we have alluded to some of the developments in credit risk management and, its convergence with CRM notwithstanding, more generally, developments in integrated risk management, the measuring and managing of credit, market and liquidity risk simultaneously, as well as operational risk, are significant. Risk management software has been at the centre of innovation and expenditure by wholesale financial institutions. This is due to the huge growth in the off-balance sheet derivatives business, the consequent rapid increase in market and credit exposures at firms, and the subsequent imposition by financial regulators of new capital adequacy and regulatory reporting requirements. A brief appraisal of how risk management technology is evolving and the key business drivers accelerating this evolution follows.

Advances in Credit Risk and Balance Sheet Optimisation

The world is riskier than it used to be, and, in order to survive in this riskier environment, many leading financial institutions have developed innovative new strategies for credit risk and broader balance sheet management. As a best practice benchmark, at JP Morgan Chase, PCs, chained together into a parallel processing supercomputer, perform billions of risk measurement calculations daily, to gauge the effect of hedges and collateral on the credit exposure from products, companies and industry sectors. Because it understands its risk position, the bank can net credit exposure across products, customers and industry sectors to ensure that risk capacity is used productively. And JP Morgan Chase is by no means the only bank that has invested in developing this risk capacity and capital optimisation capability.

Traditionally risk was managed in a very basic manner. The techniques and technology to strip out credit risk from the underlying trade simply did not exist. Consequently, credit limits had to be defined for each customer based on a credit rating, which varied periodically. The disadvantage of this approach was that the maximum size of the credit facility often exceeded the actual utilisation thereof. And although the firm extending the credit was potentially exposed to the limit, it earned a return only on the amount actually drawn down. As result, credit risk capacity was wasted. In addition, the unpredictable nature of infrequent credit events, to which the bank had to react, had a disruptive effect, and exposed the bank to the risk of creditor draw-down before the line could be adjusted.

However, the advent of liquid markets in credit risk has led to the emergence of a dynamic approach to credit risk management through continuously updated market-based measures of credit quality. Such market-based measures include the published credit prices for companies by reinsurers, such as Swiss Re. In addition, liquid credit markets have also spurred the development of innovative new credit risk management tools – credit derivatives. These may be used to diversify the credit portfolio, for example a credit risk swap can be used to exchange regional risk without affecting actual relationships. In this new dynamic environment of continuous numeric measures of risk, credit lines are no longer static, but change constantly in response to more precise and timely price signals on credit quality, credit market liquidity, and other factors. A reduction in credit lines, however, does not necessitate a reduction in the amount of business a bank can do with a customer, as hedging or laying off risk can offset the credit exposure. In other words, the decision to transact no longer implies a commitment to assume credit risk. The customer need never know, in fact, that the bank has bought credit protection to reduce exposure. This leads to efficient capacity utilisation.

Today, the outsourcing of credit risk no longer involves a lengthy underwriting process, inscrutable pricing and onerous terms. Clients demand speed, flexibility, simplicity, transparency and security from their outsourcers. In fact, industry leaders, such as Swiss Re, offer a fully transactional product and service offering online. Clients can log on, locate the company whose credit they need to hedge, enter the amount and tenor of protection needed and, with a click of a mouse, receive an indicative price.

The benefits of this new level of flexibility become especially apparent during economic downturns. Instead of increased provisions for bad debts and charge-offs, and cost cutting elsewhere, the tools now exist to buy a hedge, reduce risk concentration, or swap into a more attractive investment in risk.

Risk Management: From the Enterprise to the Universe

This section, based on analyses performed by *Risk* (2000a), continues the hypotheses that the focus in risk management is shifting from internal enterprise-wide risk management (ERM) systems to external Web-based risk services for customers within a B2B e-business strategy.

According to *Risk* (2000a), much of the growth and innovation in risk management technology over the past five years has been driven by ERM projects. These are designed to enable financial institutions to manage their capital on a risk-adjusted basis. In other words, these systems help the firm to identify and analyse its market positions, the amount of economic and regulatory capital required for these positions, the quality of profits generated by business units taking these positions, and to implement internal models to reduce regulatory capital charges and improve shareholder profitability.

Many lessons have been learnt from the successes and failures of these projects, not least of which have been the problems of integrating systems and maintaining clean data sources. While there is still much work to be done, the focus of activity, as measured by dollar spending and innovative R&D, has shifted away from ERM projects. The scope has in fact become much wider; not only do firms want state-of-the-art risk management for themselves, but they also want to provide such risk management services to the universe of counterparts. The centre of gravity has now migrated to wholesale financial institutions aiming to provide risk management services for their customers (the pension funds, institutional investors, corporates and hedge funds) within a B2B portal offering.

The reason for this, of course, is the intensifying competitive environment. Even on the Net, as a channel, the pressure to differentiate the product offering and provide a unique service is mounting. While every bank can provide market research, prices and execution, the one advantage that a bank has in an existing relationship with a customer is the fact that it holds that customer's positions and trades in its internal systems. If it can use these positions to provide value-added services to the customer, it may acquire a 'killer app'. Risk management functionality on these positions could be one of the most valuable of these features. Finally, banks have committed significant resources and expertise to managing their own risks, and huge potential benefits may be realised if these same resources were leveraged to provide a service to customers. Examples of risk functionality would be providing mark-to-market valuations, sensitivity reports, value-at-risk and stress scenario analysis for customer portfolios.

Evidence of the pervasive demand for this type of service is found in the burgeoning supply thereof. The Web portals launched by financial institutions, and new Web product announcements from software vendors and application service providers (ASPs) in many cases include risk management services at a much reduced cost, which are targeted at customers hitherto unable to afford such expertise or systems.

The provision of these services on this basis is consistent with the wider trend in software provision, which favours the ASP model. In the future, it is likely that offerings launched by financial institutions and technology firms working together in business partnerships will be the most successful. Such products will be key in attracting new types of customers to the wholesale financial markets.

This model, however, will not hold the same appeal for sophisticated market participants who trade in many markets using many different systems. For these participants, real value will be delivered through an end-to-end integration. Risk management services and broader portfolio optimisation and other e-business offerings must be designed to provide straight-through integration from multiple external front-ends to a customer's internal systems and processes. An emerging language protocol for connecting the public network to local networks or internal systems is making this increasing possible.

Protocols may also offer a solution to the broader conflicts between closed proprietary Web offerings and the open versions. The question of whether single-dealer portals will prevail or whether a few multi-dealer portals will annex all the liquidity and users may not have such an either/or answer. Again, if one accepts that Web services and system integration is a key requisite, then it will be easy for users to connect services from single-dealer portals or multi-dealer portals into a solution appropriate for their needs. This will allow a world of single-dealer or multi-dealer portals to co-exist in a symbiotic relationship. The advantage that single-dealer portals will have is a close relationship with their customers and a detailed understanding of their positions – surely an advantage that will only be magnified with the creation of new tailored derivatives contracts specific to a customer's requirements and powerful direct marketing technologies.

Having argued that most intellectual effort and innovation is focusing on risk management services within a B2B e-commerce offering, important work still needs to be done within banks on ERM systems. In fact, some of the same techniques and technologies that are shaping B2B e-commerce solutions will also have a profound impact on ERM systems.

In the same way that the power of the Internet was unleashed by standardising simple protocols and technologies, resulting in an open network, with a large number of hosts providing a wide range of services to a large number of users with very different needs, a similar architecture could radically enhance ERM systems.

In a world of increased market volatility and credit exposures, it has become critical to obtain a real-time view of the aggregated book – the position and exposure – and to know as quickly and exactly as possible the exposure to an event at the disaggregated level. This need is impossible to meet within an ERM architecture that collects all the data into a central warehouse. Implementation is too costly and too complex. It is, however, within the possibilities of distributed component architectures that manage the complexity and requirements at appropriate levels. Solutions that integrate appropriate components of source systems across the enterprise are much more achievable and powerful. Such architectures are beginning to emerge at leading financial institutions, and are being offered by vendors.

Risk management technology suffers from the fact that financial institutions continue to try and develop too much software in-house and software vendors fail to deliver quality solutions. In an industry that relies heavily on computer software technology, and spends ever-increasing amounts on this technology, the cost benefits and productivity gains from these investments are increasingly under scrutiny. The pendulum in the buy/build debate is swinging back towards software vendors, as increasing layers of functionality become a commodity and financial institutions focus on their core competencies. The challenge for software vendors in keeping the pendulum their way is to build significantly better software. The best way of achieving this is with software designed to take advantage of key technologies emerging from the Web and B2B e-commerce initiatives, and a solution architecture that collectively integrates services provided by many hosts and vendors on an open network.

The challenge of moving from ERM systems to universe-wide enterprise risk management systems (the universe being the enterprise and its customers) is at first sight a daunting one. However, it offers valuable benefits. These include realigning a financial institution's business processes within a CRM framework that delivers tailored services directly to individual customers by leveraging internal resources, data, systems and expertise. The evolution from enterprise- to universe-wide risk management undoubtedly offers huge opportunities to those firms that master the technology.

Overall, automated pricing and trading has indeed presaged the era of data analytics. As anecdotal testimony of this, one of the leading technology providers, Decisioneering, christened its risk analysis, forecasting and optimisation product 'Crystal Ball 2000'.

BACK-OFFICE AUTOMATION: THE HOLY GRAIL – STP

The trading process has changed beyond all recognition since the early days of the stock market, when 'curbstone brokers' stationed on the street shouted orders to clerks hanging precariously off the ledge of the Mills Building, and is on the precipice of more fundamental change. One of the most significant developments affecting the industry is the move by regulators to shorten the settlement process from trade-date-plus-three days (T+3) to trade-date-plus-one day (T+1) by June 2005. This move has been prompted by the growing risks borne of growing trade volumes. US institutional trade volume has risen from an average of 182,000 trades per day in 1995 to 418,000 in 1999, and recent market volatility has produced record spikes relative to that average. On 4 April 2000, for example, 4.38 billion shares were traded on the NASDAQ and NYSE, as the NASDAQ plummeted almost 250 points and the Dow Jones Industrial Average surged 300 points. The Securities Industry Association (SIA) predicts that trade volume will increase by 25% annually in the future, propelled, to a large extent, by technology (Schwab Institutional, 2000).

The increasing trading volume, under the T+3 regime, is imposing a high level of risk on participants across the entire trade cycle. The current system is increasingly overburdened, capacity is being strained, and the industry is experiencing a marked deterioration in processing efficiency. A recent study conducted by the Society for Worldwide Financial Telecommunications (SWIFT), for example, produced some alarming statistics (PaceMetrics, 2001):

- 59% of trades need to be amended, repaired or cancelled
- 10% of confirmations/settlements result in mismatches
- 15% of transactions fail to settle on time
- 20% of cross-border trades fail to settle on contractual settlement date.

Nor is the cost of fixing these exceptions insignificant. On a fixed cost of US$10 per trade, repairing instructions costs US$6, resolving mismatches costs US$16, and resolving settlement failure costs US$50+.

Furthermore, with the surge in cross-border investment, cross-border trade processing has also become one of the industry's top priorities. As previously indicated, compared with the relatively economical US system, clearing and settling cross-border trades costs upwards of ten times the cost of domestic clearing and settlement, for example. Furthermore, exposures to foreign exchange and legal risk, counterparty, and operational risk increase exponentially. Operational risks are aggravated by the lack of global conventions in settlement cycles and messaging protocols (although SWIFT and FIX are gaining dominance). According to the SIA (Global Investment Technology, 2001), it is estimated that 15–16% of all cross-border trades fail.

Consequently, there is widespread recognition among industry regulators and participants that if today's trade processes attempt to handle tomorrow's volumes, those risks and costs will become intolerable. That a shorter cycle time is absolutely critical has now gained wide currency. However, current systems will need to undergo extensive changes in order to operate efficiently and navigate risk in the future. The relatively low-tech methods being employed to execute and settle trades are both risky and inefficient, and industry participants now accept that the current trading system must be reengineered using technology to ensure that the integrity and safety of the trading process remains intact.

Specifically, achieving T+1 will require significant reengineering of trade processes and technologies to increase automation, reduce manual intervention, and thus eliminate redundant processes or manual data entry and hence reduce 'breaking points' that greatly increase the risk of trade failure. Breaking points represent a series of repetitive and inefficient interactions among trade participants that generally involve excessive manual steps (for example telephone calls, faxes and data entry).

The principles of straight-through-processing (STP) are commonly identified as the solution to today's problems and to achieving T+1. Essentially STP is about treating the trade cycle as a single unit, which necessitates migrating from today's sequential processing to an environment of 'seamless' integration among systems and processes (from execution, to settlement, to transaction reporting). There have been a number of high-profile industry forums concerned with this issue, two of the most high profile of which include the Global Straight Through Processing Association (GSTPA) and Omega (a joint venture between Thompson Financial and the DTCC). There is no doubt that firms will have to make large investments in solutions for T+1. According to the SIA (Accenture, 2001), the industry will need to spend US$8 billion to achieve it, but will realise US$2.7 billion in full year cost savings starting in year three.

Ultimately, the drivers of STP come in many forms – globalisation, technological convergence, the rise of e-business, the migration from cross-border to no borders, exploding trading volumes, the need for cost reduction, the industry move towards shorter settlement cycles, and specifically the looming regulatory requirement for a T+1 settlement cycle. All these forces are combining to drive the financial services industry towards a confrontation with the future. That confrontation is coming fast, and will mean that existing systems cannot be retrofitted or fine-tuned to meet the new demands.

OFFENSIVE STRATEGY: STRUCTURING

In tandem with the 'defensive' e-strategies, banks also need to pursue 'offensive' strategies. In the accelerated product lifecycles of today, 'today's innovations are tomorrow's commodities'. This calls for dual, yet polarised, competencies. In order to garner the high margins of early phase products, a bank needs to excel at product innovation, and to survive in the mature markets, it needs to excel at operational efficiency. Hence, focusing on the disciplines necessary for complex trade structuring (which, by nature, is not automatable, but does leverage computational power through modelling) is the natural complement to the e-trading strategy (see Figure 13.1).

In practice, this involves building up small teams of live traders and salespeople specialising in structuring and executing complex transactions with infrequent end-user customers. Such transactions tend to be high margin because institutional investors still need the advice, confidentiality and capital of market-makers to effect them. Thus, firms are continually designing new structured products, such as new asset-backed securities and new derivatives, to diversify trading revenues. The evolution of JP Morgan's derivative business provides an example of how securities firms are migrating from lower to higher margin products and benefiting from growing volumes. JP Morgan has always been a leader in the fast growing markets for over-the-counter deriv-

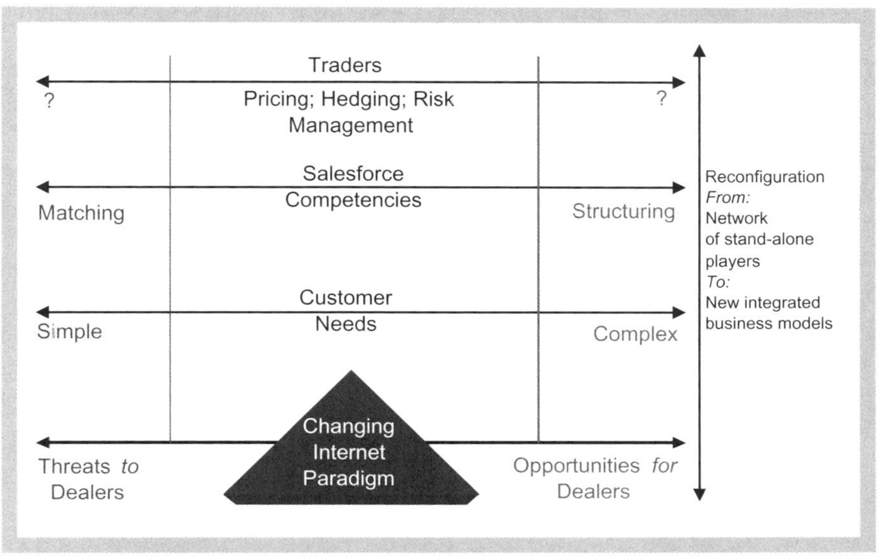

Figure 13.1 The changing Internet paradigm

Source: Wee, L.S. and Lee, J., 2000: 'Breaking Barriers', Risk, electronic trading special report, March 2000, p. 17

atives. Since the late 1980s, the overall market for OTC derivatives has grown in excess of 40% per annum, as measured by notional outstandings. This rapid growth has attracted competition and led to commoditisation of many trades. However, given the scale of JP Morgan's derivatives business, it remains very profitable, even though market-making profits have been eroded on many plain-vanilla transactions.

JP Morgan is driving down its cost of execution for more commoditised derivatives, and has cut its unit costs on these trades by almost 50% since 1996. This allows the firm to compete effectively for routine trade flows and spread costs over greater volumes. At the same time, the firm is using its global network of professionals to originate more 'structured' derivatives trades, which tend to be more profitable. Structured derivatives have grown to 50% of interest rate derivative revenues from 20% in 1997.

CONCLUSIONS

When it was first conceived, the World Wide Web was intended to democratise the flow of capital, whether it be intellectual or financial. While this process may have been retarded somewhat, with more and more investors logging on, from the rowdy day traders, to staid septuagenarians, to blue-chip institutions, eventually a more egalitarian structure is probable.

The buy-side has an insatiable thirst for cheap liquidity and over the long term will continue to seek out liquidity at a discount. For securities firms, order flow is currency, and they must therefore combat the natural tendency to preserve the status quo, or risk losing order flow. Thus, securities firms will continue to aggressively manage the forces of technology and the concomitant transparency which conspires to drive down trading margins – by automating routine trading to the highest extent possible to reduce costs, while growing volumes from a broader customer base, and warehousing complex trades. This may strain the capabilities of some firms, and operational or risk management losses are possible in this environment. However, as global capital markets deepen and trading costs fall, overall trading volumes should continue to grow, mitigating price declines. In the medium term, the advice, confidentiality and capital provided by market-makers on complex trades look difficult to automate.

CHAPTER 14

VIRTUAL REALITY BYTES

Of course, the tri-phase e-strategy plus the structuring offensive outlined above only works in theory, even the 'in practice' part is only in theory. By the business-school book, this is a strategy designed to replace man with machine, sack half the workforce, and so slash costs, pump up the volume and, through an ingenious deployment of technology, integrate businesses so that each feeds off the other, creating a virtuous or 'virtual' feeding frenzy – allowing the bank to maintain its position at the top of the food chain, milk every cash cow in perpetuity, while extending tentacles into juicy new markets. It's not even an academic work, it's a work of fiction. In reality, virtual reality bytes!

After superimposing Porter's Five Forces or any other derivation of the old 'SWOT' model to analyse the supply and demand side of the market and devising a brilliant strategy in response to what technology can do *for* and will do *to* the business of banking, many e-venturers fail to take a few first principles into account. In the first instance, network-based technologies serve to enhance market efficiencies – by reducing friction, disintermediating, facilitating a multiplicity of buyers and sellers and the free flow of information. The efficient market hypothesis taken to conclusion equals zero profit. It's hardly surprising then that many new economy ventures can't make the economic numbers add up. John L Langton, the CEO of the International Securities Market Association (ISMA), has been quoted as saying that 'the fundamental purpose of banks and securities houses is to make as much money as possible, from as many people as possible, so long as it doesn't upset the regulators'. Apparently, a few banks forgot about this *raison d'être* in conceiving their e-businesses. To be more explicit, one of the most fundamental success factors in this environment is scale. This is expanded upon below, but suffice it to say that a reinforcing three-pronged strategy comprising stakes in numerous e-markets, true STP and AI is not for the lessor specimens of the banking world.

Apart from basic economics, a few other things have gone wrong in the implementation of e-strategies. When the eminent financial journal *Euromoney* bestowed its inaugural wholesale banking Internet awards in 2000, it was with some reluctance. The tone of the journal's authors was positively scathing. They pronounced the collective efforts of the world's leading investment banks to migrate their businesses to the Internet 'a mess', citing fundamental business mistakes that would never be permitted in their traditional operations. Quoting an exasperated survey respondent, the report stated that 'Banks are spending millions and millions on their e-strategy, but they can't answer the simple question "what are you actually doing?". They will just reply "we are spending millions and millions on it".' In awarding the best Internet site in wholesale finance, *Euromoney* concluded that 'no bank comes anywhere near to deserving it this year'.

Success in e-business still requires the same basics of good business sense – a clear strategy, strong leadership and management, good communication, high-quality products across the full range of markets they serve, a strong brand, and integration with operations. According to *Euromoney* in 2000, none had put all these building blocks in place. Indeed none had come close. By 2001, some of the damage had been undone, but banks still had some distance to go. Among the many failings of banks in e-enabling themselves, the following were identified as recurring.

Poor Leadership, Confused Strategic Objectives and Strategy and a Lack of Cohesion

The random plucking of any old dealer off the dealing room floor and anointing him with a fancy e-commerce VP title and office was the downfall of many a bank's e-business division. But the misalignment with the organisational structure was even more fundamental. The relationship between technology, the trading operation, and the value creation process itself had not been clearly defined, resulting in the e-business team functioning as mere ineffectual gofers, or the technical team acting as if it were omnipotent. Fortunately, most banks have now ditched their e-business divisions and cleared up reporting lines. Almost across the board, e-business teams are no longer their own little empires, with little to show for it and no one to answer to. For the most part, e-business is being integrated into the business so that it is not out there trying to cannibalise or compete against it. This restructuring, however, has yet to bear fruit.

Poor Communication

Another problem identified was that of poor internal (as well as external) communication, leading to rumour mongering and suspicion among those potentially threatened by technology. The e-business team dubbing itself 'deathofasalesman.com', as was the case in one instance, is hardly conducive to securing critical buy-in or support. While e-business hasn't quite shaken off its 'grim reaper' stigma, and the fear felt by traders that their job is at stake to machines has not quite abated, the reality is that technology has actually caused few redundancies. The steep growth curve in many product markets has resulted in technology simply being leveraged to avoid significantly expanding headcount. Resistance is slowly being overcome, especially in the area of analytics, which is being used more by internal than external clients. In these pioneering fields, the boundaries between technology and the business are blurring, as the former becomes increasingly integral to the latter.

Channel Conflict and Migration Issues

Channel conflict and/or migration issues have also been poorly addressed. Many banks were and still are too aggressive in their migration strategies, failing to recognise that old habits die hard and that clients need to be enticed online, not bulldozed. In many instances, smaller clients who insist on doing simple trades on the phone are being slowly cut off by the bank without due accounting for the loss sustained.

Competitors, What Competitors?

In developing their online product and service offerings, banks have paid scant attention to their competitive environment. Many had no idea what rivals were doing at launch, leading to ignorance and paranoia, unsubstantiated 'World First' claims and, significantly, a lack of competitive positioning and no differentiation. And, as *Euromoney* noted, 'they think a link to the homepage of the Tokyo Stock Exchange is cutting edge technology'.

Lack of marketing orientation

Although many banks are now more clued up on what their rivals are doing, they still haven't gone back to basics on the demand side. It seems that few have developed their new products on the basis of meeting known customer needs, in fact many seem not to know who the customer is at all. Large segments of the market are currently very poorly serviced, such as the corporates and issuers. Banks have a long way to go before they can swear that they truly know what their clients want from the electronic medium.

Unresolved Co-optition/Competition Issues

As alluded to before, many banks have not distinguished between a venture capital and strategic investment with respect to consortia e-markets. In the course of the *Euromoney* surveys, it became apparent that in certain instances bank employees don't even know which consortia they're in. And at 'desk' level, many are clinging to their proprietary sites while paying lip service to the multi-dealers – which they view as a tax on business they're somehow entitled to. Moreover, the 'open' markets have been marred by politics, secrecy and a lack of plain old small business management know-how – another instance of arbitrary leadership. One anonymous survivor of an ill-fated consortium venture confided the following to the *Euromoney* investigators:

> Most platforms are set up by traders. They have no idea how to run a company. None have ever run a company or small business. The bank just plucks them off the trading floor, gives them money and says: 'Run the site'. Banks need to re-think if they want a future in the commoditised markets.

In sum, banks have travelled some way down the learning curve – and have learnt some hard lessons. By the end of 2001, some serious advances had been made in certain respects. Online analytics, for example, had come into their own. The tools that some firms now offer are impressive, bringing new levels of transparency to clients, giving them the same portfolio modelling and pricing capabilities as the banks themselves have, even for complex products. *Euromoney* identified UBS Warburg, JP Morgan Chase, Morgan Stanley and Goldman Sachs as among the best. But the Web is still not fulfilling its potential. No one bank stands out as the best overall in online wholesale finance across all disciplines – forex, equities, fixed income and derivatives – from pre-trade data, research and analytics, through to execution and settlement, and co-operates optimally with rivals on multi-bank solutions. In the interim, it is the technology vendors who are leading the way. As *Euromoney* noted, 'No matter who wins the war, the arms dealers will always make money'.

CHAPTER 15

THE NET STRATEGIC IMPACT OF TECHNOLOGY ON THE BUSINESS OF SECURITIES TRADING

To conclude this section on the strategic response of broker-dealers to this unprecedented wave of technological change, we will review the net effect of technology on securities houses' traditional lines of business: market-making, its dependent, proprietary trading, as well as institutional brokerage and corporate treasury business. The critical factors for success in the new environment and the positioning options available to larger and smaller players respectively are identified as well as the emerging competitive environment.

THE NEW ECONOMICS OF MARKET-MAKING

As noted previously, principal transactions income accounts for one-third of pre-tax profits earned by the banks rated by Moody's (2000). The agencies' favourable opinion of the business of securities trading (implied in the favourable credit ratings of banks with a skewed dependence thereon), is apparently not shared by investors, however. Investors express their low opinion explicitly in low price-to-earnings ratios. According to analysis performed by

McKinsey (Davidson et al., 2001), banks that earn a relatively high proportion of their income from trading (including market-making, brokerage and principal trading) are consistently penalised by the market, exhibiting relatively low P:E ratios.

In reality, however, the economics of market-making and brokerage compare well with those of other core banking activities, such as underwriting securities and managing assets. According to McKinsey (Davidson et al., 2001), over the past 20 years, trading revenue has grown just as fast as other sources of bank income (refer to Figure 15.1) and has been only marginally more volatile. Despite declining margins, in the aggregate, US and European securities firms have responded aggressively and succeeded in counteracting its erosion. In those markets in which profits on plain-vanilla facilitation trades are already quite low, securities firms have succeeded in cutting costs and growing volume by automating and multi-channelling. In many commoditised products, volumes are growing more quickly than margins are falling. The most prominent example of this is in the equity markets in the US and Europe, where turnover has grown at rates exceeding 25% per annum over the past decade.[1]

The success of Knight Trading Group provides anecdotal evidence of the attractive returns to be earned by providing electronic liquidity in such markets. Knight is interesting because it is essentially a 'pure' day-trading firm, deriving over 95% of its revenues from this source. Knight is also the leading market-maker on the NASDAQ with a market share of close to 20%. The firm's trading technology allows it to handle up to 1.5 million trades per day, and even as spreads on OTC stocks have compressed, Knight has enjoyed great success, as higher volumes and volatilities of stocks have presented strong trading opportunities. Knight's average revenue per trade fell from US$11.05 per trade in 1997 to US$8.51 per trade in 1999. In spite of this compression, pre-tax income rose over 400% to US$279 million, as trade volume more than tripled over the time frame.

In fact, overall, trading revenue has grown even faster than other income sources in recent years because of the global boom in securities trading. From 1995 to 1999, market-making and brokerage revenue grew at an 18% clip annually, slightly faster than the overall average revenue for the whole securities industry. At the same time, the trading of securities accounted for more than half the total revenue growth for some of the largest securities firms, as accounted for in Figure 15.2. On the whole, margins in market-making and brokerage can be just as attractive as margins in other banking activities. Some banks are realising a return on equity of well over 20% from making markets for traditional cash equities, while margins for more innovative products (such as derivatives) or for the provision of trade-related services can top 40%. This

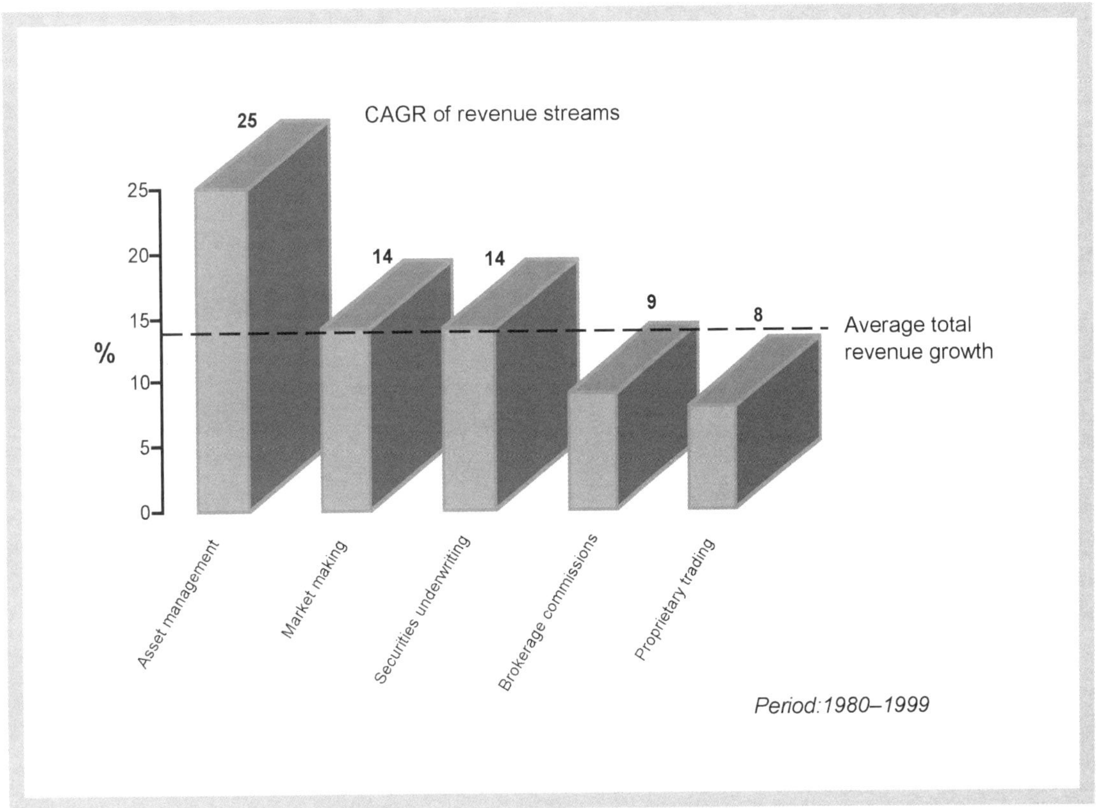

Figure 15.1 Market-making keeps pace
Source: Securities Industry Association, 2002

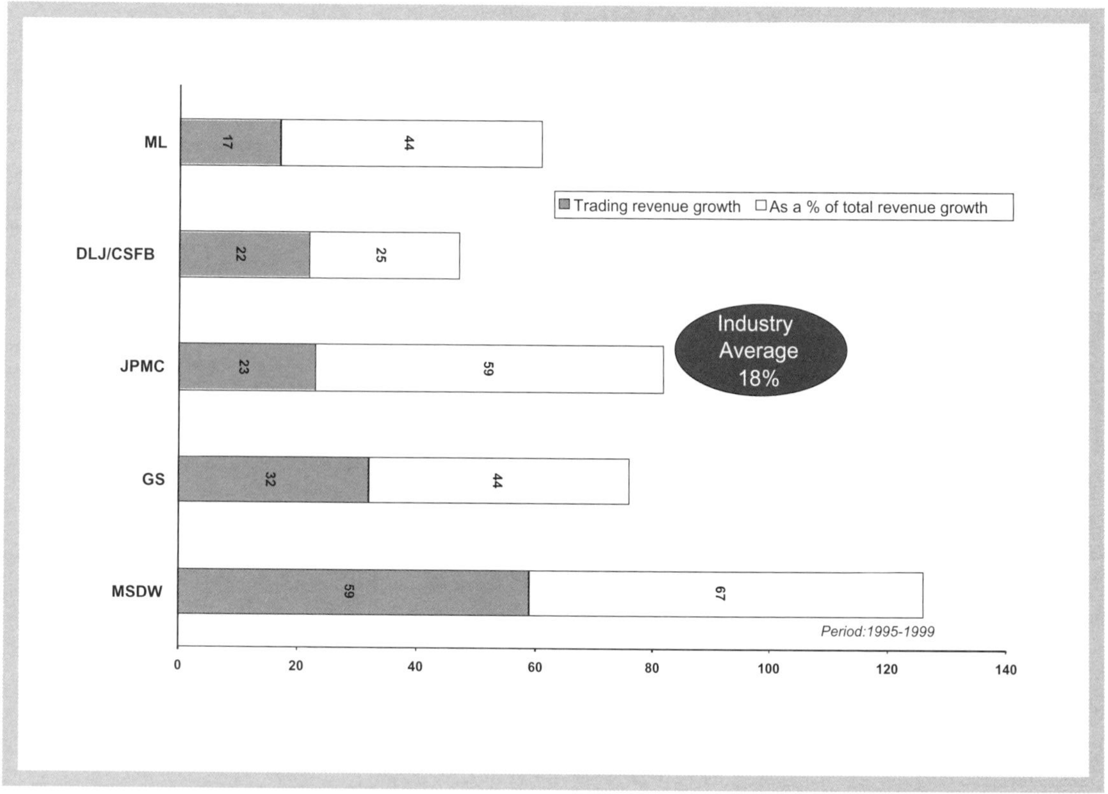

Figure 15.2 Wall Street power houses exhibit hyper-growth in trading revenue
Source: Securities Industry Association, 2002

compares very favourably with the 10–30% earned in underwriting and asset management.

As we look to the future, securities firms are predicting an even fiercer operating environment. In a survey of its members conducted by ISMA (Langton, 2001), three-quarters expected margins to have halved within three years. However, historically, trading volumes surged every time the structure and efficiency of markets improved, for example following the 1986 'Big Bang' reforms at the London Stock Exchange, and the 1997 Order Handling Rules in the US, so future prospects are good. Under the structural reformation currently underway in global markets, trade volume growth is predicted to reach over 25% annually in the aggregate. Market-making can still be attractive for participants who use technology to automate the trading process and gain scale. And herein lies the catch. All banks, whether they choose to compete fully or not, should decide how to position themselves.

CRITICAL SUCCESS FACTORS: SCALE

If market-making and brokerage is an attractive business, why do so many industry players malign it? The main reason is the schizophrenic role of technology. McKinsey asserts that far from killing the business, technology will actually save it (Davidson et al., 2001). Commissions and spreads are falling, and this trend won't be reversed. The old people-intensive business model, for the most part, no longer holds. Huge parts of the business – trading in bonds, cash equities, and standardised derivatives – are becoming commoditised. Winning in this environment will require banks to reach unprecedented scale, and a handful of them will take the lion's share of the profits. But emerging technologies will make competing in this new environment profitable for the eventual winners, allowing them to increase dramatically the volume of trades they can process while lowering their costs and increasing their profitability. The leading players will recognise that technology is an advantage, not a threat.

New systems can automate everything from front-end order capture to back-office clearing and settlement. Paradoxically, technology can also increase margins per trade. For example, new order-management software can automatically break up and manage large block trades to minimise their impact on market prices, thereby giving the customer a better price and boosting margins in the process. Provided volume is sufficient, internal matching systems enable banks to capture the full spread and avoid exchange fees; while CRM software can increase margins per account and may boost trading volumes as well. Increasingly, winning banks will need to provide services beyond trade execution, such as prime brokerage.

Investing in these new technologies obviously raises the fixed costs of any trading business. Scale, which makes the business more attractive in several other ways, will therefore be needed. Besides lowering the marginal cost per trade, a greater volume of orders cuts volatility and risk. With a larger order flow, an institution can match more of its trades internally, thereby putting up less capital in each transaction and holding a smaller inventory of securities. As a result, and as confirmed by analysis performed by McKinsey, there is a clear negative correlation between trading revenue and the value at risk (VAR) relative to trading volume (Davidson, 2001). Merrill Lynch and Morgan Stanley Dean Witter, for example, have a much lower VAR relative to their trading revenue than do firms that have smaller order flows, such as Donaldson, Lufkin & Jenrette. Bigger companies will find trading to be a more stable and profitable business.

In capturing additional order flow, players will also benefit from diversification. Institutional orders from mutual fund managers, pension funds and insurance companies are important because of those orders' size and overall share of the market. But many institutional investor segments trade infrequently and tend to base their buy and hold activities on fundamental portfolio decisions. Hedge funds are usually more active traders, with average turnover rates that are three or more times the size of their assets, so their order flow can provide valuable real-time information on market conditions. And banks can't ignore retail customers: smaller trades are easier to execute and more richly priced. Furthermore, small orders (a proxy for retail trades) now represent around 70% of all trades executed in OTC stocks, up from 57% in 1994. Orders from outside the US will also be important, given the rapid growth of global securities trading.

THE FUTURE OF PROPRIETARY TRADING

Proprietary trading has received a huge amount of well-deserved bad press of late. These activities are essentially no different from what hedge funds do, but while George Soros's investors are prepared, at least in theory, to stomach huge losses as well as gains, shareholders of blue-chip banks are not. In recent years such opportunities have been more limited, and the resulting risk of these trades is perhaps better left to hedge funds, whose investors can diversify their own portfolios appropriately.

Most major banks have now scaled down these speculative activities, but taking principal positions is a necessary and potentially lucrative part of market-making. The difference is that such positions are closely related to customer business, not speculative bets. In making markets or executing a large client trade, a bank must often take on some or most of the position for a period and stands to gain (or lose) from price movements during that time. In fixed-income businesses, trading gains (or losses) from this kind of activity can overwhelm spread or commission revenues. Naturally, banks also gain valuable information about market sentiment from market-making. They can, and should, exploit this information to manage their inventory of securities efficiently and (if risk limits are observed) to gain from taking principal positions for the bank's account.

IMPLICATIONS: COMPETITIVE ENVIRONMENT OF THE FUTURE

Clearly competing in this new environment isn't cheap and calls for very deep pockets. Consequently for banks of varying size different, and sometimes difficult, choices will have to be made. Institutions with a strong share of trading volume should move full-speed ahead. Given the scale and speed needed to win, mergers and acquisitions are the most promising way to obtain new technology and order flow quickly; relying on organic growth will be difficult. Another shortcut to growing order flow is buying it from brokerages or smaller broker-dealers. A global presence is a necessity, since much of the growth will take place outside the United States, and some new technologies, and institutional learning, can be leveraged globally. To gain a foothold in other countries, acquisitions, joint ventures and alliances will be the primary penetration strategy. Technology, scale, and skills will differentiate the best from the rest.

Goliath will Inherit the Future

The foregoing discussion of the critical factors for success in this new electronic environment and the capitalisation preconditions have some ominous implications for those who do not meet these and the likely competitive landscape of the future.

Interestingly, nearly every major innovation in market history has been the result of co-operation among powerful and well-capitalised industry rivals. In 17th-century Japan, big rice merchants protected themselves from radical price swings by inventing a futures market. In late 18th-century New York, stock operators, threatened by a law forbidding public stock transactions, established a private association: the New York Stock Exchange (NYSE). In mid-19th-century Chicago, leading merchants formed the Chicago Board of Trade to provide members with market information and later a trading floor (*The Point*, 2001).

Like their predecessors in Japan, New York and Chicago, a handful of the most dominant global financial organisations are suspending their normally fierce competition to collaborate in creating new, for-profit electronic marketplaces. This elite group of power players is well on the way to dominating trading, clearing and settlement worldwide. As these giants grow larger and stronger, small firms will either be devoured or marginalised and left to forage for viable niche segments to survive.

According to Accenture, once the transformation is complete, the giants will sit unrivalled atop (*The Point*, 2001). Regardless of their national origins, these firms will solidify their positions as vast global players. About 20 firms, mostly from the United States and Europe, may try to break into the ranks of the global giants, but most will fail. Currently, fewer than 10 institutions qualify as global players, and the number will probably shrink. Only these firms have the order flow, market power and positioning necessary to make the new electronic markets work. Liquidity begets liquidity – by establishing markets to meet their own needs, the giants command liquidity on their own terms

What of David?

In the long term, as pressures mount, firms that cannot make the transition to 'low-cost mass liquidity provider' will be forced to retreat from market-making in certain products. This will be aggravated not only by the capital entry barriers to retaining margins (through high automation and high volume), but the tolerance for negative margins by the super powers as well. Apparently, some already only remain active in certain markets in order to have access to flow information that can be used for proprietary trading.

Certain dealers may reconsider their business models – scaling down on trading in commoditised and low-margin products and outsourcing it. A withdrawal from market-making could involve an allocation of less risk capital in the aggregate. However, given the price compression that has gone on in many products, the reduced risk appetite of securities firms seems sensible.

Moreover, as dealers reposition themselves, they may use the potential for the 'unbundling' of services that electronic trading facilitates. The foreign exchange product set supplied by banks to their clients provides an example. It consists of four distinct elements. The first of these is research. This includes conventional economic research publications, flow and technical analysis, and the strategic and tactical advice given to clients by FX salespeople.[2] The second element is credit risk; the risk of counterparty default assumed in transacting any FX deal. The third element is market risk; the market-directional risk a bank effectively takes over from the client when it transacts a deal. The fourth and final element is settlement, which includes all the required confirmations and payments. Banks currently package together all these services to their clients and charge for them implicitly through the bid/offer spread in their FX prices. Electronic dealing offers the opportunity to unbundle these products and services. This would be advantageous because banks are generally effective at providing some of these elements, and less effective at providing others. One bank may be excellent at assessing credit risk on its clients, but not have the skills and resources required to manage the market risk on the FX deals those clients transact. Another bank may be excellent at market-making, but may lack the FX business volumes to justify the investment in the infrastructure required to handle settlements efficiently. Even within one of these elements, a bank may display variable abilities. For example, in managing market risk, a European regional bank may be excellent at making markets in the euro and other European currencies, but may lack similar skills in Asian regional currencies. In time, banks will focus on their core strengths and outsource the remaining functions, concentrating on some but probably not all of these four functions.

Platforms such as FXall purport to offer each member bank the opportunity to concentrate on those elements of the FX product set where it can deliver exceptional quality, and to outsource those elements more effectively handled by a third party, which will enable banks to offer their clients a full FX service of the highest quality throughout. This process is commonly known as 'white labelling'. The white labelling outsourcing model is increasingly popular in the FX market, but it is only on an e-platform that this can be exploited to the full. Using white labelling, the client need not be aware that third parties are supplying elements of the product set. For example, the FXall platform will provide an automated dealing capability whereby, if a customer can't get an FX quote in a particular currency pair from bank A, this request is seamlessly passed on to bank B. The market risk is assumed by bank B, while the credit risk is assumed by bank A.

Another example of this unbundling is the 'prime brokerage' model. This is where a client chooses to concentrate the booking of all FX deals, and the associated credit risk, with one bank, while continuing to source pricing from and deal with a number of different banks. In the previous example, the customer goes direct to bank B for the quote, then 'gives up' the settlement to bank A. The inter-bank 'back-to-back' deals required to facilitate this are today often booked in a manual and labour-intensive manner. FXall will automate this process fully. This should deliver a significant boost to the development of prime brokerage in the FX market. The fourth product, settlement, will become highly automated and much more sophisticated, with bilateral and multilateral netting becoming the norm. FXall contends that one of the clearest business principles to emerge in the past few years is the need to 'do what you do the best and outsource the rest'.

Finally, all intermediaries, but especially those adjusting their position in the food chain, have to re-evaluate their human resource management, which will change as a result of the introduction of electronic trading. For example, they will possibly require a different mix of skills from their salesforce, emphasising advice and relationship more than execution, which will also be reflected in a change from current incentives and pay structures. It is worth emphasising that while the Internet will provide straight-through-processing, it will not provide straight-through-thinking. There will always be room for the knowledge worker in the knowledge economy.

David's Survival: Guts and Glory

Finally, these platitudes aside, a few plain language observations pertaining to smaller players are warranted. In the land of the giants, 'squandering squillions' was the order of the e-mania heyday. By contrast, it was non-headline-grabbing paralysis that afflicted many of the smaller players. A business school textbook analysis of the landscape of the future thrust many smaller players into analysis paralysis mode as they struggled to find a position for themselves in the emerging topography or to find ways to overcome apparently insurmountable scale entry barriers. As the pioneering independents in the virgin e-market terrain were turned to road kill when the Wall Street superpowers steamrollered into these new territories, it provided proof-positive of the futility of avant-guardism for many smaller banks.

However, since standing frozen like a rabbit caught in the headlights has never yet proved to be an effective response to environmental changes, smaller players need to take advantage of the hiatus that the global economic slump has afforded and rethink their response. They need to grasp that the key to survival lies in a combination of guerrilla strategies rather than offensive or defensive ones. First, the evolution of existing market structures may be severely retarded in certain regions, and particularly emerging market regions. The delay may be due to technological, including raw bandwidth, constraints (a product of regulation in the telecommunications sectors), as well as because of the inadvertent protectionism afforded to banks by capital account regulation. As we have observed, regulatory stimulus is as important a catalyst to structural change as technology. The existence of exchange rate regimes, for example, may serve to prohibit locally domiciled and listed corporations and institutional investors from participating on global electronic markets in the immediate future. So for niche players with a clear regional target segment, the need to shift from closed to open trading may not be immediate. Moreover, when the stay of execution is over, and the shift does occur, these players may be well positioned to at least dominate a regional market centre that is underserved by the global platform. Alternatively, these players may be able to position further down a global food chain, by tendering to act as a regional CCP on global exchanges on an outsource basis. More broadly, the emerging markets for commodities and risk represent a real growth opportunity for smaller, regionally-based players, not least in terms of internationalising their business.

Generally, banks, especially smaller banks, are justifiably loath to attempt to venture into new markets (to trade on a proprietary basis) in which they lack some form of clear competitive advantage, such as is derived from market-making in the form of informational advantages. While data analytics may eventually serve as a substitute for data asymmetries, programme trading is, as yet, no better than punting in the dark. And while electronic trading networks now provide a reasonably inexpensive delivery channel for price-making to new markets, attracting order flow as a no-name brand lacking in infrastructure certainly isn't easy either. However, in some of the emerging product markets, smaller regionally focused banks have a real edge.

As mentioned previously, ultimately all markets are a fulcrum between risk-sellers (or hedgers) and risk-buyers (or speculators). Credit derivatives and their future derivatives provide a mechanism by which a lender can strip out and sell undesirable risk, leaving him with a relatively stable investment and potential return thereon. Similarly, it provides a borrower with a mechanism to reduce his credit risk premium and hence his cost of capital. The more risk is disaggregated over time, the more borrowers will be able to cut the number of basis points over a benchmark rate attributable to externalities, such as political risk, industrial action, catastrophes and so on. It should be obvious that such instruments are tailor-made for emerging market or developing country FDI.

In addition to product innovation for the hedging of capital market investments (equity or debt), new applications of risk derivatives are also facilitating the hedging of cash flow risk borne by the ultimate physical infrastructure investor (be it a factory, utility, mine operator, or other entity). Swaps, options, forwards and so on are now being employed in many capital-intensive heavy industries (such as steel, pulp, petrochemicals, coal, gas, shipping and so on), which tend to characterise less-developed economies.

The propulsion for the issuance of such risk hedging instruments has been the emergence of liquid secondary markets. In these second-stage product markets that are in the process of liquefying and commoditising, the electronic medium facilitates liquidity sourcing. With the birth of the Net, hedgers and speculators can be connected globally and thereby create liquid secondary markets in these innovative instruments, which ultimately benefits the primary market.

A prominent emerging market intermediary is ideally positioned in this development cycle, as it has both the source of these new issues on tap for origination and will remain linked to the end-users and underlying markets in its secondary trading activities. Over the long term, the growth in this type of market is likely to be exponential. A shortage of capital is the fundamental constraint on emerging market economic growth and, especially since the pre-millennium emerging market crisis, these economies have suffered from risk aversion by the capital exporters. With the convergence of product innovation and Net-generated liquidity in this new era, however, FDI and indirect capital inflows may surge once again.

Ultimately, smaller players need to re-evaluate their business from an electronic media perspective. They need to assess their existing target market segments in terms of their current corporate and institutional investor client base's needs, especially in terms of their international expansion and capital-raising activities. They need to estimate the threat posed by international competitors. And they need to re-evaluate the product and service and channel offering, across the supply chain, and its configuration in an environment of client-centric multidisciplinary solutions. Finally, they need to seek new business opportunities and growth potential arising out of technology, all from a perspective of imagination, not imitation. In other words, mimicking the formulae of the Goliaths will be suicidal for the Davids. These players need to position themselves in geographic or other market and product niches (such as debt origination, securitisation in lieu of factoring, distressed debt disposal, trade finance and so on) where they will retain competitive advantage through a focused value proposition and aligned set of competencies.

THE FUTURE OF INSTITUTIONAL BROKERAGE

As a somewhat separate business to market-making and proprietary trading, recent developments indicate that institutional brokerage is also poised for fundamental change over the next three to five years. The emergence of new trading technologies, new onerous disclosure regulations, the resulting decline in (per-share) commission rates and the growing importance of in-house research capabilities signal an industry in the early stages of flux. More significantly, these developments have begun jeopardising the very source of institutional brokerages' value proposition, compelling them to begin to attune to such changes, anticipate how their organisations will be affected, and formulate the most appropriate strategic response in order to serve clients in the new and more demanding environment to come.

Evaluating Brokers' Traditional Services: Research, Not Execution, is What Counts

At their core, institutional brokerages provide just two basic services to their institutional investor or asset manager clients:

1 research, and

2 trade execution capabilities.

A Reuters survey (Okin, 2001) conducted by Tempest shows that asset managers attach far greater value to research in selecting and compensating their brokers; assigning over 80% of commission dollars in respect of analysts' telephone calls and site visits, research, and support services. Especially critical is research analysts' ability to respond quickly to breaking news and to evaluate its impact on the performance of current and planned investment strategies. Only 20% of commission is assigned on the basis of efficient trade execution, and, in fact, most asset managers view trade flow simply as compensation for good research.

Closer examination of the 20% assigned to trade execution reveals only four distinct but interdependent points of value provided by brokers:

- *Anonymity*, which shields asset managers' intentions from the market.
- *Order working*, or matching, either by finding a natural match for a large order, or by executing multiple smaller orders.
- *Price improvement*, whereby brokers execute trades at the best possible price, ideally beating the volume weighted average price (VWAP) for the day.
- *Liquidity and market-making*, providing immediacy of execution by acting as the principal and accepting the market risk, or by rapidly finding a counterparty.

When all four of these points of value are fully replaced by technology, the traditional role of the institutional broker will cease.

Recent Developments Erode Brokers' Value in the Food Chain

These traditional points of value for both research and execution have already begun to weaken in the face of several recent changes.

1. The Emergence of Alternative Markets

First, the emergence of electronic communication networks (ECNs) and electronic trading networks in general, particularly the buy-side to buy-side variety, has provided institutional investors with access to faster, cheaper alternative markets, where they can trade in secret, bypassing the brokers altogether. This trading channel will become even more attractive as ECNs integrate with asset managers' in-house order-management systems, using standard industry formats or protocols to facilitate seamless order flow directly to and from portfolio managers.

2. Direct-access Order Routing Technology

Second, allied to this, the increasing penetration of technology that provides direct access to multiple electronic marketplaces is supplanting brokers in order routing.

Transaction costs, speed, anonymity and order control are the factors most often cited by next-generation stock traders when they explain the evolution and growth of so-called direct-access technology.

Direct-access software, which allows stock traders to route orders electronically and expeditiously to multiple execution destinations, without any intervention from an intermediary (see Figures 15.3 and 15.4), has been around, in various iterations, since the mid-1990s. But the technology really started to gain ground in 1997, following the implementation of SEC-mandated Order Handling Rules, which were intended to level the playing field for smaller US equity investors, and which gave rise to a plethora of ECNs (equity trade-matching engines that electronically crossed customers' buy and sell orders). Following the emergence of ECNs, which quickly seized significant market share in NASDAQ stocks, investors needed a fast and cheap electronic mechanism for routing orders to these matching engines. Consequently, direct-access vendors started to emerge, and today there are more than 20 providers of the technology.

Most of the current direct-access suppliers cater mainly to active day traders. Transaction cost savings was the benefit that initially lured them. Since these rapid-fire traders were actively buying and selling stocks throughout the course of a day, they needed an inexpensive mechanism for entering and routing orders. Direct-access vendors met that need. A recent industry study (Sales, 2002), for example, shows that direct access enables individual investors to reduce their transaction costs by up to 25 to 30 basis points. In fact, at the macro-level, direct-access order routing to ECNS is a key factor contributing to a current average trade execution cost of US$10, compared to approximately US$200 a few years ago.

Other factors – including order control and speed – have also contributed significantly to the rise of direct access. Using a direct-access system, an investor can control which execution destination their order gets routed to, such as a preferred market-maker or ECN, for example. Speedy order routing

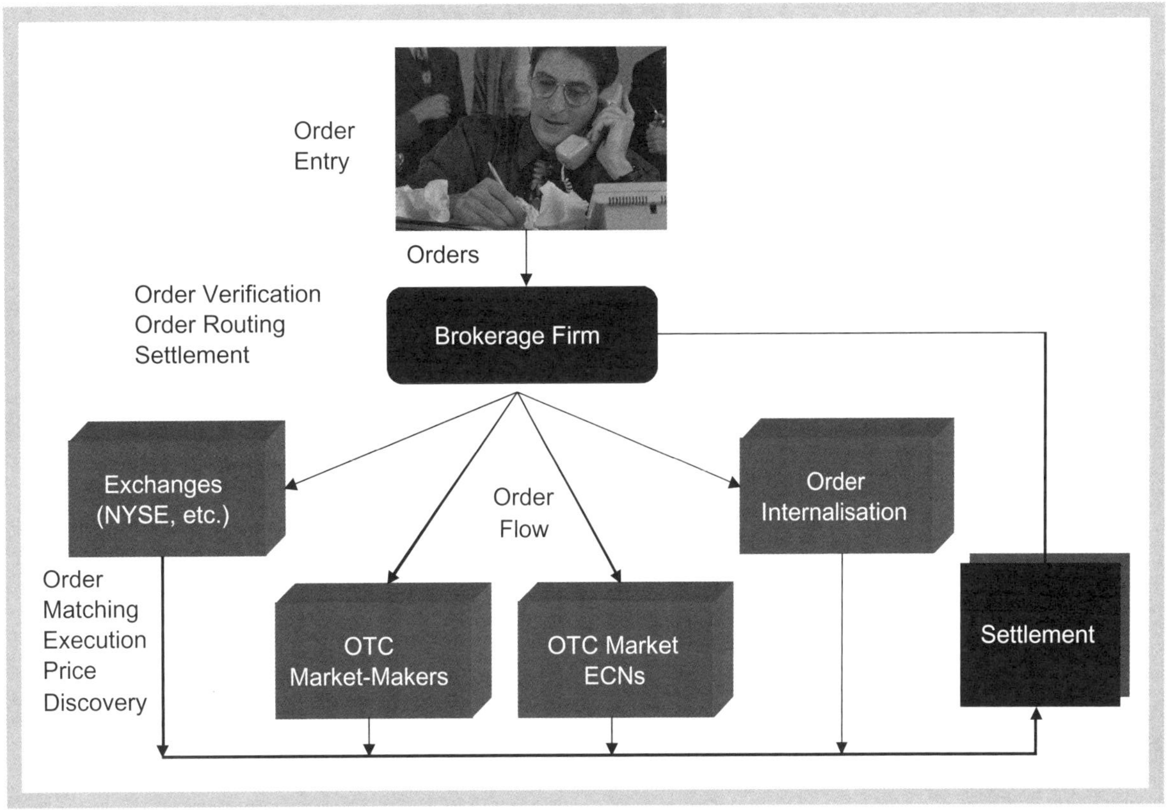

Figure 15.3 Broker-mediated trading process with multiple destinations

Source: Fan et al., 2000

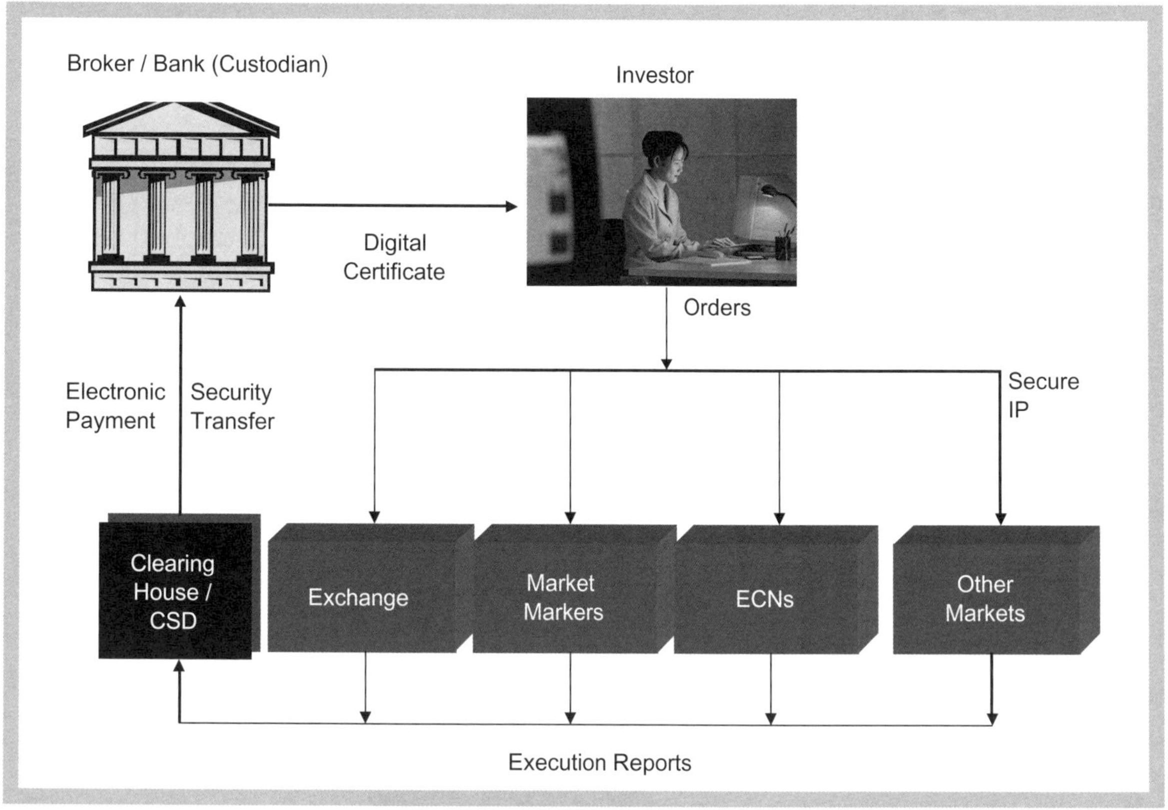

Figure 15.4 Direct trading model
Source: Fan et al., 2000

and filling is another advantage. Using direct access, an investor can route out a 50,000 share order for Cisco's stock and get filled on the Archipelago or Instinet ECN inside of 15 seconds, for example. What day traders initially discerned was that if they could execute a trade within microseconds, they could take advantage of movement, whether it be up or down, in a stock. Technology vendors provided the platform to realise that scenario. Quicker execution and control of orders ultimately enables investors to achieve a better execution price, which is again related to transaction costs.

Although direct-access trading has experienced most of its growth in the day-trading community, buy-side institutions – particularly smaller hedge funds – have developed an appetite for the technology over the past 12 months.

Buy-side traders are less sensitive about best price than active day traders because they have to execute a certain amount of large block orders in a given day and can't necessarily afford to wait for a stock to move two ticks in their direction. Hence, initially, many were indifferent to direct access. However, as buy-siders gained more knowledge about the cost and other efficiency benefits derived from the technology, they started to leverage it.

One of the reasons that the buy-side's usage of direct-access software has increased is because the number of trades institutional traders have to execute on a given day has increased significantly over the last decade. With the rise of ECNs, the number of small orders executed in the NASDAQ market began to rise. Since there were fewer large buy and sell orders to be had, institutional traders trying to complete big block orders were obliged to execute more trades. Consequently, since they needed a fast and efficient electronic mechanism for performing more 'mini-executions', institutional traders began to warm to direct access. Ultimately, of course, the technology provides a mechanism by which institutional investors can systematically access multiple pools of liquidity on an equal basis.

Another factor contributing to direct-access popularity on the buy-side is the software upgrades performed by direct-access software vendors. Today's direct-access technology is infinitely more flexible than trading software developed a couple of years ago, allowing institutions to perform more sophisticated transactions, such as:

- Electronic block order working
- Basket trading
- Program trading.

New order-management software, as we have indicated, can automatically break up and manage large trades to minimise their impact on market prices, thereby giving the customer a better price. This is particularly useful in portfolio reallocations, which entail the trading of large blocks of many different securities. Using new electronic trading algorithms, trades of 100,000 (or even a million) shares may soon be executed electronically. Although the need for manual order working of large block trades still exists, the minimum size that qualifies as 'upstairs' is increasing immeasurably. The effectiveness of asset basket trading algorithms has also improved significantly, enabling investors to trade a bundle of securities simultaneously in a virtually unified market, instead of dealing in discrete ones, helping them to balance a diversified portfolio more efficiently and effectively. Moreover, the mechanism performs the function of market intermediary, automatically recombining stock price combinations from different sellers to satisfy the buyer's request for a specific bundle. Programme trading applications linked to order routing has also become a *force majeure*, but this is beyond the scope of this book. In addition, direct access has also given buy-side firms the ability to either supplement or replace their legacy-trader order-management and portfolio management systems.

Interest from the buy-side, supplemented by the launch of aggressive institutional strategies by a range of direct-access vendors, has helped the technology sustain its growth. The number of transactions executed by direct-access traders has steadily risen and, according to Celent Communications (Sales, 2002), a research and consulting firm, is predicted to continue to rise from 155 million in 2001 to 247 million in 2004.

While there is, undoubtedly, scope for further direct-access growth on the buy-side, it is predicted that large buy-side firms will, in the future, increasingly use direct-access technology to supplement their existing relationships with broker/dealers, but are not, however, expected to terminate their relationship with the brokers altogether.

3. Effect: Disintermediation

As technology advances and participants throughout the financial markets become more electronically connected, manual execution will wane, and the proportion of trading conducted directly between institutions will continue to increase dramatically. This shift will be driven primarily by asset managers' fiduciary responsibility to reduce costs. The pressure for cost savings through automation will be greatest for unmanaged funds – historically one of the best performing classes – because their research needs are minimal and trading expenses and related costs are often the largest drags on fund performance. From an institutional brokerage perspective, these trends equal disintermediation, and in the face of the mounting challenge to retain business, brokers need to find ways to reintermediate in the new configuration, in order to remain relevant.

4. The Internet, Regulation, and the Impact on 'Info-mediation'

In addition to the erosion of the value of trade execution, the criticality of the brokers' role in 'info-mediation' is also being diluted by both technological and regulatory developments. The Internet has made tools and data such as analyst recommendations, estimates and first call revisions, news feeds, charts, trading oscillators, market forecasts and insider trading available instantly online. Once the exclusive province of leading-edge institutional traders, these tools now are readily accessible by asset managers and even small retail investors. Moreover, new best execution rules and the US SEC's ban on selective disclosure[3] will narrow the relative information and analytic advantage that brokers have enjoyed over asset managers. Brokers are being forced to upgrade their advisory capabilities in order to convince investors that they still add superior value.

5. Straight-through-processing

Institutional brokerage firms are facing pressures related to massive volume growth and deteriorating operational efficiency. This pressure is particularly acute in cross-border trading, which is growing exponentially. Consequently, the need to expand capacity, mitigate risk and contain operating costs has become urgent. At industry level, this has manifested in mandatory trade settlement cycle compression to T+1 by 2005, achievable through a high degree of automation in transaction processing – the ultimate version of which is dubbed straight-through-processing (STP).

6. Market Structure

More broadly, the unprecedented changes taking place in the macro technological and regulatory environments are altering the very structure of markets. Institutional brokerage firms function within and are directly affected by this macro-environment and therefore need to stay attuned to these changes and adapt time to new structures as they evolve.

Creating a New Future

1. Enhancing Order-routing Capability

Competition from buy-side to buy-side markets, as well as from multiple market access vendors, market fragmentation, increasing globalisation and demand for multi-asset class trading capability are inducing brokerage firms to reach an ever-increasing number of execution venues. Thus, in the first instance, firms need to boost their order-routing capabilities and maintain links to the best pools of liquidity, so that they can better compete with the vendors. These liquidity pools include the new entrants, such as ECNs, which exist across numerous asset classes, such as equities, fixed income, FX, commodities and derivatives, as well as 'electrified' traditional exchanges. While some of these platforms are competitive threats, others provide a means to increase liquidity. The dilemma is deciding which platforms will provide access to the best liquidity while remaining extant. Brokerages must also meet the need for increased foreign trading by connecting to foreign execution venues in an electronic format, developing robust multi-currency capabilities, increasing risk management capabilities to handle more complex exposures, and beefing up the back office to enable cross-border clearing and settlement. Additionally, as direct-access technology providers and new forms of crossing networks court the buy-side, broker/dealers must strive to increase anonymity and reduce slippage, leakage and front-running.

Essentially, brokers must find ways to make themselves integral to the new trade flow by adding value to it. One of the ways to achieve this, of course, is to acquire or enter into joint ventures and alliances with the order-routing technology providers. By partnering with one or more leading technology providers, brokerages could offer market-making capabilities for extended trade matching and routing solutions. This approach would also allow brokerages to provide liquidity and order working expertise for large orders, and thereby generate revenue through commissions, spreads, and return on risk capital. Additionally, brokerages could invest directly in an ECN.

There are already a number of precedents. Several of the NASDAQ ECNs are owned by an individual brokerage or a consortium of brokerages. Among the leading direct-access software suppliers, Investment Technology Group (ITG) is positioned as a hybrid broker/software vendor, that markets its own direct-access front-end Quantex exclusively to buy-side institutions, and also owns and operates the E-Crossnet electronic trading network. Interactive Brokers Group (IB) is another example. IB, which owns and operates market-making firm Timber Hill, is among the few suppliers of direct-access technology that actually originated on the buy-side. Initially, IB built its Trader's Workstation direct-access platform in support of its own market-makers, but eventually made it available to a wider market, and now the Trader's Workstation universe of users is comprised of 50% institutional investors.

2. Value-added Services

Over time, compensation for research and advice will become *unbundled* from trading compensation, leaving brokers even more vulnerable in trade execution (pursuance of the above strategies notwithstanding). To counter the continuing erosion of commission-based margins, institutional brokerages must develop new value-added and premium-priceable products to bolster their traditional fare: execution and research.

Moreover, as alluded to above, market data, and generic, static research (economic, sector, industry and company) will not be sufficient in the information age. Brokerages need to offer a suite of dynamic, customised or personalised portfolio (and, therefore, risk) management or investment decision-support services. Many of the leading Wall Street brokerages have already invested in developing a fairly sophisticated set of online tools or toolboxes in this sphere. Morgan Stanley's current offering, one of the best in equities, provides a good template. However, this is but one example of the multitude of features offered by the power brokers.

Clients access all the bank's online equity products through a single point; ClientLink. From the ClientLink site, online research via Research Link, trade execution via TradeXL and portfolio analytics via Basket Link are all just a click away.

- *Basket Link* is a pre-trade analytics tool. It allows clients to screen their portfolio for any liquidity, market impact, tracking or other risks that may be incurred from trading the constituents. The system can also optimise the portfolio to match specific targets set by the client, and can create buy and sell lists to achieve them.

- *Research Link* boasts one of the most comprehensive sets of useful functionality. Obviously, it is customisable, allowing clients to filter the research and news that greets them when they open the homepage and also the alerts that they receive via e-mail. A useful feature on Research Link is a window dedicated to the analysts' intra-day notes. This too is customisable, so that clients are not bombarded with irrelevant e-mails all day. The stock screening tool allows users to build up a selection of stocks based on an almost limitless number of criteria. It integrates all the economic, sector and stock research and allows the user to flow through a constructed argument. It also has a section designed for the dedicated number cruncher. It provides access to the bank's cash flow, earnings and balance sheet estimates plus all the operating, financial and valuation ratios derived from company modelling. Research Link is also impressive because of its intelligent use of webcasts. Opinion is divided about how useful they are – large institutional investors will still want to have direct access to the analysts – but for smaller clients the webcasts can add value. The best use of this functionality comes in displaying interviews with people that the clients wouldn't usually have contact with, such as corporate CEOs. Audio-only and slide presentations are also offered alongside the videos, for clients that may not have the necessary technology or whose firewalls don't allow webcasts.

As well as developing proprietary systems, Morgan Stanley is taking part in industry-wide initiatives. In particular it is a founding member of themarkets.com, a site that provides a single point of access to the research of nine of the leading investment banks.

- *TradeXL* provides execution functionality with some impressive complementary auxiliary services. Clients have online access to a daily statement with a summary of all trading activity and also a reference diary. The system can also be linked to risk and portfolio analytics tools, be they the client's own systems, or Morgan Stanley's Risk Link and Basket Link products. Clients can customise the system so that the live data flowing from the exchanges can be fed into trading analytics tools to update positions and manage performance and market exposure, in real time. Other functionalities on the system include the ability to see the depth of the liquidity in the markets both numerically and graphically, and the ability to track volume weighted average price (VWAP). By automating trading to a VWAP benchmark, TradeXL enables users to work the 10% most illiquid stocks manually, and then route the other 90% through an automated system, which helps to optimise users' time. On average, trading confirmation is submitted to the client within 5 to 10 minutes. Since this far exceeds the industry standard (banks are only required to confirm trades the day after they are executed), TradeXL's speed of response wins the bank a lot of mandates.
- Finally, in terms of order management and settlement tracking, Dresdner Kleinwort Wasserstein's Ops/Tracker clients are given direct access to the broker's internal systems affording real-time local environment data. The system allows clients to view, in real time, the entire lifecycle of a trade, from execution to settlement. Clients select a securities tab, then see a quick view, which shows them trades that are due to be settled on that day or the following day, trades that are open, and failed or failing trades. The aim is to allow back-office users to see what they need to do that day as soon as they log on in the morning. The site can also be used to search for specific trades or within certain time frames and it is possible to drill down through any of the trades to get further details. This has reduced the need for communications and has assisted in the management of failed and failing trades. All of the information can be downloaded on to Excel and is time stamped.

Although not many clients have the capability, files can also be downloaded into XML so that clients can upload the information into their own system.

Finally, in terms of bolstering the value-added services offering, brokerages can also find new products in the realm of technology via increased connectivity to market utilities and market data via FIX capabilities, as well as through business operations, such as outsourced clearing and settlement services.

3. Middle- and Back-office Enhancement

As firms begin to trade more globally and even domestically, with a wider array of counterparties, credit and market risk exposure management systems as well as operational risk and disaster recovery management systems need to be overhauled. Risk management systems need to be evaluated for their effectiveness as well as for their ability to interact with the rest of a firm's trading operations on a real-time basis.

Efforts to achieve straight-through-processing are necessary to comply with pending mandatory T+1 settlement cycles and to address deteriorating operational inefficiencies. Moreover, both the risk and front-office capabilities described above (especially the provision of value-added analytics) derive in large measure from a high degree of back-office automation. STP initiatives include internal work necessary to link disparate systems together and bring the operation up to real-time status, as well as external links to improve data flow both pre- and post-trade, as well as among counterparties, exchanges, clearing agents and custody providers.

As with retail firms, institutional firms must centralise e-commerce operations in order to increase efficiency. This will help organisations to leverage technology developed for one line of business across the entire operation.

Finally, firms can adopt a defensive response to these trends by focusing on a specific institutional segment – 'the human factor' segment – which comprises those investors who prefer direct human market interaction because they do not believe an automated system can ever achieve the execution prowess of a savvy trader.

4. Summary

In sum, international institutional brokerages are confronted by:

1. The proliferation of electronic marketplaces (either new electronic entrants or 'electrified' exchanges), including pure buy-side to buy-side markets,

resultant liquidity fragmentation, and multi-market access or order-routing technology, whose vendors constitute competition.

- The generic response to which is invest in an ECN and/or joint venture with a vendor to boost electronic order-routing capability to multiple execution or liquidity destinations.

2. The advent of the Internet as a research distribution channel and the consequent erosion of the value accorded to the provision of traditional research (in addition to the commoditisation of execution).

   - The generic response to which is the development of electronic personalised or customised portfolio (risk) optimisation tools.

3. Massive volume growth, particularly cross-border, and the concomitant regulatory and economic pressure to boost operational efficiency.

   - The generic response to which is the initiation of ambitious straight-through-processing initiatives.

THE FUTURE OF CORPORATE TREASURERS AND THEIR BANKS

The Demand–Supply Chasm

In the locale of online treasury and banking, currently it's a case of buy-side demand pitted against sell-side inertia. In a survey conducted by TCA Consulting, for example, over 70% of treasurers in the UK indicated that they would potentially use the Internet to buy banking services in the future, with 60% adding 'regularly' to that potential. For certain activities, such as money trading or FX, there was a widespread expectation that the Internet would eventually become a primary channel, with fewer than 10% of respondents stating that they would hardly ever use it for that purpose. The general consensus was that the Internet was of value as a delivery mechanism. Unfortunately, this expectation was misaligned with the treasurers' perceptions of their banks' current and future capabilities in this respect. In fact, only 22% felt that their banks either were using or planning to use the Internet as a primary delivery channel. According to TCA, 'few were convinced that their bank actually had an Internet strategy' (TCA, 2001). These figures indicate that banks have an expectations gap to fill.

The Reduction in the Number of Corporate Banking Relationships and How to Stay in their Number

Compounding this is a strong preference among the majority of treasurers (50% according to the TCA survey) to reduce their number of banking relationships. In order to remain in that number, banks will therefore have to differentiate from the competition. Although corporate treasurers only represent one component of banks' customer base, and the e-channel only one component of the total service offering, the deficiencies currently experienced by treasurers in this regard, contrasted with their own online expectations, makes this an obvious starting point.

It is apparent that those corporates who intend to reduce the number of banking relationships classify the banks that they retain into two distinct groups: full service global banks that will provide services such as FX and cash management, and those filling geographical or product niches. Banks will therefore have to make an effort to stay on the relationship list and will also have to decide in which capacity.

Security and Connectivity

Currently only 8% of corporates use the Web to buy banking services. The major impediments to a higher uptake are security and connectivity. Most corporates resent bank's attempts to lock them into proprietary software, which connects solely with in-house systems, their tendency to dictate data formats, and to impose the burden of building interfaces on the client.

The ability to mingle position information from several banks so that the treasury can obtain an enterprise-wide view of, for example, its cash positions, is widely demanded. There are already precedents in this respect in the area of custodial services. Furthermore, for single commoditised product transactions, such as straight forex, treasurers also expressed a desire to be connected from the single-bank/multi-product site to the multi-bank/single-product sites, so that they could obtain comparative prices from competing banks. In other words, the price versus time constraints of the single-bank/multi-product or multi-bank/single-product site structure need not be overcome in the short term by a multi-bank/multi-product alternative. Instead, a linkage system, that retains the bank as the primary point of contact (especially if the bank provides the cash management and other value-added services) may prove equally effective in meeting the client's varying needs. Over time, this may be an alternative for banks to the complete withdrawal from a commoditised market. Such a withdrawal incurs the risk associated with relinquishing any degree of contact and opportunities to cross- or up-sell.

In addition, real value, in terms of cost savings and higher service quality, will be realised only when proper connectivity is provided through to the back office. To this end, banks need to provide clients with standardised interfaces for data translation and dedicated integration teams for setting up and maintaining automated data transfer between the banks and clients' back offices. This task has been made appreciably easier for banks in the wake of Y2K. Since Y2K, many corporates use ERP (enterprise resource planning) and accounting systems from a small number of vendors that use well-defined standardised formats. The time and cost can be further reduced if banks outsource this to external integration specialists. The provision of transaction visibility through back-office connectivity, using online workflow tracking/monitoring systems, would also help both parties to free up resources.

Client Relationship Management

The challenge for banks will be to decide on a client by client basis which services are best suited to commoditised Internet delivery and which require a more personalised approach. CRM solutions will help manage this process, protecting both commoditised and value-add business, and the position as primary point of contact. CRM will automate the key client information collation process, supplanting the people who currently perform this task more cost efficiently, and extending the scope. Profitability will be better measured, helping the bank to discriminate better between clients reserved for personal service even for low-margin products if preferred. It will enable the bank to become more proactive in meeting needs (for which clients express a strong preference) or at least stop annoying clients with unsolicited pitches for products that don't serve their needs. Ultimately, the days of a 'one size fits all' approach is over. In the new era, there is a pronounced need for banks to shift from supply to demand-led psychology. A recurring theme with treasurers is that banks are too focused on their own internal product-based structure, and aren't able to be responsive to clients' needs across the full range of dealings with the bank.

Conclusions

As corporates start to make greater use of the Web for gathering information, such as the pricing provided on multi-provider portals, the risks for Internet laggard banks will increase. Some have become increasingly dependent on a lack of transparency and information flow to retain clients. At present some treasurers are clearly still unaware of the opportunities available to them, but this will change – particularly as they start to receive more approaches from non-bank suppliers of commoditised products. Over 60% of corporate treasurers polled reported that they had been approached by non-banks for the provision of wholesale financial products or services over the Internet (compared to only 40% who reported that they had been approached by banks). And these potential competitors were not only thinly capitalised start-ups of whom customers may be wary, but players of substance too, such as institutional investors and major insurers. Already sites such as Currenex have begun to have an impact by wooing large corporations, such as oil majors. Under these conditions, playing the 'high level service' card for commoditity transactions that the treasurer does not wish to expend time on anyway will quickly be trumped. The market is fast approaching the end of a long period of stasis.

The above notwithstanding, not all banks have failed to offer a decent online service to the corporate client segment, however. Both Citibank and JPM's Corporate Treasury Portal number among the rare and impressive exceptions.

SAMPLE ONLINE BANKING SERVICES:

- Money trading/FX
- Letters of credit
- Bonds
- Custodial services
- Deposits
- Lending
- Clearing services
- Equity underwriting/securities
- Debt underwriting
- Cash management
- Portfolio valuation

CONCLUSION: TECHNOLOGY INVESTMENT IS THE KEY TO THE FUTURE

The securities industry is in a period of fundamental transition and broker-dealers are facing many new threats to their business. In fact, all aspects of the sell-side's business – trading intermediary, proprietary trading, information provider – are being contested. Following many years of economic bounty, a global slump is putting additional pressure on their business. How will broker-dealers respond to these events to retain their position, which is more fragile than ever?

According to a recent TowerGroup/SIA survey (2001), the vast majority of broker-dealers' believe that the future success of their operations largely depends on the astuteness of their technology investments. Broker-dealers believe that 'the critical decisions they make in the next few years will drive their success in the next few decades'. The almost universal new sell-side paradigm calls for 'opportunity that is generated by technological advances'. Only through continued investment in systems will broker-dealers position themselves to seize those opportunities.

Business Drivers

Thus, rather than cut back, the majority of sell-side firms are increasing their commitment to technology, extending their IT budgets for nearly all functions and locations. Broker-dealers are using technology to optimise their trading positions, maximise operational efficiency, and mitigate the many kinds of risk evident in the markets today. Furthermore, in this era of globalisation, securities trading has become a truly global activity, leading broker-dealers to use technology to expand geographically into multiple new markets, which represent great opportunities for growth, and to derive the optimum business product/market mix. As a result, spending on IT by location is becoming more balanced as the sell-side's commitment to Asia and Europe reach the same level as in North America.

Risks and Action Items

Recognising that trading margins are shrinking, the broker-dealers' decisions to increase technology spending may be compromised by their reduced revenues. TowerGroup urges broker-dealers to continue to invest in technology, even as market conditions erode their profit margins.

> In this new millennium, the new business models created by technological advances will be the driving force behind the creation of the next big opportunity.(TowerGroup, 2001)

Thus broker-dealers' commitment to technology as a remedy to adversity indicates that they do recognise the opportunity that will arise from it. To succeed, it is imperative that broker-dealers accelerate their drive towards upgrading their customer systems while improving their efficiency.

Taxonomy

Technology budgets, as a representation of the overarching positioning strategy in the evolving marketplace, may be apportioned among the following:

1. e-business initiatives in order to extend customer service and reach
2. Front-office applications in order to optimise the risk and return of trading decisions
3. Back-office system upgrades and the reengineering of securities processing technology in order to efficiently handle increasing transaction volumes and pending regulation
4. International initiatives to advance broader international efforts in order to capitalise on the integration of disparate global markets.

Finally, broker-dealers must determine the appropriate mix of in-house development versus what can be generically termed 'outsourcing'.

Notes

1 This growth in volume has been stimulated by growth in the base of investors, in turn due to both new technology and strong bull markets (by contrast, the long-suffering Japanese equities markets have seen only 3% growth in turnover during this time frame). Hence, the downturn over the past year may erode some of the gains secured by securities firms.

2 Research, however, as a value-added service, adds less value in the corporate market, in particular, since the core need is simply to hedge exposure, not to analyse conditions for position-taking purposes.

3 The fair disclosure rule prohibits the practice of company officials providing material information to select Wall Street analysts. Essentially, it levels the playing field among analysts and investors. Market moving information, if it is disclosed, must be broadly distributed. The Internet will be an important vehicle for distribution of company information in this context.

CHAPTER 16

CORPORATE LONGEVITY

To conclude, it is once more appropriate to distance ourselves from the trees of securities trading in order to see the woods. For, in the end, Darwinian-style adaptation and survival in this new electronic environment depends not on the soundness of the cause–effect model as outlined in this book. In fact, the actual strategic analysis and emergent strategy and even implementation are very secondary to the underlying psyche that informs this process.

As a starting point, but continuing the overarching theme of evolution and lifecycles, let us look at the sobering realities of corporate life expectancies. This subject has been analysed in some depth by Royal Dutch/Shell. Arie de Gues presented their findings in a 1997 *HBR* case study entitled 'The Living Company'. Since Shell was celebrating their centenary, they took the opportunity to re-evaluate their future in the context of the past. They observed that in the world of institutions, corporations are relative newcomers. They have only been around for about 500 years, a mere moment in the course of human civilisation. In that time, as the producers and custodians of material wealth, they have achieved immense success. However, compared with what they could be, most corporations exist at an early stage of evolution, and exploit only a fraction of their potential.

Consider their high mortality rate. By 1983, fully one-third of the 1970 *Fortune* 500 companies had been acquired, or broken up, or had merged with other companies. How do we know that many of the deaths are premature? Because we have evidence of much greater corporate longevity. Japan's Sumitomo has its origins in a copper-casting shop founded by Riemon Soga in 1590. Sweden's Stora, currently a major chemical and pulp manufacturer, began as a copper mine in Sweden more than 700 years ago. Examples such as these suggest that the natural life span of a corporation could be many centuries. However, company birth, death and population registries in the northern hemisphere indicate that the average life span is well below 20 years. Even those that survive the high infant mortality rate continue to live only another 20 years on average. The implications are depressing.

The high corporate mortality rate seems unnatural. No living species suffers from such a discrepancy between its maximum life expectancy and the average span it realises, and few other types of institution – churches, armies, or universities – have the abysmal record of the corporation. What can explain this longevity gap? Mounting evidence suggests that so-called 'living corporations' excel at management for change, to use a modern cliché. They understand that, as an organisation of human beings, they are in business – any business – to stay alive, and are therefore able to survive in a world in which endurance depends on the ability to adapt and to evolve. Stora, the most dramatic example, survived the Middle Ages, the Reformation, the wars of the 17th century, the Industrial Revolution, and the two world wars of the 20th century. Its core business has shifted from copper, to forestry, to iron, to hydropower, to pulp and chemicals manufacturing, and it continues to adapt to an unpredictable world.

THE OPERATIONAL EFFICIENCY DEATH MARCH

So what's wrong with the rest? In a recent *McKinsey Quarterly* article, the authors postulate that, for historical reasons, corporations have been designed to operate – to produce goods and services – rather than to evolve (Foster and Kaplan, 2001). Creation and destruction – the two key elements of evolution – are missing. Moreover, as the rate and pace of change accelerates over time, companies' survival rates are worsening. The first Standard & Poor's index of 90 major US companies was created in the 1920s. The companies on that original list remained there for an average of 65 years. By 1998, the average anticipated tenure of a company on the expanded S&P 500 was 10 years. If history is a guide, over the next quarter century no more than a third of today's major corporations will survive as an entity with an identity in an economically important way. This deterioration is precisely because most corporations' response to accelerated change has been to get better at operating, not at evolving.

In a 1996 *HBR* article entitled 'What is Strategy?', author Michael Porter makes the observation that over the last decade, under pressure to improve productivity, quality, and speed, managers have embraced tools such as TQM, benchmarking and reengineering – whatever the name, the goal is the same, to get better at what you're already doing. Dramatic operational improvements have resulted, but rarely have these gains translated into sustainable profitability.

Operational efficiency shifts the productivity frontier outwards, effectively raising the bar for everyone. But although such bases for competition produce absolute gains, they lead to relative gains for no one. Consider the $5 billion-plus US commercial printing industry. The major players – RR Donnelley, Quebecor, World Color Press and Big Flower Press – are all competing head-to-head, serving all customer segments, offering the same range of printing technologies, investing heavily in the same new equipment, running their presses faster and faster, and reducing crew sizes. But the resulting productivity gains, rather than being retained in superior profitability, instead accrue to customers and suppliers. Even industry leader Donnelley's profit margin, consistently higher than 7% in the 1980s, fell to less than 4.6% in 1995.

This pattern is playing itself out in industry after industry, both new and old. According to Warburg Dillon Read in an April 2000 report on e-brokerage (Serra, 2000), for example:

> the market is becoming hyper-competitive with a pricing structure close to marginal cost for the low end of transaction values . . . this fierce price war due to lack of differentiation has actually damaged the long-term structural profitability of the industry.

The reason why improved operational efficiency leads to this end-state is a side effect that has been christened 'competitive convergence', and it is subtle and insidious. The more benchmarking companies do, the more they look alike. The more that rivals outsource activities to efficient third parties, often the same ones, the more generic those activities become. As rivals imitate one another's improvements in quality, cycle times or supplier partnerships, strategies converge and competition becomes a series of races down identical paths that no one can win.

Competition based on operational efficiency alone is mutually destructive, leading to wars of attrition that can be arrested only by limiting competition. The recent wave of industry consolidation through mergers and acquisitions makes sense in the context of operational efficiency-driven competition. Driven by performance pressures but lacking strategic vision, company after company has no better idea than to buy up its rivals. The competitors left standing are often those that outlasted the others, not companies with real advantage.

After a decade of impressive gains in operational efficiency, many companies are facing diminishing returns. Continuous improvement has been drilled into managers, but its tools unwittingly draw companies toward imitation and homogeneity. Gradually, managers have let operational efficiency supplant strategy. The result is zero-sum competition, static or declining prices, and pressures on costs that compromise companies' ability to invest in the business for the long-term. In an 1999 *HBR* article entitled 'Bringing Silicon Valley Inside', author Gary Hamel dubbed this 'the efficiency death march'.

WHEN CORPORATE CULTURE KILLS

While not many corporations have reached Porter's and Hamel's conclusions, there is a growing appreciation that operational efficiency is necessary but insufficient. In a McKinsey survey (Foster and Kaplan, 2001) of over 1000 companies, many reported that while they are now satisfied with their operating prowess, they are dissatisfied with their ability to implement change. 'How do the excellent innovators do it?' they ask, presuming that excellent innovators exist, and, most fundamental of all, 'How do we find new ideas?' This failure to adapt and innovate stems from the inherent conflict between the need for corporations to control existing operations and the need to create the kind of environment that will permit new ideas to emerge and old ones to die a timely death. Ironically, the root of this conflict lies embedded in the organisation's own lifecycle. In 'Creative Destruction', Foster and Kaplan (2001) observe the phenomenon of 'cultural lock-in' that emerges during its course.

Cultural lock-in is the last in a series of 'emotional' phases in a corporation's life, a series that mirrors, remarkably, that of human beings. In the early years of a corporation, just after its founding, the dominant emotion is passion – the sheer energy to make things happen. As the corporation ages, passions cool and are replaced by 'rational' decision making, often simply the codification of what has worked in the past. Eventually, rational decision making reveals that the future potential of the business is limited. Often, at this point, threatened by the prospect of a bleak future, the corporation goes into defensive mode to protect itself, just as defensive emotions emerge in our lives when we sense impending distress. Decisions are made to protect existing businesses. The fear of discarding the old for the new often effectively shields the corporation from the perception of future danger – as well as the need to act – for a long time and paralyses creative destruction. Thus, cultural lock-in is the inability to change the corporate culture even in the face of clear market threats, which explains why corporations fail to respond to the signals of the marketplace.

Cultural lock-in stems from the formation of hidden sets of rules, or mental models. Mental models are the core concepts of the corporation, the belief system, the cause and effect relationships, the values and assumptions, the guidelines for interpreting language and signals, the war stories repeated within the corporate walls. Mental models are invisible in the corporation, they are neither explicit nor scrutinised, but they are pervasive. Well-crafted mental models allow management to forecast the future, make efficient and effective decisions, and solve problems. But once formed, mental models are extremely difficult to change; they become self-reinforcing and self-sustaining, which results in the gradual ossification of the invisible architecture of the organisation.

Mental models manifest themselves in corporate-control and decision-making systems designed to ensure predictability; of cost control, the control of capital expenditures, or the control of the deployment of key people. Corporate-control and decision-making systems undermine the ability of the organisation to innovate. For example, the case for creating a new business can be rejected, since its probable success cannot be quantified in advance. Under these circumstances, it is more likely that ideas based on the incremental growth of current capabilities and mental models will be encouraged. Worse, these systems can also create 'defensive routines' in organisations, including the failure to challenge the status quo, the failure to encourage a diversity of opinions and so on. Leaders with genuine vision are suppressed. People who try bring about adaptive change are silenced. On occasion, they are killed.

And the corporations most vulnerable to cultural lock-in? Why, those companies that have reached the end of their first generation. The first time growth starts to stagnate, corporations are susceptible to shifting into operational efficiency and acquisition gear at the expense of anything else. The first handover of the reins to a successor of the founders often engenders a corporate identity crisis, handled by entrenchment in 'the way we do things' as a substitute for 'who we are'. Failure to perceive the dangers that lie ahead results. Change becomes impossible.

Unfortunately, the very assumption of predictability or continuity represents a disconnection with reality, and when mental models are out of sync with reality, corporations lose their early warning system. It dampens a company's ability to innovate or cast off operations with a less exciting future. Moreover, it signals the corporation's inexorable decline into inferior performance. Once cultural lock-in guides a company's decisions, in the absence of some great external shock, the corporation's fate is sealed.

HOW THE MARKETS ENABLE CHANGE

Why is this so? Because cultural lock-in manifests itself in three general fears – the fear of cannibalisation of an important product line, the fear of channel conflict with important customers, and the fear of earnings dilution that might result from a strategic acquisition or investment. The consequences are dire, because as reasonable as all these fears seem to established companies, they are not fears that are in the market. And so the market moves where the corporation dares not.

Markets, lacking culture, leadership and emotion, do not experience the bursts of desperation, depression, denial and hope that corporations face. The market has no lingering memories or remorse. It has no mental models. The market does not fear cannibalisation, customer channel conflict, or dilution. It simply waits for the forces at work to play out – for new companies to be created and for acquisitions to clear the field. The markets silently allow weaker companies to be put up for sale and leave it to the new owners to shape them up or shut them down. Actions are taken quickly on early signs of weakness. Most of the time, the market simply removes the weak players and, in removing them, improves overall returns. Lacking productivity-oriented control systems, markets create more innovation than do corporations.

THE ROAD AHEAD

So, how can corporations make themselves more like the market? The market itself has pointed the way to a solution. In an era of increasingly fast economic change, there are certain kinds of firm – particularly private equity firms – that have demonstrated the ability to change at the pace and scale of the market, and they have earned sustained superior returns for doing so. The two kinds of private equity firms – principal investing firms and venture capitalists – are quite different from each other, but each looks somewhat like the holding companies of the late 19th century. It is possible to imagine that private equity firms will form the seeds of the industrial giants of the 21st century.

These newly important firms have been able to outperform the markets for the last two to three decades, longer than any other kind of company we know of. These financial partnerships have discovered how to engage in creative destruction at the pace of the market, exactly as Joseph Schumpeter envisioned. Created around the fundamental assumption of discontinuity, they have then determined how best to incorporate continuity. The difference is profound:

1. These firms never buy any company to hold forever. Rather, they focus on intermediate (three- to five-year) value creation. Corporations, in contrast, concentrate on the very short term (less than 18 months) for operations and the very long term (greater than eight years) for research.
2. Private equity firms make as much money by expanding the future potential of their assets as they do by increasing the assets' operating income. When a private equity firm invests in a company or buys all the equity, the firm buys it with a 'take-out' strategy in mind: management knows what it

must do in the next three to five years to build the property so that it has long-term value for the next buyer.

3. Finally, private equity companies think of their business as a revolving portfolio of companies in various stages of development. They realise that they will sell some of their properties each year and buy others. They keep the pipeline full of new properties at the front end and supplied with buyers at the back end, cultivating both simultaneously (a skill at which they excel).

These firms differ from conventional corporations in their divergent thinking. They differ in the depth and speed of their research activities. Moreover, private equity firms allow each of the companies they buy to retain its own control systems. This allows the private equity firm to concentrate on creation and destruction to a far greater extent than do traditional corporations and even to a greater extent than a private equity firm's own wholly or partially owned subsidiaries do.

REDESIGNING THE CORPORATION

Long-term corporate performance has not matched the performance of the markets, because corporations do not adapt as fast as the markets do. Markets perform better than corporations because markets allow new companies to enter more freely, and they force the elimination of those companies without competitive prospects more ruthlessly than corporations do. Moreover, markets do these things faster and on a larger scale than do corporations.

This is due to the way that corporations evolve. Redesigning the corporation to evolve quickly rather than to operate well requires more than simple adjustments; the fundamental concepts of operational excellence are inappropriate for a corporation seeking to evolve at the pace and scale of the markets. One cannot just 'add on' creation and destruction, one has to design them in. And only if the corporation is redesigned to evolve at the pace and scale of the markets will long-term performance improve.

Royal Dutch/Shell identified four distinct traits of the so-called living companies, who seem designed to renew themselves over many generations (de Gues, 1997).

- The first is the manner in which they risk capital. These companies do not risk capital gratuitously, but they understand the meaning of money in an old-fashioned way, that is, having money in the kitty, when their competitors do not, to pursue attractive new opportunities, without having to convince third-party financiers thereof.

- The second is their sensitivity to the world around them. They excel at staying attuned to and adapting to the constant changes in the world around them, by valuing and rewarding those engaged in these activities as highly as those engaged in continuing existing businesses, that is, those who live to sign the next deal.
- The third is their awareness of their identity.
- The fourth is a tolerance for new ideas. These companies tolerate activities at the margin: experiments and eccentricities that stretch them. They understand that new businesses may be entirely unrelated to existing businesses and that the act of starting a business need not be centrally controlled. The case studies of these 30 or so veterans cast light on many other such practices, but making the point suffices for now.

Gary Hamel (1999) notes that the average-sized venture capital firm in Silicon Valley gets as many as 5000 unsolicited business plans a year, and poses the rhetorical question to corporate CEOs: 'How many did you get?' He asserts that until senior executives spend as much energy fostering wealth-creating innovation as they do efficiency and conserving existing businesses, and until individuals believe they have the opportunity for substantial wealth creation, the marketplace for ideas will remain closed.

THE LONGEVITY OF SECURITIES TRADING IN AN ELECTRONIC AGE

It is in this context that we need to chew over what it will take for securities traders to survive in the coming years. The world of financial markets is a pulse-racing one and was never for the faint-hearted, yet it will demand ever higher levels of adrenaline in the future. Through the financial media, always a sucker for sensationalism, the story of the emerging electronic markets of the future unfolds like a protracted episode of *Star Wars*. Yet the response has been less like prospecting by true pioneers on the new frontier and more like panic and knee-jerking or, worse, inertia which will soon turn to rigor mortis. The laggards, especially, seem less paralysed by fear and more by an obtuse perception of the danger and possibilities that lie ahead. Yet a select few have begun to explore those possibilities and it is to these intrepid souls that the laggards will surrender the future.

Kenichi Ohmae summed up the new paradigm in *The Invisible Continent* (2000) when he stated that 'It is vital for the CEO of your organisation to also be your CIO'. While he conceded that a separate CIO position may also exist, he stressed that the CEO should have the 'knowledge ... and passion to double as CIO at any time'. Why? According to Ohmae, information technology and the like have become so central to corporate strategy that the 'life or death' of the company may depend on the judgement of senior leaders in this respect, particularly as companies get ever-more involved in e-business. If the company must be reorganised to fulfil the cyber-imperatives on the invisible continent, as most large established corporates will, then that reorganisation should be informed from a technologically savvy perspective. For all these reasons, the CEO should be keenly, personally aware of these trends. Interestingly the anecdote related by Ohmae to underscore this concerned a bank:

> This point came home to me in the early 1990s when Walter Wriston, then chairman of Citigroup, selected his successor, John S Reed, whose background was in technology not in traditional banking. When asked why he had chosen him when there were so many other potential heirs apparent, Wriston replied: 'The future of banking is going to be determined in nano seconds. It's a technology game, and its very, very hard to teach bankers the technology'. (Ohmae, 2000, p. 59)

Look where Citi is today.

Ultimately, the electronic economy is manifest first and foremost in the purest markets of all: the markets for money and capital. These are tending towards the eventual establishment of a virtual, single, global marketplace. In this as yet unformed mega-market in the ether, survival will depend on the response born of those two most basic of instincts: fear and greed. Fast forward the future!

GLOSSARY OF TERMS

Financial Terminology

Access	Eligibility to participate in a market.
Anonymity	Non-disclosure of counter-party identity (pre-trade or post-trade).
Architecture (market)	Broadly, key features of market structure such as participation arrangements, venues, trading protocols.
Back office	Operational unit of an organisation responsible for post-trade activities such as *clearing* and *settlement*.
Bid-ask spread	Difference between buying and selling price quoted by a *dealer*.
Block trade	Large, potentially price/market-moving trade.
Broker	A firm which operates in a market on behalf of other participants to mediate transactions, (generally) without being a party to the transactions itself (cf *dealer*).
Bundle matching	An *algorithm* that matches orders for securities in bundles and provides *price discovery*.
Call market	An order-driven market where orders are processed at discrete points in time, being matched by a particular *algorithm*.
Centralisation	Tendency for trading, price formation and information exchange to be concentrated in a single marketplace.
Clearing	The process of transmitting, reconciling and confirming instructions to transfer instruments prior to *settlement*.
Consolidation of trading	Bringing together aspects of the trading process (*order routing, execution*) into a smaller number of markets (cf *fragmentation of trading*).

Continuous market	Market that trades on an ongoing basis (cf *call market* or periodic market).
Counterparty credit risk	The risk that the market participant on the other side of a transaction will default.
Dealer	Firm whose primary business is entering into transactions on both sides of wholesale financial markets and seeking profits by taking risks in these markets (cf *broker*).
Dealer market	Market where orders for *execution* pass to an intermediary (*dealer*) who executes them from their inventory.
Demutualisation	Process of exchanges converting from a co-operative organisation owned by member *dealers* and *brokers* to a for-profit company.
Depth	Quantity of outstanding orders pending (possibly at different prices) on either side of the market.
Derivative	A financial contract whose value depends on the value of one or more underlying reference assets, rates or indices.
DVP	Delivery versus payment. Simultaneous exchange of instruments and payment.
Economies of scale	Situation where unit costs drop as volume increases.
Efficient market	Market where prices balance underlying supply and demand and adjust as smoothly as possible, without discontinuities or excessive volatility unrelated to fundamentals.
Electronic order routing	Delivery of orders to *execution* system.
Electronic trading	In broad terms, this refers to any use of electronic means of sending orders (bids and offers) to the market, *electronic order routing*, automated centralised *execution* and subsequent dissemination of price and volume information.
End-users	Market participants who provide the underlying supply and demand in a market. They range in size from individual retail traders to institutional investors and large corporations.
Execution	The matching of orders or trade proposals which turns them into actual trades.
Explicit trading costs	Costs such as market access fees, commissions, tax, *clearing* and *settlement* costs and staff and IT overheads (cf *implicit trading costs*).
Fragmentation of trading	Division of some aspects of the trading process (*order routing*, *execution*) between different markets (cf *consolidation*).
Front-running	Illicit practice of *dealer* using information from a customer order to trade before that order is executed.
Gapping	Large discontinuous movements in prices.
Hidden order	An order invisible on the *order book*.
IDB	Inter-dealer broker, specialist *broker* who acts as intermediary between *dealers*.
Iceberg order	See *hidden order*.

Immediacy	Ability to execute an order immediately.
Implicit trading costs	The bid-ask spread and impact on market price of a trade (cf *explicit trading costs*).
Indication of interest (IoI)	An investor's stated, but non-binding, desire to purchase securities at a given price.
Information asymmetry	Tendency for some market participants (for example banks, *brokers*) to be better informed than others (for example customers).
IPO	Initial Public Offering; the initial sale of shares in a new company.
Limit order	Order to buy a specified quantity up to a maximum price, or sell subject to a minimum price (cf *market order*).
Liquidity	The ability to transact in a market without markedly moving prices. Three aspects of liquidity are *tightness*, *depth* and *resiliency*.
Market impact cost	Cost of a trade resulting from an order moving the price against a trader. Such costs are smaller in a market with high *liquidity*.
Market-maker	*Dealer* obliged to quote buy and sell prices in return for certain privileges within a market (sometimes used to refer to anybody who provides quotes).
Market order	Order to buy (or sell) a specified quantity at the prevailing price (cf *limit order*).
Multilateral interaction	Price formation by more than two market participants.
Order book	A centralised market where prices are determined by an order execution algorithm from participants sending firm buy and sell orders (cf *quote-driven* or dealer driven).
Order routing	Delivery of messages from *end-users* to the *execution* destination.
Orderly trading	Conditions under which similar orders execute at similar prices.
OTC	Over the counter. Bilateral transactions not conducted on a formal exchange.
Price discovery	Determination of prices in a market.
Price formation	The incorporation of new information in the pricing process. It is influenced by specific market rules.
Quote-driven	A usually decentralised market where a class of participants, possibly *market-makers*, post bid and ask quotes, often indicative, with prices being determined through bilateral negotiation.
Resilient market	Market which continues to function in an *efficient*, *liquid* and *orderly* manner at times of great price uncertainty and market stress.
Settlement	Completion of a transaction by exchange of instrument and funds.
Tightness (market)	A measure of *liquidity* derived from the bid-ask spread (difference between buying and selling quotes).
Trader	Employee of *dealer* or *end-user* paid to operate in financial markets.
Transparency	Ability of market participants to observe (pre-trade) quotes, (post-trade) prices and volumes in a timely fashion.

Strategy Terminology

First mover advantage	Possible ability of first entrant to a market to achieve a dominant position for example by setting standards or through establishing a dominant brand name.
Outsourcing	The practice of a firm contracting a non-core activity to a third party.
Unbundling	Separate provision of (and charging for) products and services previously offered jointly.
White label	Arrangement whereby an intermediary makes available transaction services to its customers under its own brand, while channelling the resulting transactions through another organisation, with a view to saving costs. The provider of the white label product may specialise in transaction services and may be in a better position to benefit from economies of scale.

Technology Terminology

Algorithm (order execution)	Rules to determine the method by which orders are matched.
Extranet	Linked network of *intranets* or part of a company's *intranet* that is extended to users outside the company. They may be used to share securely part of a business's information or operations with suppliers, vendors, partners or customers.
Inter-dealer system	ET network between *dealers*, sometimes involving obligations on them to act as *market-makers* (for example BrokerTec, eSpeed, EuroMTS).
Internet	An open worldwide communication infrastructure consisting of interconnected computer networks and allowing access to remote information and the exchange of information between computers.
Intranet	An *internet*-like system only operating within a single organisation.
Killer-app	Killer application. Jargon referring to an electronic application that enjoys a high level of demand.
Multi(ple) dealer system	System allowing customer to examine quotes from a number of dealers simultaneously (for example TradeWeb).
Network effect/ externalities	Tendency for liquid markets to attract further *liquidity* as market participants want to trade where others are already actively trading. Sometimes referred to as 'demand side economies of scale'.
Open architecture	System design based on publicly available and standardised software, enabling easy interlinkage (cf *proprietary system*).
Outage	Interruption to operation of a market.
Pricing engines	Automated order/quote generating systems that automatically generate prices and/or orders.
Proprietary system	System that can only be used with a specific market or dealer (cf *open architecture*).

Scalability	Ease with which increasing volumes of participants or transactions can be accommodated.
Single-dealer system	ET system offered by one dealer to its customers which only provides access to information/facilities offered by this single dealer.
Smart agent	An enhanced search engine that can compare across different sites to find the best deal.
STP	Straight-through processing: the capture of trade details directly from front office systems to *back office*. Completes automated processing of confirmations and settlement instructions without the need for rekeying or reformatting data.
Tipping	Tendency for a system provider that has achieved a dominant market share to move to (a near) monopoly.
VPN	Virtual private network. A private data network that uses public networks but maintains security through tunnelling protocols and security procedures such as access control and encryption.

REFERENCES

Accenture (2001) 'T+1 Business Case', *Accenture*, Presentation to the *Wall Street & Technology* Drilling Down on STP Conference, 24 May.

Adams, C., Mathieson, D.J., Schinasi, G. and Chadha, B. (1998) *International Capital Markets: Developments, Prospects and Key Policy Issues*, International Monetary Fund, World Economic and Financial Surveys, Washington DC.

Arthur Andersen/Risk Publications (2000) 'Bandwidth: Optical Illusion or Genuine Commodity?', *Risk* and *Energy and Power Risk*, Bandwidth Special Report, July.

Arthur, W.B. (1996) 'Increasing Returns and the New World of Business', *Harvard Business Review*, July–August.

BIS (Bank for International Settlements) (2001) *The Implications of Electronic Trading in Financial Markets*, BIS, Committee on the Global Financial System, Basle.

Bloch, B. (1997) 'Business Cycles: Psychology and Speculation', *The South African Journal of Economics*, **63**(3) 398–418.

Caprio, G. and Klingebiel, D. (1996) *Bank Insolvencies: Cross Country Experience*, World Bank, Policy Research Working Papers 1620, Washington DC.

Chote, R. (1998) 'Capital Flows Must Be Handled With Care', *Business Day*, 8 September.

Davidson, C. (2000) 'How to Keep the Customer Satisfied', *Risk*, Technology Risk Supplement.

Davidson, J.A., Grepin, L.M. and Hogg, C.M. (2001) 'Remaking Market Making', *McKinsey Quarterly*, (3).

Davidson, J.D. and Rees-Mogg, W.R. (1997) *The Sovereign Individual*, New York: Simon & Schuster.

de Geus, A. (1997) 'The Living Company', *Harvard Business Review*, March–April.

De Soto, H. (2000) *The Mystery of Capital*, New York: Basic Books.

Demirguc-Kunt, A. and Detragiache, E. (1998) *Financial Liberalisation and Financial Fragility, International Monetary Fund*, Working Papers 83, Washington DC.

Economist, The (1995a), 'The Myth of the Powerless State', *The Economist*, 7 October, pp. 3–4.

Economist, The (1995b) 'The World Economy: Who's in the Driving Seat?', *The Economist: The World Economy*, 7 October, pp. 5–7.

Economist, The (1997) 'The Future of the State', *The Economist: The World Economy*, 20 September, pp. 1–56.

Economist, The (1998) 'Turmoil in Financial Markets: The Risk Business', *The Economist*, 17 October, pp. 21–4.

Economist, The (1999) 'Farewell to the Floor?', *The Economist*, 7 August, p. 62.

Economist, The (2001a) 'The Rise and the Fall', *The Economist*, 3 May.

Economist, The (2001b) 'Is Government Disappearing?', *The Economist*, 27 September.

Economist, The (2001c) 'Globalisation and its Critics', *The Economist*, 27 September.

eFX (2001) 'Frank Feenstra, Greenwich Associates', *eFX*, Autumn, p. 54.

Fan, M., Stallaert, J. and Whinston, A. (2000) 'The Internet and the Future of the Financial Markets', *Communications of the ACM*, **43**(11): 83–8.

Financial Times (1998) 'Frail Orthodoxy of Financial Systems', *Financial Times*, 21 October, pp. 1–4.

Fishman, C. (1999) 'This is a Marketing Revolution', *FastCompany*, May, p. 204.

Foster, R.N. and Kaplan, S. (2001) 'Creative Destruction', *The McKinsey Quarterly*, (3).

Global Investment Technology (2001) 'Messaging Standards Continue to be Key to T+1 as Industry Falls in Tune with Market Realities', *Global Investment Technology*, 19 March.

Hamel, G. (1999) 'Bringing Silicon Valley Inside', *Harvard Business Review*, September– October.

IMF (International Monetary Fund) (1997) *World Economic Outlook, 1997*, International Monetary Fund, World Economic and Financial Surveys, Washington DC.

Kiley, K. (2001) 'Online Investment Banks Ponder What Went Wrong', *KPMG Analysis: Banking Insider*, 11 July.

Kindleberger, C.P. (1989) *Manias, Panics and Crashes: A History of Financial Crises*, 2nd edn, Basingstoke: Macmillan – now Palgrave Macmillan.

Langton, J.L. (2001) 'Securities Trading in the New Economy: Surviving the e-Revolution', *International Securities Market Association*, Speech to e-Securities Forum, 12 February.

Lascelles, D. (1998) 'Reduce Risk: Learn To Love Speculation', *Financial Mail*, 23 October, pp. 42–3.

Lee, P. (2000) 'Banks Struggle to Deliver on their Internet Promises', *Euromoney*, July,
p. 135.

Liebenberg, L. (1999) *Implications for South Africa of the Redesign of the International Monetary System*, University of the Witwatersrand, Faculty of Management, South Africa, Johannesburg.

Lindgren, C.J., Garcia, G. and Saul, M (1996) *Banking Soundness and Macroeconomic Policy*, International Monetary Fund, World Economic and Financial Surveys, Washington DC.

Mandel, M.J. and Foust, D. (1998) 'How to Reshape the World Financial System', *Business Week*, 12 October, pp. 47–50.

McCormick, F. (2001) *Currenex and the Rise of Online FX*, Celent Communications, Wholesale Banking and Institutional Trading, Report, 6 November.

Moody's (2000) *The Impact of Alternative Trading Systems on Market-making at Securities Firms*, Moody's Investors Service, Global Credit Research, Special Comment, July, New York.

Oakley, T. (2001) 'Greenwich Urges Uptake of e-Fixed Income', *euromoney.com*, 30 May.

Ohmae, K. (1999) *The Borderless World*, rev. edn, New York: HarperCollins.

Ohmae, K. (2000) *The Invisible Continent*, New York: HarperCollins.

Okin, H. (2001) 'Emerging Trading Technologies Create Serious Value Challenges for Institutional Brokerages', *Accenture, Outlook*.

PaceMetrics (2001) *A Quantum Leap in Operational Efficiency for STP and T+1*, PaceMetrics, London.

Plexus Group (1998) 'The Official Icebergs of Transaction Costs', *Plexus Group Inc., Commentary No. 54*, January.

Point, The (2001) 'Land of the Giants', *Accenture, Outlook: The Point*, **1**(4).

Porter, M.E. (1996) 'What is Strategy?', *Harvard Business Review*, November–December.

Rafalaf, A. (2000) 'The Death of the Inter-Dealer Broker', *Wall Street & Technology*, 1 June.

Risk Publications (2000a) 'Risk Management: From the Enterprise to the Universe', *Risk*, Technology Risk Supplement.

Risk Publications (2000b) 'How to Keep the Customer Satisfied', *Risk*, Technology Risk Supplement.

Risk Publications (2001) 'Back to the Future', *Risk*, Derivatives Exchanges Special Report, May, p. S8.

Rosberg, M. (2001) *Achieving Cross-border Trade Processing Goals*, Securities Industry Association, Research Reports, Vol. II, No 3, New York.

Sales, R. (2001) 'Online Bond Consortiums', *Wall Street & Technology*, 16 May.

Sales, R. (2001) 'The Fight to Attract Listed Equities Order Flow', *Wall Street & Technology Online*, 10 December.

Sales, R. (2002) 'A Journey from Active Day Traders to Institutions, *Wall Street & Technology*, 7 January.

Sanders, C. (2001) 'Small Investors Warming up to Bond Buying on the Web', *Reuters*, Special Report, 25 July.

Sanders, S. (2001) 'BrokerTec Uses Incentives to Build Bond Trade Volume', *Wall Street & Technology*, 5 December.

Schmerken, I. (2001) 'Cooperation or Collusion?', *Wall Street & Technology*, 11 January.

Schwab Institutional (2000) 'The Changing Trading Environment: T+1, Straight Through Processing and What it Means to Independent Investment Advisors', *Schwab Institutional*, Market Knowledge Tools, Industry Report, October.

Securities Industry Association (2002) *Securities Industry Income Statement*, SIA, Online Publications, (Quarterly) Financial Results. www.sia.com, April.

Securities Industry Association (2002) *SIA's Securities Industry Databank*. www.sia.com, April.

Serra, D. (2000) 'European e-Finance', *Warburg Dillon Read*, Global Equity Research, Europe Banks: e-Finance, April.

Smithers, A. (1999) 'Why Markets Will Fall', *The World in 1999*, p. 137.

Soros, G. (1998) *The Crisis of Global Capitalism*, London: Little, Brown.

Tanzi, T. (1998) *The Demise of the Nation State?*, International Monetary Fund, Working Papers 120, Washington DC.

TCA Consulting (2001) *Corporate Treasurers and their Banks*, TCA Consulting, New York.

TowerGroup (2001) *Securities Industry Spending Trends: Recognising the Need to Invest in the Future*, TowerGroup, Massachusetts.

TowerGroup/SIA (2001) *Technology Trends in the Securities Industry 2001: Investing in Tomorrow's Infrastructure*, TowerGroup, Massachusetts.

Tully, S. (1999) 'Will the Web Eat Wall Street?', *Fortune*, 2 August, p. 114.

United Nations (1998) *World Economic and Social Survey*, United Nations, New York.

US General Accounting Office (2000) *On-line Trading: Better Investor Protection Information Needed on Brokers' Web Sites*, US General Accounting Office, GAO/GGD-00-43, Washington DC, May

Vartanian, T.P. and Ledig, R.H. (1999) *21st Century Money and Banking*, New York: Fried Frank Harris Shriver & Jacobson.

Vinzant, C. (1999) 'So We Need a Stock Exchange?', *Fortune*, 22 November, pp. 251–60.

Weatherford, J. (1997) *The History of Money*, New York: Three Rivers Press.

Wee, L.S. and Lee, J. (2000) 'Breaking Barriers', *Risk*, Electronic Trading Special Report, March, p. 17.

Wirth, G. (2000) 'After Taking Heat for its Dutch Auction Model, WR Hambrecht May Have the Last Laugh', *Investment Dealers Digest*, 11 December.

Wright, B. (2001) 'Online Markets Disappoint in Credit Derivatives', *euromoney.com*, 26 June.